**People** weekly

PRIVATE
LIVES

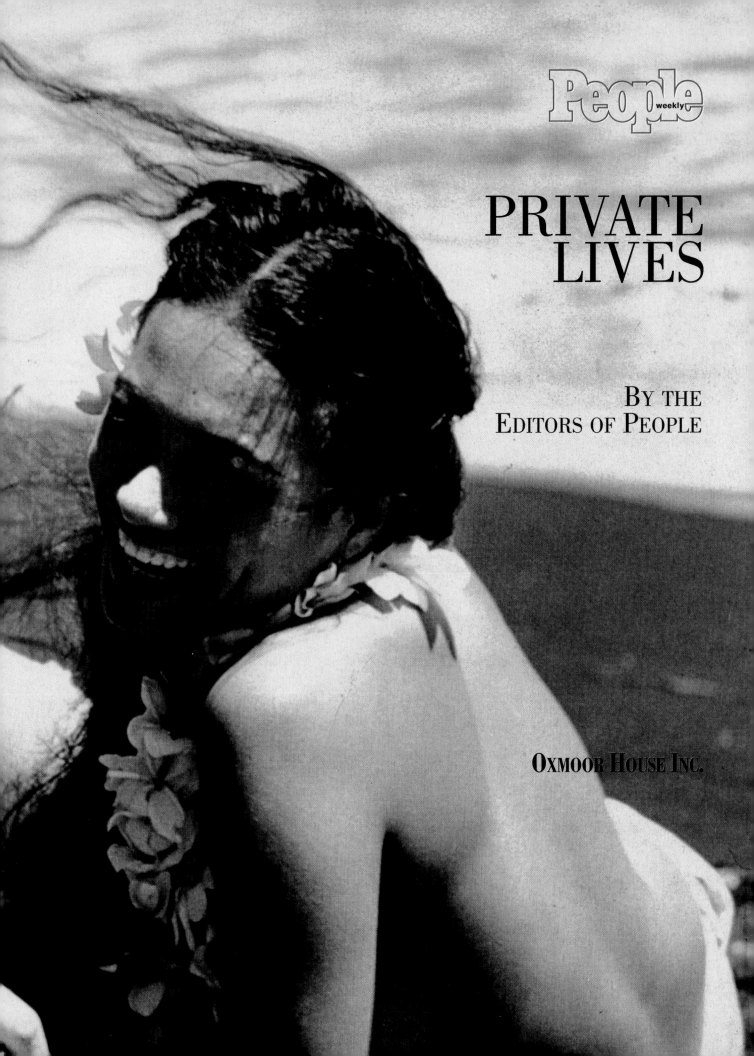

People weekly

# PRIVATE LIVES

By the
Editors of People

Oxmoor House Inc.

Copyright 1991 The Time Inc. Magazine Company

PUBLISHED BY OXMOOR HOUSE, INC.
1271 AVENUE OF THE AMERICAS
NEW YORK, NEW YORK 10020

ISBN: 0-8487-1024-X
Library of Congress Catalog Card Number: 90-64375

Manufactured in The United States of America
First Printing 1991

PRIVATE LIVES
SENIOR EDITOR: Jane Kagan Vitiello
    EDITORIAL ASSISTANTS: Stacey Harmis, Roxana Lonergan
    RESEARCHER: Denise Lynch
    COPY EDITOR: Ben Harte
DIRECTOR OF PHOTOGRAPHY & RESEARCH: Geraldine Howard
    PHOTO EDITORS: Zoe Moffitt, Marthe Smith
    PHOTO ASSISTANTS: Jan Baxter, Mary Burns, Norma Mandt
PRODUCTION MANAGER: Jerry Higdon
    ASSOCIATE PRODUCTION MANAGER: Rick Litton
DESIGNER: Bob Cato

Special thanks to Senior Editor Morin Bishop for his generous production expertise, to Dick Burgheim and Hillie Pitzer for their support, and to Karin Grant and Mary Carroll Marden, PEOPLE Photo Department, and the staff of the Time Inc. Magazines Picture Collection for their cooperation.

COVER PHOTOGRAPH: Ron Galella

TO ORDER PEOPLE WEEKLY, write to:
PEOPLE WEEKLY
Subscription Service Department
P.O. Box 30603
Tampa, Florida 33630-0603

PRIVATE LIVES IS BASED ON THE EFFORTS OF THE EDITORIAL STAFF OF PEOPLE WEEKLY.

MANAGING EDITOR Landon Y. Jones Jr.
EDITOR, SPECIAL PROJECTS Richard A. Burgheim
ASSISTANT MANAGING EDITORS Ross Drake, John Saar, Hal Wingo
SENIOR EDITORS Lee Aitken, Mark V. Donovan, Cutler Durkee, Dick Friedman, Jack Friedman, Eric Levin, Ralph Novak, Joseph Poindexter, Richard Sanders, Susan Toepfer, Roger R. Wolmuth, Jacob Young
ART DIRECTOR John Shecut Jr.
PICTURE EDITOR Mary Carroll Marden
CHIEF OF REPORTERS Nancy Pierce Williamson
DEPUTY CHIEF OF CORRESPONDENTS Irene Kubota Neves
ASSOCIATE EDITORS Paula Chin, Daniel Chu, James S. Kunen, Kristin McMurran, Leah Rozen, Maria Wilhelm
SENIOR WRITERS Ron Arias, Steven Dougherty, Mary H.J. Farrell, Michelle Green, David Grogan, Ken Gross, Bill Hewitt, David Hiltbrand, Kim Hubbard, Bonnie Johnson, Michael J. Neill, Jeannie Park, William Plummer, J.D. Reed, Susan K. Reed, Marjorie Rosen, Susan Schindehette, Elizabeth Sporkin, Joyce Wadler
STAFF WRITERS Tim Allis, Peter Castro, Charles E. Cohen, Patricia Freeman, Eileen Garred, Tom Gliatto, Cynthia Sanz, Karen S. Schneider, Joyce Wansley
WRITER-REPORTERS Andrew Abrahams, Sue Carswell, Toby Kahn, J.D. Podolsky, Lisa Russell
REPORTERS Peggy Brawley (Deputy Chief), Rosemary Alexander, Veronica Burns, Maria Eftimiades, Ann Guerin, Mary S. Huzinec, Denise Lynch, Hugh McCarten, Sabrina McFarland, Gavin Moses, Khoi Nguyen, Gail Nussbaum, Vincent R. Peterson, Marge Runnion, Mary Shaughnessy, Ying Sita, Maria Speidel, Leslie Strauss, Robin Ward
PICTURE DEPARTMENT Beth Filler (Deputy Editor), Holly Holden, Maddy Miller (Associate Editors), Mary Fanette, Mary Ellen Lidon, Sarah Rozen (Assistant Editors), Betsy Young (Negative Reader), Karen E. Lipton, Eileen Sweet, Anne Weintraub, Blanche Williamson (Research), Stan J. Williams (Picture Desk), Alison Sawyer, Karin Grant (Photo Chief, L.A.), Jerene Jones (London), Francesca d'Andrea (Paris)
ART DEPARTMENT Hillie Pitzer (Associate Director, Special Projects), Angela Alleyne (Assistant Director), Mary M. Hauck (Designer), Tom Allison, Sal Argenziano, Allan Bintliff, Brien Foy, Joseph Randazzo, Ching-Yu Sun, Richard G. Williams, Thelis Brown
COPY DESK Sue Aitkin (Chief), David Greisen, Will Becker, Marcia Lawther (Deputies), Dolores Alexander, William Doares, Judith I. Fogarty, Ben Harte, Rose Kaplan, Patricia R. Kornberg, Alan Levine, Mary C. Radich, Muriel C. Rosenblum, Janet Scudder, Sheryl F. Stein (Copy Editors), Deborah Hausler, Jessica Foos Jones, Lillian Nici, Eric S. Page, Patricia Rommeney (Assistants)
PRODUCTION Betsy B. Castillo, Geri Flanagan, David Luke, Gloria Neuscheler, David J. Young (Managers), Guy Arseneau, Catherine Barron, Kalen Donaldson, Bernadette DeLuca, Patricia Fitzgerald, George Hill, Robin Kaplan, James M. Lello, Maria Teresa Martin, Anthony G. Moore, Kathleen Seery, Karen Silverman, Karen J. Waller, Anthony White, Paul Zelinski
EDITORIAL TECHNOLOGY Amy Zimmerman, Janie Greene
COPY PROCESSING Alan Anuskiewicz (Manager), Anthony M. Zarvos (Deputy), Michael G. Aponte, Soheila Asayesh, Donna Cheng, Denise M. Doran, Jayne Geissler, Charles J. Glasser Jr., Nelida Granado, Key Martin, Jennifer Paradis-Hagar, Barbara E. Scott, Ellee Shapiro, Larry Whiteford
EDITORIAL BUSINESS MANAGER Sarah Brody
ADMINISTRATION Susan Baldwin, Bernard Acquaye, Christina Basch, Marge Dodson, Angela Drexel, Nancy Eils, Joy Fordyce, Deirdre Gallagher, Diane Kelley, Mercedes R. Mitchell, Margaret Pienczykowski, Jean Reynolds, Pauline Shipman, Michael Tanner, Martha White, Maureen S. Fulton (Letters Manager)
NEWS BUREAU William Brzozowski, Charles Guardino
NATIONAL CORRESPONDENTS Lois Armstrong, Garry Clifford
TELEVISION CORRESPONDENT Alan Carter
DOMESTIC BUREAUS BOSTON, Dirk Mathison; CHICAGO, Giovanna Breu, Barbara Kleban Mills, Champ Clark; DETROIT, Julie Greenwalt; HOUSTON, Kent Demaret, Anne Maier; LOS ANGELES, Jack Kelley, Michael Alexander, Lorenzo Benet, Thomas Cunneff, Todd Gold, Kristina Johnson, Robin Micheli, Craig Tomashoff, Florence Nishida, Monica Rizzo; MIAMI, Meg Grant; NEW YORK, Victoria Balfour, David Hutchings; SAN FRANCISCO, Dirk Mathison; WASHINGTON, Jane Sims Podesta, Margie Bonnett Sellinger, Barbara Lieber
EUROPEAN BUREAUS. Fred Hauptfuhrer (Chief), Jonathan Cooper, Laura Sanderson Healy (London); Cathy Nolan (Paris)
SPECIAL CORRESPONDENTS BOSTON, S. Avery Brown; CHICAGO, Civia Tamarkin; CINCINNATI, Bill Robinson; CLEVELAND, Ken Myers; INDIANAPOLIS, Bill Shaw; LOS ANGELES, Doris Bacon, Eleanor Hoover, Mitchell Fink, Nancy Matsumoto, Vicki Sheff; MEMPHIS, NASHVILLE, Jane Sanderson; MIAMI, Linda Marx; MINNEAPOLIS, Margaret Nelson; MONACO, Joel Stratte-McClure; MUNICH, Franz Spelman; NEW YORK, Michael Small; ORLANDO, Sandra Hinson; PHILADELPHIA, Andrea Fine; PITTSBURGH, Jane Beckwith; ROANOKE, Lelia Albrecht; ROME, Logan Bentley; ST. LOUIS, John McGuire; SAN DIEGO, A.F. Gonzalez; SAN FRANCISCO, Dianna Waggoner; TEL AVIV, Mira Avrech; WASHINGTON, Katy Kelly, Linda Kramer
CONTRIBUTING PHOTOGRAPHERS Marianne Barcellona, Harry Benson, Ian Cook, Tony Costa, Mimi Cotter, Alfred Eisenstaedt, Stephen Ellison, Evelyn Floret, Henry Grossman, Kevin Horan, Steve Kagan, Christopher Little, Jim McHugh, Robin Platzer, Neal Preston, Co Rentmeester, Raeanne Rubenstein, Steve Schapiro, Mark Sennet, Peter Serling, Terry Smith, Barry Staver, Stanley Tretick, Dale Wittner, Taro Yamasaki
EDITORIAL SERVICES Christiana Walford (Director), Jennie Chien, Benjamin Lightman, Peter J. Christopoulos, Beth Bencini Zarcone

# CONTENTS

# INTRODUCTION

**I**n the last decade before the end of a century, thoughts turn from what was, to what is, to what will be. It's a natural time to take stock. We've created, here, a keepsake of noteworthy people of 1990—a record of triumph and tragedy, landmarks and sitzmarks, hijinks and low notes. We present them in all their nobility and folly, passion and perseverance.

These are the inside stories—provocative, enlightening, moving, scandalous, and occasionally appalling. For better or worse, we think these people and their stories worth preserving.

The Editors of PEOPLE

# 1990... In the Limelight

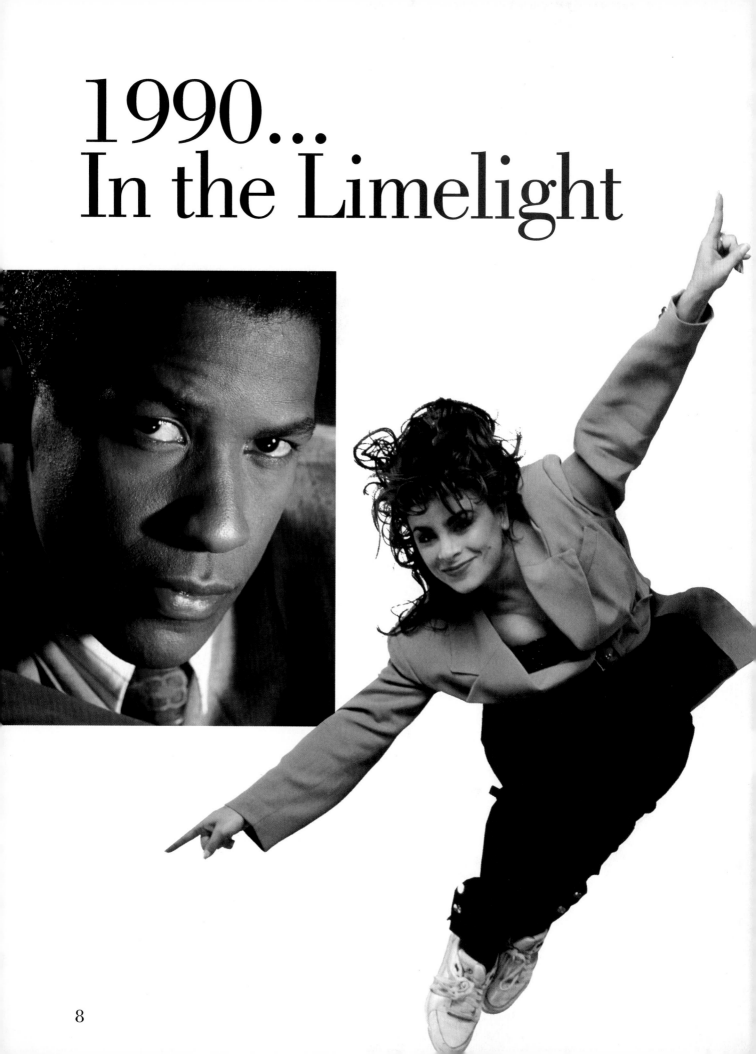

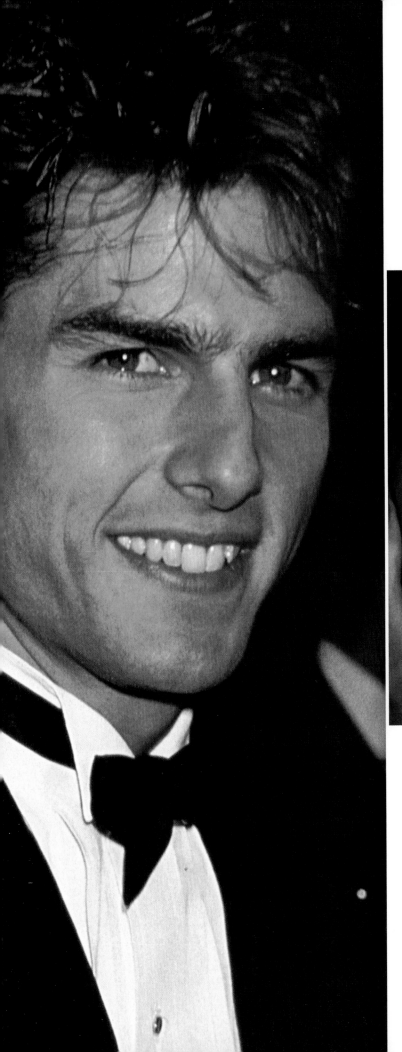

# IN THE LIMELIGHT

# MOVIES

**D**ANIEL DAY-LEWIS—Day-Lewis, who won an Oscar for portraying the indomitable Irish painter, poet and novelist Christy Brown, a cerebral palsey victim, in *My Left Foot*, has shown a versatility in his previous roles that invites comparisons with his countryman Alec Guinness. He played a London street tough in *My Beautiful Laundrette*, the effete Cecil Vyse in *Room with a View*, the sexy brain surgeon Tomas in *The Unbearable Lightness of Being* and the panicked British art appraiser Henderson Dores in *Stars and Bars*. (Not to mention a successful run as Hamlet with the Royal National Theatre in London.) The 33-year-old actor is the son of England's late poet laureate C. Day-Lewis and the actress Jill Balcon. His grandfather Sir Michael Balcon was production chief of Ealing Studios and discovered Alfred Hitchcock.

**J**ESSICA TANDY—Luminous acting legend Tandy won an Oscar for Best Actress for her performance as the acerbic Miss Daisy. The 81-year-old London-born actress, who made her professional stage debut when she was 16, probably remains best known as the original Blanche Du Bois in Tennessee Williams's *A Streetcar Named Desire*. Tandy has been married to actor Hume Cronyn for 48 years.

**D**ENZEL WASHINGTON—Winner of Best Supporting Actor for *Glory*, Washington admits that before he read the film's script he had been unaware of the important role that black soldiers played in the Civil War. "That's probably the thing that really made me decide to do the picture," he said.

This year, the 35-year-old actor dropped out of *Love Field*, Orion's interracial love story in which he was to have co-starred with Michelle Pfeiffer. He said the part wasn't developed as he had envisioned it. Rumor had it that after dropping out, Washington had a change of heart and asked for an 11th-hour meeting with the film's director, Jonathan Kaplan. A source close to Kaplan said the director chose not to meet with Washington and instead sent back word that his services were no longer required for the film. Kaplan himself denied the story; Washington's agent did not return calls. *Love Field* was filmed with Eriq LaSalle as Washington's replacement.

**T**OM CRUISE—Superstar Cruise can make a hit by just showing up. His blockbuster portrayals of red-blooded, all-American youths struggling for glory have made him one of Hollywood's most bankable names and reportedly upped his fee to nine million dollars per picture. Cruise, at 28, has a boyish but pulsating intensity. Each of his succeeding brushes with movie peril has chiseled another notch of experience into his clean-cut sensuality, so that he has become darker, handsomer and PEOPLE's choice for SEXIEST MAN ALIVE in 1990.

The Syracuse-born Thomas Cruise Mapother IV once toyed with the idea of taking a vow of celibacy and becoming a priest. Moving from town to town because of his parents' jobs (his father was an electrical engineer, his mother a teacher), Tom received a disjointed education, which was further impeded by his inherited dyslexia. His mother and three sisters, said Cruise, nurtured him through a mostly fatherless adolescence (his parents divorced when he was 11) and taught him sensitivity to women. At 14, he spent one relatively stable year at a Franciscan seminary in Cincinnati but then changed his mind about the priesthood. By the time he finished high school in Glen Ridge, New Jersey, he had discovered a new calling: acting.

Within months of moving to New York City, he landed a small part in the 1981 Brooke Shields vehicle *Endless Love*, impressing the film community enough to win a larger role that year as a fanatic military student in *Taps*. As a greaser in Francis Ford Coppola's 1983 film, *The Outsiders*, he displayed early signs of his feverish devotion to character preparation, having a cap from his tooth removed and skimping on showers for several weeks. By the end of that year, he was a box office draw in *Risky Business*, playing an enterprising young pimp-for-a-day.

Cruise is very focused, a trait which serves him well as he chases his hotdogging pursuits. Before filming 1986's *The Color of Money*, he spent seven weeks perfecting poolroom stunts. To portray Vietnam

10

Tandy

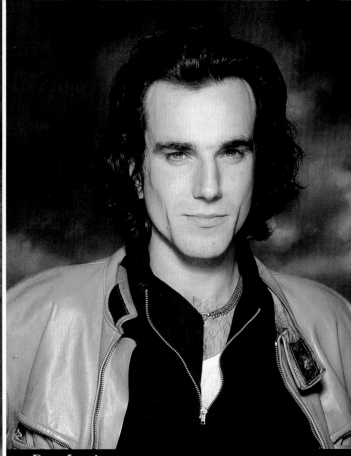

Day-Lewis

Washington

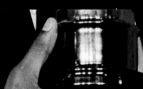

vet Ron Kovic in *Born on the Fourth of July*, he spent entire days in a wheelchair and agreed to ingest a serum that would paralyze him for two days—until the movie's insurers balked. The film won him an Oscar nomination for Best Actor.

Cruise separated from his wife of two-and-a-half years, actress Mimi Rogers, late in 1989. It was toward the end of filming *Days of Thunder*, said members of the crew, that Cruise hooked up with his Aussie co-star, Nicole Kidman. His divorce from Rogers became final in the fall and Cruise and 23-year-old Kidman were married on Christmas Eve.

---

MORGAN FREEMAN—Despite his loss of the Best Actor Award to Daniel Day-Lewis, nominee Morgan Freeman of *Driving Miss Daisy* said he was thrilled by the four Oscars—including Best Picture—the movie won. Freeman, 52, who once played "Easy Reader" on PBS's *Electric Company*, said he was "still floating six inches off the ground."

---

PAULA ABDUL—The Oscar show choreographer Abdul is Hollywood's hottest newcomer. Only two years ago, the diminutive Syrian-Brazilian-French-Canadian-Jewish-American was a respected, if strictly behind-the-scenes choreographer for the likes of Janet Jackson and George Michael. Thanks in part to the power of her saucy, sexy and sometimes salacious videos, the 27-year-old former L.A. Laker cheerleader is selling more records than Madonna. She has had four No. 1 singles, an album that went No. 1, and has won an Emmy for her choreography on the *Tracey Ullman Show*. Abdul has also won four MTV Awards, two American Music Awards and a Grammy and was nominated as Best Female Pop Vocalist.

---

SPIKE LEE—Director Lee, whose controversial film *Do the Right Thing* gained him the Chicago Film Critics award for best picture and best director, was displeased at not getting Oscar nominations for those same categories. "We are disappointed about the Academy, but you know, they're old," said Lee of the members of the Academy of Motion Picture Arts & Sciences. Lee, who noted he had not gotten around to seeing the other race relations film, *Driving Miss Daisy*, which attracted nine Academy Award nominations, went on to say, "I suppose Americans want to be nostalgic, remembering a time when black men knew their place. That saddened me."

The Academy may have slighted Lee, but that hasn't undercut the director's well-earned Hollywood authority. Lee keeps adding to his entourage—and his budget. He made 1986's *She's Gotta Have It* for $175,000. His fourth film, *Mo' Better Blues*, which opened in 1990, cost $10 million.

Spike's sister Joie Lee, 28, who has had a role in each of Lee's movies, co-starred in *Mo' Better Blues*, and his father, Bill, a jazz bassist and composer, was

back again to score the film. The family veterans were joined by Best Supporting Actor Denzel Washington and Charlie Murphy, brother of Eddie. Though Spike's feud with Eddie has been well chronicled, the director did not indicate that Charlie's presence represented a truce, but simply said he was the best person for the job.

The movie's plot spun off Washington as a trumpet player named Bleek Gilliam, torn between his love of music and his desire for two women: an aspiring jazz singer, played by newcomer Cynda Williams, and a Harlem schoolteacher, played by sister Joie. Spike cast himself as Giant, Washington's unsavory manager. While hyping the film, Lee criticized *Bird*, Clint Eastwood's 1988 homage to jazz legend Charlie Parker, for being a narrow treatment of a black artist by a white filmmaker. Asked about Lee's remarks, Eastwood said being white and doing a story about black people, or the reverse, had no bearing: "Mr. Lee is certainly welcome to do a story on Beethoven, and it might be brilliant."

---

TEENAGE MUTANT NINJA TURTLES
Having fallen into a slick of radioactive sewer slime, four turtles emerge as intelligent, humanlike, martial-arts experts with a taste for pizza....

The craze began in 1984 when the turtle brothers, Leonardo, Donatello, Michaelangelo and Raphael were hatched—and crawled to cult popularity—in the black-and-white comic books produced by former free-lance artist Peter Laird, now 36, and ex-short-order cook Kevin Eastman, 27. Four years later they invaded morning cartoons and the consciousness of America's preteen—and, most dramatically, pre-school—mainstream, shrieking, "Cowabunga!" (the Turtles' favorite war cry, stolen from Howdy Doody's Chief Thunderthud) and badgering, "Hey, Dude!" (their surfer-style greeting of choice).

The Turtle cartoon series was followed by Turtle videos, action figures, trading cards, computer games, frozen pizzas, cereal and yogurt—all of which could rack up as much as $600 million in retail sales in 1990.

Then came the movie, which grossed $25.4 million in its first weekend, making it the largest spring opening ever. Its reptilian heroes were real actors wrapped in elaborate neoprene costumes designed by Jim Henson's Creature Shop. Their facial expressions were controlled electronically by off-camera puppeteers.

The cartoon show now broadcasts in dozens of countries from Brazil to Australia. The Turtles will soon show up in Italy, Germany and Holland (to name just a few). When the Turtles made a July appearance at a Singapore airport, 30,000 children showed up yelling, "Yo, Dude!" Even Lee Kuan Yew, the country's Prime Minister—but more important, a devoted grandfather—is a reputed Turtle buff.

Why should a goofy tale of turtles trained in combat by a sage old rat have so completely seduced America's—and the world's—teen-and-under crowd?

_Freeman_

_Lee_

_Cruise and Rogers_

_Abdul_

Perhaps because unlike conventional superheroes, they are silly and behave essentially like children. The Ninja Turtles squabble with their siblings, live for pizza and understand life through TV.

Cowabunga!

KIM BASINGER—When she made *Batman*, Basinger was romantically paired, at least in the press, with 43-year-old producer Jon Peters and then with 32-year-old Prince, who supplied much of *Batman*'s music. Given the wisdom of hindsight, PEOPLE came to the conclusion that the latter relationship had less to do with romance and more to do with a calculated attempt on Basinger's part to learn everything she could from Prince about the recording process.

Now ensconced romantically with Alec Baldwin, her co-star in Disney's *The Marrying Man* (in which she plays a lounge singer), 36-year-old Basinger signed a recording contract with Hollywood-based Giant Records. Professionally, the word was that her singing of '40s torch ballads "blew away" Michelle Pfeiffer's singing in *The Fabulous Baker Boys* and Basinger was expected to enter the studio for her first album early in 1991. Don't look for Prince to make a guest appearance on it. Sources say His Purpleness and Kim don't speak anymore.

The romance between Basinger and Baldwin seemed to be moving ahead quite nicely. Baldwin, who is 32, is now living with Basinger at her San Fernando Valley home.

JULIA ROBERTS—Whether she's playing the fiery Portuguese waitress in 1988's *Mystic Pizza*, the gold-hearted hooker in this year's blockbuster *Pretty Woman* or a cerebral medical student in *Flatliners*,

22-year-old Julia Roberts has managed to make a once-in-an-era kind of splash. Her luminous on-screen presence now gets her one million dollars a picture, but her appeal seems to go beyond sheer box-office clout. Her rangy good looks—guileless gaze, and incandescent smile—have put her on two most-beautiful-woman-in-the-world lists and on too many magazine covers to count.

It does seem incredible that five years ago the only role Roberts had ever played was Elizabeth Dole in the Campbell High School annual mock-election campaign. Yet she waited only three days after collecting her diploma before she left her hometown of Smyrna, Georgia (population 32,246), to move to New York City, where she bunked in with actress sister Lisa, two years her senior. Older brother Eric, then 30, had already picked up an Oscar nomination for 1985's *Runaway Train*. He suggested her for the part of his sister on a low-budget drama he was set to film. Other parts followed. Her performance as the doomed Shelby in *Steel Magnolias* won both a Golden Globe award and an Oscar nomination—and it was just her third major exposure.

In Hollywood she has a reputation for getting affectionate with colleagues: She once lived in Venice, California, with her *Satisfaction* co-star Liam Neeson (the title character in *Darkman*) and was later engaged to Dylan McDermott, who played her *Magnolias* screen husband. But her friendship with 23-year-old Kiefer Sutherland, whom she met on the set of *Flatliners*, is the one that seems to have stuck. Since Sutherland filed for divorce from his wife of three years, Camelia Kath, 36, he and Roberts have been spotted steadily around Hollywood and various film locations. A "friendship ring" that was a gift from Sutherland has led to speculation that the two plan to marry.

## ACADEMY AWARDS

**Best Picture: DRIVING MISS DAISY**

**Best Director: OLIVER STONE for Born On The Fourth Of July**

**Best Actor: DANIEL DAY-LEWIS for My Left Foot**

**Best Actress: JESSICA TANDY for Driving Miss Daisy**

**Best Supporting Actor: DENZEL WASHINGTON for Glory**

**Best Supporting Actress: BRENDA FRICKER for My Left Foot**

**Best Original Score: ALAN MENKEN for The Little Mermaid**

**Best Original Song: ALAN MENKEN and HOWARD ASHMAN for Under The Sea**

**Best Costume Design: PHYLLIS DALTON for Henry V**

**Best Foreign Picture: CINEMA PARADISO**

*Teenage Mutant Ninja Turtles, with their leader Master Splinter*

*Roberts*

*Baldwin and Basinger*

# MUSIC

**B**ONNIE RAITT—Raitt capped her 1989 comeback by winning all four Grammys for which she was nominated. *Nick of Time*, produced by Don Was of Was (Not Was), was named Album of the Year over pre-award favorites Don Henley and the Traveling Wilburys. The album also earned Grammys for Raitt in the Female Rock Vocal and the Female Pop Vocal categories. Raitt and veteran bluesman John Lee Hooker shared Best Traditional Blues honors for their "I'm in the Mood" track on Hooker's *The Healer* album.

The daughter of Broadway musical star John Raitt, Bonnie made her acquaintance with folk music at a Quaker summer camp in upstate New York. Music remained a hobby through two-and-a-half years at Radcliffe, where she devoted most of her time to community organizing and majoring in African studies. Gradually, however, she became absorbed in the Cambridge, Massachusetts, folk music scene and developed a club following. She dropped out of school, and aided by what she calls "the gimmick of being a girl blues guitar player," she became "your all-around opening act. I wasn't too ugly, I wasn't too pretty, I wasn't too threatening, I wasn't too bad."

This was the first time in Raitt's 20-year career that she had earned any major Grammy nominations, let alone won. The last decade was difficult for 40-year-old Raitt, who fought drug and alcohol abuse and was dropped from her longtime label before being signed by Capitol. *Nick of Time* is her tenth album.

---

## JOHN LEE HOOKER—"The blues is the only music," Hooker said with a low growl. "Everything else they's doing—rock and roll, pop—it all comes from there. Somethin' 'bout a woman. Somethin' 'bout a man. Somethin' 'bout a man and a woman. That's the blues. I don't try to figure it out too much though. Just is."

Hooker is something of an elemental force himself. At 71, he has become the grand old man of a music tradition he inherited growing up in the Mississippi Delta town of Clarksdale. Now enjoying an old-age roll, he won his first-ever Grammy this year for a duet with Bonnie Raitt, one of several blues disciples who appeared on *The Healer*, Hooker's first LP in a decade. "John Lee has maintained his swampiness after all these years," Raitt said. "He's never lost his primal roots. He's remained as foreboding sounding and looking as you'd expect from an old bluesman."

"I don't play a lot of fancy guitar," Hooker said by way of self-analysis. "I just got this heavy, good rhythm, you know. I play a heck of a funky beat. What I do is soulful, it's the feeling."

It's a feeling he discovered as a boy growing up in the Delta flatlands, a region that in the 1920s was rich not just with cotton but with gritty, itinerant bluesmen. Their music found little acceptance with his father, William Hooker, a Baptist minister. "You know how those preachers are," said John Lee. "They think it's the devil's music." But Hooker, the fourth of 11 children, gained a formidable ally at age 12 when his sharecropper parents split and his mother, Minnie, married Will Moore, an amateur blues singer and guitar player who performed at local fish fries. "My style today is what he taught me," Hooker said gratefully. "If it wasn't for him, I would have been just a regular unknown person forever."

At 14, Hooker joined the Army. Stationed in Detroit, he was booted out after just three months when the Army learned his real age. Faced with the hard labor of sharecropping at home, Hooker headed back north, in search of stardom.

After drifting through Memphis and Cincinnati, where he made a name for himself as a gospel singer, he landed back in Detroit in 1943. Working as a janitor in a Chrysler plant by day, he played to black audiences in local bars at night. He was still sweeping up at Chrysler when he was discovered by the owners of the Modern Records label in 1948. That year he released his first single, "Boogie Chillen," an immediate hit that brought him to the attention of white audiences for the first time. When his "I'm in the Mood" sold an astonishing one million copies in 1951, he hung up his broom for good.

16

John Lee Hooker

Bonnie Raitt

*Crosby and Dylan*  *Neville and Ronstadt*

Hooker, who eventually recorded more than 100 albums, was a legend by the early 1960s when a young Bob Dylan and the then fledgling Rolling Stones opened his concerts. As happened so often to the blues performers who were rock's progenitors, Hooker never enjoyed the enormous financial rewards reaped by his young imitators. "I was happy just to be out there playing," he said philosophically.

And although he never got rich, Hooker didn't go broke either. "I've always kept my head above water," he said. "I'm very conservative with money. I learned it ain't what you make, it's what you save."

Now, with his reputation secure, he forsaw less roadwork and more time in his La-Z-Boy. "I'm gonna retire real soon," he said, insisting he had recorded for the last time. Johnny Winter, a fan since childhood, said, "When John Lee goes, it's going to be the end of an era." But Hooker doesn't see it that way. "As long as there's people on this planet," he said, his eye glinting with the wisdom of years, "somebody's gonna be alone and have the blues."

---

## AARON NEVILLE/LINDA RONSTADT
It was an unlikely pairing: Aaron Neville, vocalist for the gifted siblings who perform their distinctive "voodoo gumbo" version of New Orleans rhythm and blues as the Neville Brothers, and Linda Ronstadt, the smooth-voiced queen of pop-rock, who sings just about anything but. The two met years ago during a New Orleans concert; Aaron Neville dedicated a song to Ronstadt, then invited her up onstage for an impromptu doo-wop medley. Their voices clicked, and the rest is history. "Don't Know Much" is a cut from Ronstadt's, *Cry Like a Rainstorm—Howl Like the Wind* album. The song won a Grammy for Best Pop Vocal in 1990.

---

## THE ROY ORBISON BENEFIT—Three
nights after Bonnie Raitt won her four Grammys last February, she turned up at Los Angeles's Universal Amphitheatre for an all-star tribute to the late Roy Orbison. "There will never be another singer like Roy," said Raitt, who performed solo and also fronted for the Femme Fatales, a one-night-only girl group that featured k.d. lang, Emmylou Harris and others.

The show, a benefit for the homeless, drew an odd-lot assortment of performers, including Dwight Yoakam, B.B. King, Patrick Swayze, former Byrds Roger McGuinn, Chris Hillman and David Crosby, and Bob Dylan. Most sang Orbison hits.

"Roy and I often discussed why so many people were homeless," said his widow, Barbara, 38, who wanted to link the tribute to a worthy cause. "He identified strongly with them."

---

## YOUNG M.C.—In the swaggering, in-Yo!-face
world of rap music, Marvin "Young M.C." Young is a true eccentric. The 22-year-old rhymer is soft-spoken, polite and even frugal. The singer shuns gold chains, partly because he's chary of the possibility of helping the South African economy, and partly because as a University of Southern California economics graduate (1988) he considers the metal a poor investment.

Young doesn't drink or smoke or even party much. About the only thing that he has in common with his precocious peers is a flair for language and a love of the big beat. He has already proved, by co-authoring Tone-Loc's monster rap hit "Wild Thing," that the genre can take a joke. With a Grammy for his own hit single "Bust a Move" and a platinum LP, *Stone Cold Rhymin'*, Young is rap's next great hope to broaden the music's commercial appeal.

Born in London to Jamaican parents who moved to New York City in 1970 (his father is a telephone company executive, his mother a nurse), Young grew up in Hollis, Queens, home of rap stars Run-D.M.C. and L.L. Cool J. Michael Ross, co-owner of Delicious Vinyl Records, signed Young after hearing him rap over the phone in 1987.

18

*Young M.C.*

"My mother said, 'You can do this record thing as long as you're self-sufficient,'" explained the rapper. "She doesn't want me living with her when I'm 35."

NEW KIDS ON THE BLOCK—There's Joe McIntyre, 17, Jordan Knight, 20, brother Jonathan Knight, 21, Donnie Wahlberg, 20, and Danny Wood, 21—together they're breaking hearts and banking zillions. Performing for some two million screamers in a summer-long, 63-date tour, the vocal group New Kids on the Block is riding the crest of the most frenzied pop-music phenomenon since Beatlemania.

Okay, the Beatles did write their own songs, play their own instruments and spearhead a cultural revolution. But give the Kids credit: Nobody beats them when it comes to marketing. Dell Furano, the Kids' merchandising wiz, reckons that the vast New Kids product line, spewing everything from posters to sleeping bags, would gross $400 million this year alone. Add revenues from their best-selling authorized bio, three million-selling long-form videos, plus concert-ticket and record sales, and figure these Kids won't be wanting for lunch money.

Last summer three albums of their Motown-derived, funk-lite music ranked in Billboard's list of best-selling records. The LP *Step by Step* had already sold more than three million copies two months after its release. *Hangin' Tough*, the group's breakthrough 1988 LP, has sold eight million.

The mastermind of everything having to do with the New Kids on the Block is the group's creator, composer and songwriter, Maurice Starr, né Larry Johnson. A Floridian who moved north and found his own career stalled—he and brother Michael never made it as the Johnson Brothers—Starr, 36, was the creative force behind New Edition, a black vocal group from Boston that had a string of R&B hits in the mid-'80s. After losing the group in a bitter contract dispute, Starr, who is black, set out to create "a white New Edition."

In the summer of 1984, Starr sent Boston talent agent Mary Alford to scour the city's racially mixed inner-city neighborhoods for white playground break dancers, rappers and singers. In Dorchester she discovered Donnie Wahlberg, then 14, one of nine children of a divorced working mom and a bus driver. "Mary heard about me from some other kids, who kept telling her, 'You got to meet Donnie,'" said Wahlberg, whose sense of responsibility almost cost him the opportunity of his life. "She came to my house, but I couldn't talk because my father said I had to mow the lawn. But she came back, and two hours later I was at Maurice Starr's. When I told him I needed some music, he started clapping his hands. I did one of my best spontaneous raps ever. Then here's Maurice Starr, this famous guy, telling me, Don Wahlberg, a goof-off kid on food stamps, that I was one of the best rappers he ever heard. I mean, it was like, 'Are you serious?'"

Wahlberg recruited a few former classmates from William M. Trotter Elementary, in predominantly black Roxbury, where he, Wood and the Knights were bused to school. Two original members, Wahlberg's little brother Mark and a friend named Jamie Kelly, dropped out. Alford's search for "a young, Michael Jackson-type kid led to Joe McIntyre, then a 12-year-old community theater veteran.

It took a bumpy year as Nynuk, Starr's original name for the group, for the boys to gel. America didn't see the Kidiacs until the summer of 1988, when the group's sweet, R&B flavored single, "Please Don't Go Girl," helped get them a national tour, opening for dream teen Tiffany.

Critics dismiss them as singing puppets manipulated by Svengali Starr. "People get us wrong," Jordan said, in the thick, wrong-side-of-the-harbor Boston accent all Kids share. "They think we're white kids from white neighborhoods who liked rock and roll and then here comes some black guy from the ghetto and we're like, 'Gee, how do you sing like Luther Vandross? Teach me how to dance like you black guys.' It wasn't like that. We're city kids. I've been break dancing and listening to rap since I was a little kid."

*New Kids on the Block*

19

*Bowie and Jagger*

"We love our fans," said Donnie. "Smart, feisty little white girls from the suburbs who stand up for us when critics put us down."

DAVID BOWIE—Ticket sales for the American leg of David Bowie's Sound + Vision tour were not going well. Despite the 43-year-old rocker's uncanny ability to reinvent himself in any number of stage personas, he couldn't seem to invent enough ticket buyers to make this section of the tour a financial success. Generally negative reviews for Sound + Vision in Europe and the fact that *ChangesBowie*, his current album, was a best-of collection rather than a new studio effort, might have compounded the problem. But all that changed. According to a source close to the rock star, sales picked up "considerably" after Bowie's ex-wife, Angela, 40, said on Joan Rivers's syndicated talk show that she had once walked in on Bowie and Mick Jagger in bed together. Both men strongly denied her story.

THE KNEBWORTH BENEFIT—The crowd was humongous, friendly and not too environmentally minded. As a parade of fortysomething rock legends—including Paul McCartney, Elton John and Eric Clapton—took their turns during a 12-hour concert at Knebworth House, an estate north of London, 120,000 fervid fans showed their enthusiasm by clapping, performing stadium waves and, in an unusual tribute, hurling thousands of plastic plates and bottles into the air.

Clearly, this wasn't Earth Day. But the much-hyped, $52-a-ticket festival did benefit worthy causes, notably Britain's Nordoff-Robbins Music Therapy Center, which helps autistic and mentally handicapped children. Emcees and guests included Timothy Dalton, Prince Albert of Monaco, MTV's Martha ("I begged all the executives to introduce me to Jimmy Page") Quinn and Rob Lowe. The actor explained that he caught the celebrity-cause bug several years ago when he pitched in at Farm Aid II. "It was great fun,"

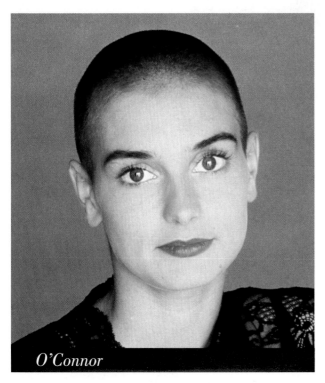

*O'Connor*

said Lowe, "so I called up and said, 'If you need me, I'm in Europe.'" Keep that name in mind, Helmut Kohl. *Rob Lowe.*

Best of show? The consensus: McCartney.

---

SINÉAD O'CONNOR—Close-cropped Sinéad O'Connor, the feisty Irish pop singer who refused to appear on NBC's *Saturday Night Live* with comedian Andrew Dice Clay on the grounds that his act was degrading to women, also refused to permit "The Star-Spangled Banner" to be played before a concert on her U.S. tour.

O'Connor informed personnel at the Garden State Arts Center in New Jersey that she would not perform if a national anthem—*any* national anthem, including her own—was played. (In an attempt to appease her, the Garden State Arts Center, which has a 23-year tradition of playing "The Star-Spangled Banner"

before shows, offered to play the Irish national anthem as well.) In the interest of crowd control and safety at the nearly sold-out concert, O'Connor's request was accommodated, and the show went on.

In a statement issued later, O'Connor clarified her position: "This was not meant as a snub of Americans. I sincerely harbor no disrespect for America or Americans, but I have a policy of not having any national anthems played before my concerts in any country, not even my own, because they have nothing to do with music in general. I am concerned, though, because today we're seeing other artists arrested at their concerts, some threatened with having their albums taken off the shelves or not even released at all. There is a disturbing trend toward censorship of music and art in this country, and people should be alarmed over that far more than my actions...."

O'Connor recently left her husband, drummer John Reynolds, 20, with whom she has a three-year-old son, Jake, for Hugh Harris, 25, the British rock singer who served as her opening act during the recent concert tour of America.

O'Connor, who is 23, grew up in Ireland and had been living in London.

---

THE RAINFOREST BENEFIT—Sting's Beverly Hills fund-raiser for the Rainforest Foundation and the Environmental Media Association brought in donations totaling more than one million dollars from the 900 stars—including Goldie Hawn, Chevy Chase, Kevin Costner and Tom Selleck—and industry bigwigs who attended. Underwritten by department store heir Ted Field and his wife, Susie, the bash re-created a rain forest, complete with flora and humidity, in a 12,000-square-foot tent pitched behind the Fields' enormous neo-Florentine estate. Dinner was a festive Brazilian feast of chicken, rice with shrimp and scallops, and fried bananas.

Emcee Billy Crystal announced that "Art Buchwald couldn't be here tonight, but you should all know that this was his idea." The high point of the

*Sting with Brazilian rainforest friend*

*Hammer*

evening was the entertainment. Backed by Herbie Hancock on keyboards and Branford Marsalis on sax, Sting invited "the greatest garage band ever"—Bruce Springsteen, Bruce Hornsby, Don Henley and Paul Simon—onstage for a one-hour hoot.

## M.C. HAMMER

M.C. HAMMER—It would take a trip to the sun to get any hotter than 27-year-old rapper M.C. Hammer is right now. His second album, *Please Hammer Don't Hurt 'Em*, has sold more than four million copies and is only the third rap LP in history to land at the top of the pop charts. It also headed the R&B charts for three months. The album's second single, "U Can't Touch This," entered the charts higher than any single since "We Are the World."

Hammer, whose real name is Stanley Kirk Burrell, dismisses rap's usual minimalism in favor of extravagant live shows that feature familiar melodic hooks, 32 performers, cutting-edge costumes and some of the flashiest footwork being done today.

Offstage, M.C. is all business and the business is Bust It Productions, the music factory that Hammer started in 1987. At its studio headquarters in Fremont, California, 30 miles from his Oakland home, Hammer grooms and produces 10 groups.

Hammer was raised in Oakland, one of eight children born to a secretary and the manager of a legalized gambling club who divorced when M.C. was five. His nickname came when Oakland A's owner Charley Finley saw him dancing in the parking lot of the Oakland Coliseum and hired the 11-year-old as a batboy and gofer. Named by the players after "Hammerin'" Hank Aaron, he spent seven years traveling the country with the team during school breaks (the M.C., rapese for master of ceremonies, came later).

A failed pro tryout with the San Francisco Giants and financial troubles that cut short his college career led him to join the Navy. Back home after a two-year tour, Hammer borrowed money from Oakland A's outfielders Mike Davis and Dwayne Murphy to form Bust It. He was neither a schooled singer nor could he play an instrument, but his first L.P. *Let's Get It Started*, spawned three Top 10 singles, and his one-man company grew to nearly 100 people. Some employees have been hanging with Hammer since grade school, others are "people I know who are fresh out of prison, and I say that proudly. I want an established business that can employ people from my community, where they can come and get a fair shot."

His compassion doesn't extend to competitors, however. "Rappers are like boxers—everyone's a rival," he said. "They're the most egocentric people in the music business." But Hammer knows who he is. "I'm the man," he said. "*The* man. There isn't one of them who sells as many records as I have, who makes as much money as I do, or who has a future that is going to be bigger."

## GRAMMY AWARDS

**Best Album of the Year: NICK OF TIME, Bonnie Raitt**

**Best Female Rock Vocalist: BONNIE RAITT, for the album Nick of Time**

**Best Female Pop Vocalist: BONNIE RAITT**

**Best Traditional Blues Song: "I'M IN THE MOOD," Bonnie Raitt and John Lee Hooker**

**Best Song of the Year: "WIND BENEATH MY WINGS"**

**Best Male Rock Vocalist: DON HENLEY, for the album The End of Innocence**

**Best Male Pop Vocalist: MICHAEL BOLTON, "How Am I Supposed to Live Without You"**

**Best Rock Vocal, Duo or Group: TRAVELING WILBURYS VOLUME ONE**

**Best Pop Vocal: "DON'T KNOW MUCH," Linda Ronstadt and Aaron Neville**

**Best New Artist: MILLI VANILLI***

**Best Rap Music: YOUNG MC, "Bust a Move"**

**Best Music Video, Long Form: "RHYTHM NATION," Janet Jackson**

**Best Music Video, Short Form: "LEAVE ME ALONE," Michael Jackson**

*Since rescinded. See Outrageous, p. 98

THE JUDDS—On October 19, country music's the Judds—mother Naomi, 44, and daughter Wynonna, 26—called a Nashville press conference to announce that they would be ending their seven-year career together at the conclusion of their 1991 concert tour. For many of their fans, the news was as startling as it was dismaying. Just 11 days earlier the Judds had walked away with their sixth consecutive duo-of-the-year award on the nationally televised Country Music Association Awards show, and their eighth album, *Love Can Build a Bridge*, had soared to No. 1 on the country charts. But despite her apparent vitality during dozens of 1990 concert appearances, Naomi was battling an insidious illness. She told reporters her health was forcing her to call it quits, leaving Wynonna to go it alone.

Naomi's ailment, finally diagnosed in March as chronic active hepatitis, is a severe liver ailment that affects 75,000 Americans a year. Though its symptoms may vary, and the disease can be treated with anti-viral and anti-inflammatory drugs and in some cases, as a last resort, a transplant, some patients fail to survive.

For Naomi, who is fighting the disease with characteristic faith and a powerful will, retirement is a poignant end to a magical career. The daughter of an Ashland, Kentucky, gas station owner, Diana Ellen Judd married her high school sweetheart at 17 and gave birth four months later—the week of her high school graduation—to daughter Christina Claire Ciminella. In 1968, the family moved to Los Angeles, but the marriage ended in divorce after eight years and the birth of a second daughter, Ashley, now 22. The young mother took jobs as a secretary and advertising model in Los Angeles before returning to Morrill, Kentucky, in 1976, to enter nursing school. Battling bill collectors and struggling to raise her two girls alone, the longtime amateur singer made a kitchen-table demo tape with Christina, then talked the father of a hospital patient into arranging an RCA audition. Soon after, the Judds—renaming themselves Naomi and Wynonna—were born.

Propelled by Wynonna's soulful lead vocals and Naomi's sweet-as–Moon Pie harmonies, their first single, in 1983, broke into country music's Top 20, and their second, "Mama, He's Crazy," went to No. 1. Fourteen more hit singles followed, along with four platinum albums and four Grammys.

Naomi managed to achieve personal happiness as well with her second marriage, to Larry Strickland, 44. According to Naomi, Strickland is her "own personal, custom-designed-for–Naomi Judd Prince Charming." Strickland, who sang with the J.D. Stamps Quartet when they met, is now a farmer, working on their place near Franklin, Kentucky. Naomi and Larry are devoutly religious members of Christ Church Pentecostal, where they were married. It is their combined faith—and the strong will of this remarkable woman—that is seeing them through the present crisis.

"I'm a child of God, and it tells you in the Bible all you have to do is ask and you shall receive," said Naomi. At one point during her illness she called together Larry, Wynonna, Wynonna's fiancé, Tony King, and the elders of Christ Church Pentecostal. "We met that night at the church. We did some rockin' and rollin' at that prayer healing, and I totally surrendered to God.... I believe that you can reverse illnesses by putting yourself in the Lord's hands. Miracles do happen, and I'm looking for one. I believe in it."

At last word, Naomi Judd seemed to be right.

KATHY MATTEA—Whenever country singer Kathy Mattea performed her hit "Where've You Been"—which tells the story of an aged, ailing married couple who are reunited in a hospital room—it caused considerable emotion. Early on she had considered it an unlikely hit. "I didn't know how it would play on the radio," she said. "When you're driving to work in the morning, do you want to hear about your dying grandparents and people in the hospital?"

A sentimental army of record buyers answered yes. "Where've You Been" became this year's country weeper, turning her *Willow in the Wind* LP to gold. Thanks to its success, the 31-year-old West Virginian won the Country Music Association Award for Best Female Vocalist and for Best Single. Her husband, Jon Vezner, who co-wrote the tune with Nashville's Don Henry, waltzed off with a Song of the Year trophy as well.

Vezner, 39, conceived the song after an incident involving his own grandparents several years ago. Both were in their 90s; his grandfather had had a brain seizure, and his grandmother seemed to be failing fast with problems of her own. "My grandmother didn't acknowledge anybody," said Vezner. "I found my grandfather hadn't seen her since they arrived at the hospital, so I loaded him into a wheelchair and took him to her room. Her eyes followed him as he picked up her hand, stroked her hair, and as if nothing had happened, she asked, 'Where've you been?'"

Although "Where've You Been" gave Mattea more visibility than any earlier song, she had hits before—six No. 1 singles, including "Goin' Gone," released in 1987, and the 1988 truckers' anthem, "Eighteen Wheels and a Dozen Roses." But her success came slowly. The only daughter among three children born to a chemical-plant worker and his homemaker wife, she grew up in Cross Lanes, West Virginia, listening to folk, rock, church music and "whatever was around." At West Virginia University, she studied engineering and chemistry but began singing in a bluegrass band at night. "Naive and 19," she quit college, tied a mattress to her car, hung out a sign that said NASHVILLE OR BUST and gave herself five years to cut her first record.

While she worked to win a recording contract, Mattea paid the bills by waiting on tables at a Nashville restaurant and by leading tours through the Country Music Hall of Fame & Museum. She lived above a music publisher, where Jon Vezner worked as a staff writer. One day she discovered that

The Judds

her car wouldn't start, and Vezner came by with jumper cables and lent a hand. On their first date, Mattea flatly announced she was not interested in a relationship. They were married in 1988 on Valentine's Day.

With a greatest-hits album in the stores and another single, a duet with Tim O'Brien titled "Battle Hymn of Love," doing well, Mattea seems to have made her name. Even so, come suppertime she often wears an apron around her kitchen emblazoned with the words CAPITANA POTATO. It's a joke, she said, from the time a friend came to pick up a backstage pass Mattea had left, only to be told there was no Captain Potato performing that night. "You know what they say about this business," she said. "You have to have the soul of a poet and the skin of a rhinoceros."

*Mattea*

GEORGE STRAIT—The Country Music Association's Entertainer of the Year, Strait is something of a throwback. With his blend of lilting guitar licks, keening fiddles and taut, lonesome cowboy vocals, Strait, a 37-year-old, fourth-generation Texan, would have fit right in with some of the old-time musicians he admires most, like Hank Williams and Bob Wills.

CLINT BLACK—Newcomer Black, the goodlooking 28-year-old Texan whose first album, *Killin' Time* was No. 1 on the Billboard country best-seller list for 31 weeks, won Best Male Vocalist at the Country Music Association Awards. Black, who writes or co-writes his material, said, "We've got so much to celebrate, we'd still do it even if I didn't bring home an award." He toasted his good year by flying his entire family up from Houston. Not that Black *wasn't* pleased to be honored. "This is a dream come true," he said, "and it's nothing like you could imagine."

GARTH BROOKS—On his first trip to Nashville, singer-songwriter Garth Brooks "pulled in expecting to see my name on every water tower in the place." It wasn't. Then 24, Brooks may have been the pride of Stillwater, Oklahoma, but he soon learned he was nothing in Nashville, where wannabe country stars tend to outnumber the parking meters.

Four years later, Brooks is hot. He returned to Nashville in 1988 and within 10 months had signed with Capitol Records for his first LP. That debut album, *Garth Brooks*, launched four No. 1 country singles, sold more than a million copies and raised Brooks from honky-tonker to concert headliner almost overnight. He landed five nominations from the Country Music Association, winning the Horizon Award for most promising newcomer and the award for best video.

Onstage, Brooks's show mixes soft laments and raucous cowboy rock, but on record it was that heart-tug quality that infused his first No. 1 single, "If Tomorrow Never Comes," co-written with Nashville veteran Kent Blazy.

Brooks, raised in Yukon, Oklahoma, grew up the youngest of six children fathered by an oil-company engineer. His mother, Colleen, was a 1950s country singer who recorded briefly and performed on TV with Red Foley's Ozark Jubilee. After high school Brooks headed for Oklahoma State University on a track scholarship, and while he studied for a degree in advertising by day, he supported himself playing pickup gigs and doing odd jobs. During a stint as a bouncer in a Stillwater club, Brooks was called to help a young woman who had stuck her fist through a plywood wall in a women's-room scuffle. Brooks helped free her hand.

The young woman, Sandy Mahr, turned out to be a fellow university student, and she and Brooks began dating. Their romance, interrupted only briefly by his first ill-fated trip to Nashville, resumed soon after, and in 1987 they married. "Sandy's a great woman who's every bit a lady," said Brooks. "But she don't take nothin' off nobody— especially me. I owe everything to God and her."

"Everything" in Brooks's case, includes performing 160 concerts a year, songwriting and "getting to do what I love and getting paid damn good for it."

*Strait*

*Black*

# COUNTRY MUSIC ASSOCIATION AWARDS

**Entertainer Of The Year: GEORGE STRAIT**

**Best Male Vocalist: CLINT BLACK**

**Best Female Vocalist: KATHY MATTEA**

**Horizon Award: GARTH BROOKS**

**Best Duo: THE JUDDS**

**Best Album: PICKIN' ON NASHVILLE, Kentucky Headhunters**

**Best Single:"WHEN I CALL YOUR NAME," Vince Gill**

**Best Song: "WHERE'VE YOU BEEN," John Vezner and Don Henry**

**Best Group: KENTUCKY HEADHUNTERS**

**Best Vocal Event: KEITH WHITLEY and LORRIE MORGAN**

**Best Musician: JOHNNY GIMBLE**

**Best Video: "THE DANCE," Garth Brooks**

# TELEVISION

MATT GROENING

**J**IMMY SMITS—He played a rebel in the film *Old Gringo* and a tough chief of surgery in *Vital Signs*, but it was for his television portrayal of attorney Victor Sifuentes in the Emmy-winning drama *L.A. Law* that Smits, 35, made his name. The New York City-born actor, whose exotic good looks come from a Puerto Rican mother and a Surinamese father, won an Emmy for best supporting actor in a drama series.

THE SIMPSONS—The five Emmys won by Fox's *The Simpsons* were all craft awards given out the day before Fox's nationally televised Emmy broadcast. The Simpson family (including Bart, above) took to the podium—thanks to a production technique similar to the one used in the making of *Who Framed Roger Rabbit?*— on *the* night to present the Emmy for Best Actor in a Comedy Series.

KEENEN IVORY WAYANS—The Fox network's hit comedy show *In Living Color* is a family affair. The mild-mannered 32-year-old executive producer, head writer and star, Keenen Ivory Wayans, is aided and abetted by an eight-member cast that includes his brothers Dwayne, 33, Damon, 29, Shawn, 19, and his sister Kim, in her 20s. (According to Damon, just being one of the 10 Wayans kids doesn't

Smits

necessarily guarantee a spot on the show. "The ones in the family who are not comedically talented know it, and if they don't, Keenen and I will tell them," Damon says laughingly. After the premiere of the mostly black, totally irreverent ensemble show, critics tripped over their adjectives with praise, evoking comparisons with *Saturday Night Live*. Overnight—yes, literally overnight—Keenen became one of Hollywood's most bankable young stars, black or white.

*In Living Color*'s half-hour episodes crackle with parodies of prominent black figures like beleaguered Washington, D.C., Mayor Marion Barry, Arsenio Hall and Mike Tyson, uncannily rendered by a (cosmetically) gap-toothed, mousy-voiced Keenen. Hot dance numbers by Rosie Perez, who choreographed *Do the Right Thing*, enhance the ethnic sizzle.

Many of the show's original characters, like the two likable hoods who peddle stolen goods on "The Homeboy Shopping Network," come straight out of Wayans's childhood playacting in Manhattan's Fulton housing projects.

At 22, Wayans lent an ear to the call of comedy and quit engineering school to work New York City's Improv comedy club. When he moved to Los Angeles later that year, he found that being a poor unknown was a relatively minor obstacle compared with being black. Frustrated with the narrow roles available to blacks onscreen and off, Wayans and Robert Townsend, a friend from the Improv, set out on their own to make *Hollywood Shuffle*, a stinging parody of Hollywood's stereotyping, that opened in 1986. Later that same year, Wayans co-wrote and co-produced the concert film *Eddie Murphy Raw*. But it was 1989's *I'm Gonna Git You Sucka*, a fresh attack on Hollywood's ethnic tunnel vision, that attracted the notice of Fox TV brass. "I really wasn't interested in television," said Wayans. "But they said the magic words, 'You can do anything you want.'"

CANDICE BERGEN—According to Bergen, who won an Emmy for Best Actress in a Comedy Series for playing ace TV journalist Murphy Brown in the Emmy-winning sitcom of the same name, she has received advice from several leading newsmen on possible plots. "Mike Wallace said it would be good to have a journalist go to jail," said Bergen, and CBS anchorman Dan Rather "suggested a show on dieting and hair color." The 44-year-old actress is married to French director Louis Malle.

TED DANSON—The 42-year-old libidinous barkeep of *Cheers* has traversed the money-fame minefield of the '80s with all his passions and priorities intact. On Christmas Eve, 1979, his wife, Casey, suffered a paralyzing stroke during the birth of their first child. Despite a career-igniting performance in *The Onion Field*, Danson left acting for six months to nurse her back to health. His social conscience also runs deep. He and Casey, 52,

*Wayans as Arsenio Hall*

30

*Bergen*

*Danson and Casey*

*Williams, Goldberg and Crystal*

Lynch

Midler as Mother Earth

founded the American Oceans Campaign in 1987 to foster a responsible coastal resources policy. Danson's reverence for nature dates to a Flagstaff, Arizona, childhood among the Hopi Indians. His father, an archaeologist, taught him that the past must be preserved as a legacy. Danson brings a refreshing tolerance to a central quandary of the '90s: how to reconcile domestic values with the pursuit of careers and causes.

COMIC RELIEF—"It's a shame we have to do this," said Robert Klein after the end of HBO's fourth *Comic Relief*, which raised $7.5 million for America's homeless. "It's sad to think that this is necessary so that someone can *eat*."

The four-and-a-half-hour show, live from Radio City Music Hall, boasted co-hosts Whoopi Goldberg, Billy Crystal and Robin Williams and a lineup of more than 40 comics, including Elayne Boosler, Richard Lewis, Bob Goldthwait and Steven Wright. Audrey Meadows basked in the nostalgic glow of a reunion with fellow Honeymooners Joyce Randolph and Art Carney but lamented the absence of the late Jackie Gleason.

DAVID LYNCH—Despite 14 nominations, producer-director David Lynch's quirky series *Twin Peaks* failed to win any of the year's top Emmys. The only two *Twin Peaks* got were for costume

design and for editing. Lynch was philosophical about it. "It wasn't just that we lost," he said, "but that we lost so spectacularly. As the evening wore on, I began thinking of the event as a sort of Theater of the Absurd. I couldn't get upset about not winning, because the concept of absurdity is something I'm attracted to."

No argument. Since his first feature-length film, *Eraserhead*—a nearly silent black-and-white tragicomedy about a hapless father trapped in a room with his wailing, mutant newborn—Lynch has been serving up worlds in which the bizarre lurks just below the surface of the mundane. *Blue Velvet*, voted 1986's best film by the National Society of Film Critics, was a surrealistic murder mystery that was set in motion with the arresting sight of a severed ear in a field. Lynch's disquieting, dreamlike style was less pronounced in *The Elephant Man*, which earned eight Oscar nominations, and *Dune*, his only directorial flop. *Wild at Heart*, which opened in August starring Laura Dern and Nicolas Cage, may be Lynch's weirdest offering yet. A "violent comedy, a love story in a twisted world" (by Lynch's description), it includes freak-show cameos and a fatal head bashing to heavy metal music. It won the Palme d'Or at Cannes in the spring.

But it was the brazenly offbeat *Twin Peaks* that helped turn the 44-year-old avant-garde director into the hottest, busiest talent in town. Despite this, the former Montana Eagle Scout still exudes a disarming heartland earnestness. He dresses like an overgrown schoolboy, in khakis, cap and long-sleeved shirts buttoned to the neck. "I have an eerie kind of feeling about my collarbone," he once said, explaining the buttoned-up look. "Just a breeze on it is sometimes too much for me."

EARTH DAY—Never had the stars been more down to earth. Every peril on the planet seemed to have acquired a star to call its own. Sting and Ted Danson set up foundations to save rain forests and oceans. Robert Redford, Peter Guber and Jon Peters looked into films about slain Amazon rain-forest defender Chico Mendes. Meryl Streep testified on Capitol Hill against the pesticide Alar. Madonna and Sandra Bernhard headlined at a Don't Bungle the Jungle! benefit, and Morgan Fairchild made herself an expert on the ozone layer and acid rain. Should any stars still be in need of ecological alignment, there were two new organizations, the Earth Communications Office (ECO) and the Environmental Media Association.

It all came to fruition April 22, when hundreds of earnest celebrities, from Tom Cruise to the Teenage Mutant Ninja Turtles turned out to promote Earth Day at rallies in Washington, D.C., New York City, Boston, Chicago and Los Angeles. ABC aired *The Earth Day Special*, a two-hour eco-variety show starring Bette Midler, Kevin Costner, Barbra Streisand, Robin Williams among others, including the casts of *Cheers* and *The Cosby Show*.

Seasoned environmentalists reacted to Hollywood's newfound ecological zeal with both enthusiasm and skepticism. Said Bob Hattoy of the Sierra Club: "For years we've been trying to publicize the dangers of pesticides, pollution and toxins. It's wonderful that celebrities can bring glamor and media attention to these issues the public has long ignored." But Hattoy minced no words about the environmental impact of Hollywood's prevailing culture. "Life-styles of the rich and famous are often life-styles of the wasteful and indulgent," he said. "It's not enough to attend a fund-raiser, get into your gas-guzzling limo and head home to your 40-room house that consumes more energy than a small village in the Third World. Yes, celebrities have begun to speak out, but speaking out isn't enough."

## EMMY AWARDS

**Best Comedy Series: MURPHY BROWN**

**Best Drama Series: L.A. LAW**

**Best Miniseries: DRUG WARS: THE CAMARENA STORY**

**Best Variety, Music or Comedy Series: IN LIVING COLOR**

**Best Actor in Comedy Series: TED DANSON, Cheers**

**Best Actor in Drama Series: PETER FALK, Columbo**

**Best Actor in Miniseries or Special: HUME CRONYN, Age-Old Friends**

**Best Actress in Comedy Series: CANDICE BERGEN, Murphy Brown**

**Best Actress in Drama Series: PATRICIA WETTIG, thirtysomething**

**Best Actress in Miniseries or Special: BARBARA HERSHEY, A Killing in a Small Town**

**Best Supporting Actor in Comedy Series: ALEX ROCCO, The Famous Teddy Z**

**Best Supporting Actor in Drama Series: JIMMY SMITS, L.A. Law**

**Best Supporting Actor in Miniseries or Special: VINCENT GARDENIA, Age-Old Friends**

**Best Supporting Actress in Comedy Series: BEBE NEUWIRTH, Cheers**

**Best Supporting Actress in Drama Series: MARG HELGENBERGER, China Beach**

**Best Supporting Actress in Miniseries or Special: EVA MARIE SAINT, People Like Us**

# IN THE LIMELIGHT

# ETCETERAS

*Turner and Fonda*

## JANE FONDA & TED TURNER

At first it sounded like another one of those mythical movieland romances. Jane Fonda and Ted Turner? Hanoi Jane and Captain Outrageous? But think about it: Each is an attractive, athletic, twice-married, media-savvy, politically active, environmentally conscious very rich person with an aborted college education who went into his or her father's business. As Fonda herself said, "The relationship is a natural."

It wasn't long ago—when a conservative young Ted was piecing together his television empire and a hot-headed Jane was crisscrossing the States speaking out for feminists, Black Panthers and Native Americans, among others—that a love affair, even a *friendship*, would have been out of the question.

According to a colleague, when Turner read the news last year that Fonda was calling it quits with fellow '60s radical Tom Hayden, her husband since 1973, Turner put down the newspaper and said, "Now, there's a woman I'd like to go out with." In his characteristically direct fashion, he got his hands on Jane's number and called her.

Tom Hayden, 50, and Jane Fonda, 52, divorced June 10. On Election Day, Turner and Fonda went to the new Tiffany store in Beverly Hills, where they picked out an opal (her favorite gem) engagement ring, with two diamonds thrown in for good measure.

Turner, 52, did not slip the ring onto Fonda's finger until December 21, the day she turned 53. Her publicist said the couple would not wed before June, when Fonda and Hayden's son, Troy, will be graduated from high school.

---

**CHER**—It's been a busy year for Cher. Her long-delayed movie, *Mermaids*—delayed, her publicist Lois Smith said, "because the movie was playing bouncing directors"—opened in December. Cher's 41-city U.S. tour, which began last March 31 in Dallas, closed in the summer with concerts at the Mirage Hotel. And in her spare time, the 44-year-old superstar went out and bought Jeunesse, a company that manufactures a line of skin care products.

---

**HARRY HAMLIN**—The storybook Hollywood marriage of Hamlin, 38, the litigating heartthrob of *L.A. Law*, and Laura Johnson, 33, formerly of *Falcon Crest*, ended in a nasty divorce skirmish. When Hamlin filed for divorce from Johnson in September 1989, he cited irreconcilable differences. That was putting it mildly. In court papers containing some of the most vitriolic marital invective in recent Hollywood memory, Johnson alleged that Hamlin, in the months after filing for divorce, emotionally abused and harassed her, interfered with her acting career and called her "a slut" and "a whore." For his part, Hamlin insisted, "I have made every effort to conduct myself honorably."

Ultimately, Johnson agreed. Through a publicist, Johnson said she and Hamlin had reached "a complete agreement dealing with all matters relating to their divorce." Without disclosing details, she said, "There were private matters which Harry could have made public, which would have been upsetting to me … and I appreciate and respect his integrity for keeping private matters private."

Not so private is Hamlin's current engagement to *Knots Landing*'s resident tease, Nicollette Sheridan.

---

**WARREN BEATTY**—Beatty and Madonna made very public displays of necking on the set of *Dick Tracy*, trotting off together to Los Angeles restaurants, cuddling at Hollywood gatherings and showing up hand in hand at *Dick Tracy*'s Washington, D.C., premiere. Cynics dismissed the odd coupling as nothing more than a publicity stunt. But Beatty's predilection for wooing his co-stars gave credence to the idea of a real offscreen romance with the ambitious blond.

For Beatty, Madonna was only the latest in a conga line of lovers. After breaking up co-star Natalie Wood's first marriage to Robert Wagner during his 1961 film debut, *Splendor in the Grass*, Beatty made a career of sweet-talking his leading ladies, right through *Ishtar*'s Isabelle Adjani in 1987, with stops along the way for long-term liaisons with Julie Christie (*McCabe & Mrs. Miller, Shampoo, Heaven Can Wait*) and Diane Keaton (*Reds*). Beatty also was

Cher

Madonna and Beatty

Kennedy

Sheridan and Hamlin

Gurdon and Webber

linked with Joan Collins (to whom he was engaged in 1961), Leslie Caron (in whose 1965 divorce from Peter Hall, then director of the Royal Shakespeare Company, Beatty was named co-respondent), Vivien Leigh, Susan Strasberg, Michelle Phillips, Carly Simon, Barbra Streisand, Britt Ekland and Joyce Hyser (briefly Jimmy Smits's love interest on *L.A. Law*), plus enough lesser-knowns for a supermarket tabloid to have offered women not yet heard from a $50 bounty for tales of their dalliances with him. Woody Allen once longed "to be reincarnated as Warren Beatty's fingertips."

*Dick Tracy* is over, and so is Beatty's fling with the Material Girl. What now? His next leading lady—onscreen, that is—is Annette Benning. She had a showy scene in *Postcards from the Edge* and a starring role in *The Grifters*. Benning and Beatty are slated to begin shooting *Bugsy*, a film about Bugsy Siegel, the gangland leader credited with inventing Las Vegas. Beatty will portray Bugsy; Benning plays his girlfriend....

## ANDREW LLOYD WEBBER—Webber

couldn't have been unaware of the parallels between his second marriage and the most opulently romantic of his musicals, *The Phantom of the Opera*: A less-than-handsome maestro woos a young, unknown singer—Sarah Brightman was 20 when she entranced the composer with her sweet, slightly brittle soprano—and sets about transforming her into a star. He writes an ambitious *Requiem*, giving his new bride one of his most melting melodies. Then he casts her in a magnum opus, *Phantom*, and won't allow his musical to come to America unless Actors' Equity relents and lets his leading lady sing and act the part he has written especially—only—for her. The Phantom would have applauded such romantic hubris.

But the Phantom would never have torn himself away from his organ arpeggios to do what Lloyd Webber, 42, did—have his publicist fax a separation announcement to the British press.

It seemed he had developed a relationship with Madeleine Gurdon, 27, a top-notch equestrian who rides in Princess Anne's set. "Gurtie" Gurdon, the convent-educated daughter of a retired brigadier, has been a high-profile three-day event rider for almost a decade. She is as chic as she is swift, designing an exclusive line of leather-and-suede clothes. Princess Anne, reportedly, is a customer.

Speaking of Brightman, Lloyd Webber said, "My admiration for her as an artist is undimmed." Brightman, sounding somewhat dimmed, said that the end of their six-year duet was "not something I either wish for or have sought." She added, "I believe I can continue to have a professional association with Andrew." That's a belief worth keeping. Brightman may figure prominently in plans for the movie of *Phantom*, which its composer will reportedly produce. She took the lead in Lloyd Webber's most recent Broadway offering, *Aspects of Love*, in December.

One theory behind the breakup was that although Brightman joined Lloyd Webber in the world of parties and first nights, she didn't share his growing fondness for the country squire life-style. Another was that she was unwilling to provide him with a family—although he has two children, Imogen, 13, and Nicholas, 10, by his first wife, also named Sarah.

Brightman, 30, was granted a divorce in London on grounds that their marriage of six years had suffered an "irretrievable breakdown." Her consolation prize was a reported settlement of nearly $12 million. Lloyd Webber quickly announced plans for a February 1991 wedding to Gurdon.

## JOHN F. KENNEDY JR.—Failing the bar

exam for the second time in seven months had to be embarrassing for any law school graduate. But when the Junior in your name comes after John Fitzgerald Kennedy, the problem is compounded by a noisome public spectacle. Imagine waking up to headlines shrilling THE HUNK FLUNKS on the front pages of all three New York City tabloids. That's how last May Day started for the 29-year-old Manhattan assistant district attorney.

Most young men do not have to labor under the sobriquet of "the Sexiest Man Alive" (as PEOPLE called him on a 1988 cover), not to mention the onus of following in the path of the 35th President and his brothers. At 29, John's father was already a Congressman from Massachusetts, and Uncle Bobby was chief counsel for a Senate subcommittee. At 30, Uncle Teddy won his U.S. Senate seat. A year ago sister Caroline passed the bar on her first try, albeit at the comparatively advanced age of 31. Law-practicing cousins Bobby Jr., Kathleen, Michael and Kerry Kennedy, Chris Lawford and Steve Smith are also members of the bar in good standing.

To many observers, JFK Jr. seems more his mother's son than his father's. Although he clearly has the Kennedy zest for rough-and-tumble games, John has so far passed through life at a stately pace, minding his manners, avoiding unpleasant encounters with the press and police and growing up normally.

America's uncrowned prince was a profile in unflappability as he gamely confronted a horde of reporters who surrounded him outside his office. "Hopefully, I'll pass it in July," he said, flashing his trademark killer smile and vowing to keep taking the exam "until I'm 95," if necessary. Then, with a shrug of those brawny shoulders, he conceded with beguiling modesty: "I'm clearly not a major legal genius."

Maybe not. But the legal eaglet did pass the New York State bar exam on his third try. JFK Jr. also passed the bar exam (considered to be less rigorous) in neighboring Connecticut. Had he failed the New York exam for a third time, Kennedy would have had to resign his $30,000-a-year post as a Manhattan assistant district attorney. Now he keeps his job, pockets a $4,000 raise and may soon see some courtroom action.

MICK JAGGER—Supermodel Jerry Hall, 34, after 13 years of togetherness, two children and countless fits of giggling on talk shows when the question of marriage came up, reportedly received a megacarat rock from Mick Jagger, 47. They were married in Bali on November 21.

Hall, the Texas-born, onetime fiancée of British rocker Brian Ferry, first went out with Jagger in 1977. Jagger was in the midst of a bruising—and expensive—breakup with first wife Bianca Jagger. Although Hall initially seemed to share Jagger's disdain for marriage, she changed her tune four years later. Miffed at Jagger's reluctance to be wed or be a father again (he had already fathered two daughters, Karis, now 20, with singer Marsha Hunt, and Jade, 19, with Bianca), Hall decamped for several months before Jagger's pleading brought her back. Daughter Elizabeth Scarlett was born in 1984 and son James in 1985.

In early '87, just after her acquittal on a marijuana charge in Barbados, Jerry claimed to have prevailed on the marriage front, but nothing happened. The breakthrough came in January 1990. "For the first time, we both think marriage is a good idea," Hall announced in London. Jagger, who was working in the Caribbean, didn't offer a denial. It wasn't until the close of the Stones' 18-month world tour in August that Jagger whisked his family off for a tour of the Far East and settled on Bali for the nuptuals. The peripatetic duo said their "I dos" before a Balinese priest. They devoted 36 hours to a quickie honeymoon, after which Hall returned to their London home, while Jagger jetted to the States.

BILL WYMAN—Just one day after Mick and Jerry were pronounced husband and wife, fellow Rolling Stone Bill Wyman, 54, said he was breaking up with his wife, model Mandy Smith, 20. They married 17 months before, after a six-year courtship. In 1984 Wyman first bedded the 13-year-old Mandy. "I knew it was a crazy thing, and I know I was at fault," he recently told an interviewer. "My emotions took over, and from that day onward I've been accused of being a pedophile."

There had been rumors of trouble in the marriage ever since Mandy's mum, Patsy, accompanied the pair on their honeymoon. Postsplit, the British tabloids presented theories to explain the parting. One was that Wyman, after spending only five days with his bride since the June 1989 ceremony, finally lost patience with the "mysterious wasting disease" that has kept Mandy in a London hospital since the summer. (The illness, which left her stick thin, was clearly serious, though of late she seems to be improving.)

An alternate theory was that Mandy was stung by Wyman's seeming preference for life on the road to staying at home with her. Publicly at least, Wyman's reputation as a ladies' man—he once boasted of having slept with a thousand women—did not figure into the split.

*Jagger and Hall*

*Smith and Wyman*

# pri·vate lives

n., not public; secret existences: celebrity high-jinx, royal battles, notorious infidelities and lurid revelations.

The Donald.

# THE TRUMP AFFAIR

**I**n a decade of glitz, they were the glitziest; in a decade of greed, they were the greediest: he the scrappy investor who made a fortune wheeling and dealing real estate, she the gregarious, Czech-born outsider who charmed and clawed her way into New York's most refined social circles. They fashioned an empire in their own image—and plastered their name on nearly every piece of steel, brick and glass they owned. Only six weeks into 1990, Donald and Ivana Trump announced they were calling off their 12-year marriage. It seemed the perfectly scripted end to a decade of flash and cash.

Rumors of the seismic marital rift whipped round the social circuit for months. The February 11 edition of the *New York Daily News* broke the story with the front-page headline LOVE ON THE ROCKS, citing Donald's roving eye as the reason. Trump, in Tokyo for the Tyson-Douglas boxing match, tersely confirmed the split. By next morning lawyers were lining up to do battle over the couple's lengthy prenuptial agreement, updated in December 1987.

The mysterious "other woman" in the raging divorce was a small-town Georgia peach named Marla Maples. A bit-part actress, the 26-year-old Maples catapulted into the world of the rich and famous from Dalton, Georgia, the "carpet capital of the world." Suddenly she was the biggest headliner in New York City—but not for any role she played on stage or screen.

By most accounts, the ailing marriage took its fatal downhill plunge during Donald and Ivana's stormy Christmas holiday in Aspen, where the couple was seen arguing on the slopes and outside Bonnie's, a popular restaurant on the mountain. Another vacationing skier reported that Ivana became enraged when she learned that Marla Maples was also at the resort. Two days later, according to one witness, when Maples walked out of Bonnie's, Ivana confronted her, demanding, "You bitch, leave my husband alone." Trump, who was sitting within earshot putting on his skis, took off down the mountain. Wrong move: Ivana is an excellent skier; Donald is not. When the formidable Czech pushed off in hot pursuit, fascinated observers swore they saw her whip in front of The Donald, as she calls him, and then ski backwards down the slopes, wagging her finger in his face.

---

News of Trump's impending financial ruin topped the front page of the June 4 *Wall Street Journal*.

His father, Fred Trump, built—with his own hands, at first—a substantial fiefdom of low- and moderate-income housing in New York City's outer boroughs. Donald took over a $20 million real estate empire from him, but that wasn't enough. "If I ever wanted to be known as more than Fred Trump's son," Donald once observed, "I was eventually going to have to go out and make my own mark." He dared to build his fortune where others feared to tread, scarfing up Manhattan property from the ruined Penn Central Railroad in the near-bankrupt New York City of 1974. He bought the rundown Commodore Hotel and, with the help of the enormous tax breaks he demanded, turned it into the glittering Grand Hyatt Hotel, the first and last major project he failed to name after himself. Like an attention-starved graffiti artist, he proceeded to emblazon his name on anything that stood still (Trump Tower, Trump Plaza, Trump Parc, Trump Palace, Trump Castle) and some things that didn't (his Trump Princess yacht and the Trump Shuttle airline).

His grandest edifice to date, the 120,000-square-foot Trump Taj Mahal Casino—with three-and-a-half times the floor space of its namesake in India—opened in April. He planned bigger things still. Trump City, to rise on abandoned railway yards on Manhattan's Upper West Side, was to include 11 60-story buildings grouped around the world's tallest building, a 150-story skyscraper—"the ultimate symbol," he called it. When nearby residents objected that they would be shrouded in shadow and choked by traffic, he replied, "What they think doesn't matter. They have no power." Community opposition stymied Trump's attempts to secure zoning and building permits and the plot still lies fallow.

But in this year of his 44th birthday, Trump's marriage fell apart, and his empire was crumbling. Condo sales stalled, the Atlantic City casino business was saturated—by him—and tightening credit markets made it harder to raise money to cover his debt on such high-price properties as the Trump

*Ivana.*

Castle Hotel and Casino. Owing $2 billion to banks and $1.3 million in payments to bondholders, he missed $73 million in payments due in June. In a last-minute deal to save him from default and bankruptcy, and thus protect their investment in him, the banks extended Trump a new $65 million loan, but there were strings attached. Much of his income would flow straight to his creditors, and he was to clear important business decisions with them. Particularly irksome was the requirement that Trump limit his personal living expenses to $450,000 a month, which meant cutting back by more than $100,000 his monthly outlay.

Wall Street sources said that the purpose of the bailout was not to get Trump up and running, but merely to buy time for the banks to oversee the sale of virtually all of his assets. Donald Trump's empire, once valued at $3 billion, might be as good as gone, and even his private wealth was at risk. His debt was said to include $500 million in personal loans, and though he claimed to be worth more than that, some analysts assayed his net worth at less than zero.

Trump was never a serious contender for the title of Most Venal New York Developer; indeed he was often generous. But in his business dealings, he could be brutal.

In the booming '80s, Trump's lack of restraint only helped him. He was buying into a rising market, and even if a property's income didn't cover interest expenses, demand for real estate would drive its price up. Then he would borrow against its rising value to buy more.

Trump, apparently assuming the boom would never end, forgot the very rules he set out for himself in his own book. "The point is that you can't be too greedy.... What you should never do is pay too much... sometimes your best investments are the ones you don't make.... I try never to leave myself too exposed." Famous last words.

Some hopeful fans remained. Insisted Roger Stone, a longtime business associate: "He's audacious, he's imaginative, and given a fair chance, he'll kick ass again."

———

Ivana was born in the factory town of Zlin, the only child of Milos Zelnicek, a construction designer, and Marie, a telephone operator. At 21, while studying physical education at Charles University in Prague, Ivana was in love with fellow skier Jiri Syrovatka, who helped her arrange a quickie wedding in 1971 to an Austrian friend, Alfred Winklmayr, in order to get an Austrian passport and a ticket to freedom. Syrovatka emigrated to Canada in 1971; Ivana stayed behind in Prague to complete her schooling (she was already earning money as a model). In 1973 Ivana emigrated to Canada to join Syrovatka. (She also divorced Winklmayr that year; he is now remarried and sells real estate in Sydney.)

Ivana, working as a model, met Trump at a Montreal party in 1976. Nine months later they were married. Donald was on the brink of buying his first hotel. The couple lived in an eight-room co-op apartment on Fifth Avenue, and Ivana bore three babies (Donald once said he wanted six). In 1984 the Trumps bought a Greenwich, Connecticut, weekend house for $3.7 million. The next year they picked up Mar-a-Lago, the former Marjorie Merriweather Post estate, for $10 million. The pseudo-Moorish architectural white elephant, which has 58 bedrooms and 33 baths, required a million dollars in annual upkeep and a staff of 32 in season. For a city dwelling, The Donald took the top three floors of his Trump Tower upon its completion in early 1989, polishing it off with an 80-foot living room and a wall-size waterfall backed with translucent onyx.

Ivana, chief executive officer of Trump's Castle casino for nearly three years, commuted back and forth by helicopter. In 1988, when Trump bought the venerable Plaza Hotel, he installed Ivana as president. Fashion became her business as well as her pleasure, and not just because she collected all but $1 of her annual salary in dresses. As a gesture to the American fashion industry, Ivana stopped her Concorde flights to the European shows and began to buy American.

"I never intend to look a day over 28," Ivana, 41, once said, "but it's going to cost Donald a bundle." After a highly unflattering photo of her appeared on the May 1989 cover of the cheeky *Spy* magazine, Ivana started keeping a very low profile. When she reappeared, that profile had changed. So had the cleavage.

The skier turned hotelier officially filed for divorce from her billionaire-downgraded-to-millionaire husband on November 2.

It was granted after a 10-minute session on December 11 in the Manhattan chambers of State Supreme Court Justice Phyllis Gangel-Jacob, who upheld Ivana's claim against Trump of "cruel and inhuman treatment," including his highly visible relationship with Marla Maples. The Donald issued a statement wishing Ivana well.

The Trumps won't reach a final financial settlement until after April 11, 1991, their next date in court. Ivana expects to maintain custody of Donald Jr., 12, Ivanka, eight, and Eric, six. (Child support remains to be determined.) And she wants to break that famous, frequently updated pre-nuptial agreement. If she succeeds, she could win up to 40% of Donald's worth. If she fails, she gets $10 million (not $25 million as often reported), the house in Greenwich, one month annually at the Palm Beach estate Mar-A-Lago, and the Trump Tower triplex.

Ivana, who found an evening escort in Oscar de la Renta executive Boaz Mazor, continues her day job as president of the Plaza Hotel, a prime Trump property. There, her future is uncertain. "She has a contract," says a friend, "but she can be fired for spite."

"When you ski down a mountain 100 miles an

hour," Ivana once said, "you are your own salvation. You must look out for yourself. That's how I live my life."

———

In 1989 the *New York Post* ran a blind item linking Marla, an aspiring actress and Ford agency model, with "one of New York's biggest business tycoons, a married man." But once columnist Liz Smith broke the Trump story, the fiercely competitive New York City tabloids were off and running.

BEST SEX I'VE EVER HAD shrieked the *Post*, alleging that was Marla's boast to her pals about Donald. (The next day, Marla denied saying any such thing, calling the quote a blatant lie.) The same paper reported that "the shapely blond … supposedly goes around to all the stores in Trump Tower saying, 'Charge it to Donald.'"

TV stations unearthed tapes of Maples, from a jiggly Marla workout video to a giggly beauty-pageant interview to clips of her movie walk-ons.

Marla comes from the same small Georgia town as *Today* show anchor Deborah Norville (which led the *Washington Post* to headline a story THE HOMETOWN OF THE KILLER BLONDES). She was raised by real estate developer Stan Maples, 48, and his wife, Ann, 50. (Divorced 10 years ago, Ann is now remarried to David Ogletree, a carpet-plant manager. Four years ago Stan took a bride a year younger than his daughter.) Like Ivana, Marla loves sports. According to her Northwest Whitfield High School coach, she was a star athlete. Her résumé lists juggling and the trampoline as special skills.

Once a face in the crowd, Marla became the year's most memorable face, but as an actress she was still waiting in the wings. Marla *did* endorse No Excuses jeans. Although sources said the deal was arranged by Trump, Maples's spokesman, Chuck Jones (who was also on Trump's payroll—as a consultant, he said, to the developer's planned megaproject, Trump City) denied it. Jones said No Excuses paid Maples an unspecified fee and that she agreed to do the campaign only after No Excuses promised ads promoting environmental issues.

What began as a chorus of denials, disclaimers and equivocal statements on the exact nature of Trump's relationship with Maples—and his intentions—became only slightly less murky when Ivana filed for divorce in November. Shortly after, Marla admitted that the $575 Cartier classic rolling ring that she wore on her left hand was bestowed by The Donald, but strictly in the name of "friendship."

Meanwhile, Donald was seen cavorting with Rowanne Brewer, 23, a model and former *Star Search* contestant, described by Donald as a "nice woman and a top model." "She more or less fits the bimbo image," said Maples's publicist.

*Marla.*

# JODY CARSON

There was nothing glamorous about Jody Wolcott Carson. She certainly didn't look like the former wife of one of America's highest-paid celebrities. A nomad who reckoned that she had lived in 28 places in the last 30 years, she owned little save two knit dresses, a handful of books and three shopping bags crammed with flotsam from former lives. In one was a squirrel's nest of tabloid clippings about the man Jody married at 22, the father of her three sons, and whom she has not seen—except on television—since the mid-'60s.

Jody allowed that people were usually skeptical when she said she was the first of Johnny Carson's four wives. "Nobody ever really believes me," she said.

A recluse who said that she loathed talking about herself, Jody was speaking out on the advice of Raoul Felder, the high-profile New York City divorce lawyer who was suing Carson on her behalf. Claiming that she couldn't live on the $13,500 yearly stipend that she now receives from Carson, she was petitioning him to up the ante to $120,000—a modest sum, she said, given his $40 million a year income. "I'm just so worried about my future," she said.

Felder—who has represented such ex-wives as Robin Givens and Lisa Gastineau—was banking that public sympathy would be with Jody. "There's nothing attractive about paying the mother of his three children $13,500 a year," he said.

Legal entanglements with his ex-wives are nothing new to Carson; take-my-wife jokes have become a *Tonight Show* standard. Both his 1972 split from Joanne Copeland and his 1985 divorce from Joanna Holland were attended by heated negotiations: Reportedly, Joanne received a lump sum of $160,000, a valuable art collection and $75,000 a year; Joanna walked away with more than $20 million in cash and property. Carson refused to speak about Jody's suit.

Jody Wolcott was 21 and an art major at the University of Nebraska when she met John Carson. She soon began working as an assistant in the magic act that he took to milkmen's conventions and American Legion halls. In 1949 John and Jody were married and settled in Omaha, where the ambitious Carson plugged away as a disc jockey and talk show host. In 1951, when they moved to Los Angeles with their year-old son, Chris, the pace—and their marital tensions—stepped up. The pregnant Jody began to suspect that he was seeing other women. She charged in her recent court filing that after second son Rick was born in 1952, Carson engaged in repeated physical violence against her. (Carson refused to comment.)

By 1957 the couple had three boys. But the abuse and the infidelity continued, she claimed. Jody obtained a Mexican divorce in 1963, and she was granted $15,000 a year in alimony, $7,500 in child support and 15 percent of Carson's gross earnings over $100,000. But she claimed that Carson continued to threaten to seek full custody of their children, and she was beset by anxiety attacks. After contemplating suicide, Jody spent three weeks at a psychiatric hospital, then moved to a halfway house in Warren, Connecticut, for one year. In 1970 she wed New York City art director Don Buckley—in part, she said, to strengthen her case if Carson sued for custody. Shortly before her remarriage, she contacted her lawyer, who struck a deal with Carson's attorneys. It appeared that she had agreed to give up her claim on his earnings in return for $160,000 plus $13,500 a year until 1999. Said Felder, whose attempts to modify this arrangement were based on the fact that the Carsons were divorced in Mexico: "She gave up millions and millions of dollars." The suit was filed in New York Supreme Court. The judge is reserving decision because of Jody's second marriage.

According to Jody, the years since her 1973 split from Buckley have been lonely. She is long since estranged from sons Cory, 36 (a guitar player who lives in Hawaii), Rick, 37 (who has worked in TV), and Chris, 39 (an erstwhile golf pro who lives in Florida). "We've sort of lost touch," she said of the boys, who reportedly each receive $50,000 a year from Carson. Even so, Jody said she was probably a lot happier than most people she knew: "I'm not married to a man I don't like. I don't have a job I don't like. I'm pretty free...."

*John and Jody Carson in the late '50s.*

# ATHINA ONASSIS ROUSSEL

**V**illeny, a tiny hamlet south of Paris, was unaccustomed to such excitement. French entrepreneur and pharmaceuticals heir Thierry Roussel and 38-year-old Swedish former model Gaby Landhage were finally formalizing the 19-year relationship that produced their two children, Sandrine, three, and Erik, four. But the main motive for the press horde congregating in the town square was a rare public appearance by Roussel's far more famous progeny, five-year-old Athina, the richest little girl in the world.

Athina is Roussel's daughter from a rocky three-year marriage to the late heiress Christina Onassis that ended in divorce in 1987. She has lived with her father since her mother's 1988 death in Buenos Aires. The burden of administering Athina's financial affairs is shouldered by four Onassis factotums who, with Roussel, serve as trustees of her future empire. But Roussel, 37, is the primary overseer of her personal life up to the age of 18. He draws a $1.42 million annual stipend from Christina's estate (and is said to have complained that it is not enough), but even those who see the worst in him concede his genuine concern for Athina.

Can this superrich motherless child, who is being brought up under the varied scrutiny of trustees, family retainers, watchful bodyguards and a scandal-prone father, escape the Onassis Curse? (Athina's mother died at 37 from an apparently accidental overdose of diet pills and tranquilizers; Athina's uncle, Alexander, perished in a 1973 plane crash at 24; in 1974 Athina's grandmother Tina died of pulmonary edema amid rumors that she had overdosed on sleeping pills.) How will this innocent fare in the hands of a man who fathered two illegitimate children during his on-again, off-again marriage to her mother?

Roussel met Landhage when she was living in Paris, where she worked as a fashion model and translator. The two became lovers, and the affair continued after she returned to Sweden. Even after Roussel took up again with Christina in 1984—he had first romanced her on Skorpios in 1972—he made frequent trips to Malmö to visit Gaby.

It was in 1984 that the lovestruck Christina pressed Roussel to marry her. According to an unnamed friend of Onassis's, who spoke to her French biographer, Christina told Roussel that she would give

him all the money he could ever imagine. Roussel explained to Gaby that it would be better for his business affairs if he was to marry Christina, and Gaby agreed. "He told her nothing would separate him from her—and marriage certainly did not."

Despite her unhappiness, Christina generously befriended the woman Roussel loved. Landhage has said that Christina often invited her to parties and bought presents for her children.

"Christina accepted that Athina had a brother and sister," said Christos Korontzis, her personal photographer for 10 years. "She wanted Athina to know them."

The formal wedding took place at Villeny's 17th-century Church of Saint Martin, where Gaby arrived chapelside suitably radiant—and paparazzi chanted, "Athina, Athina!" When the little lady did arrive, she waved brightly to the crowd before taking her place near the altar with Erik and Sandrine beside their parents' red velvet chairs. The congregation included family, friends and Christina's nanny-maid-confidante, Eleni Syrros, who was at her side during her fatal heart attack.

Back at Roussel's secluded country estate, Brazilian dancers, a mariachi band, chefs and florists capped two weeks of preparation for the evening's reception. That night, 550 guests, hailed by trumpeting red-coated hunters, drove down a flare-lit winding drive to a peach-and-blue tent decorated with 28,000 pink roses and a tiered, 10-foot high wedding cake topped with a spun sugar chapel. After a lavish spread of caviar, fresh fish, lobster and roast lamb, guests gathered outside for a 12-minute fireworks display.

Athina sat at the bridal table and minded her manners. "She had the 'only-child syndrome,' and she was self-centered because of the way Christina had raised her," said one intimate, "but Gaby and Thierry are very good at bringing her back to reality if she gets too full of herself."

The little girl, who already has an annual income of $4.25 million and who will inherit the bulk of her mother's $1 billion fortune when she turns 18, spent most of the afternoon playing quietly on the château's front lawn with her mother's former nanny—and charming her fellow guests. "She's really incredible. I heard her saying that little children should not be given lots of things," marveled one of the dazzled, "because then they're *spoiled*."

# PRIVATE LIVES

# THE BRITISH ROYALS

**Q**ueen Elizabeth is a figurehead, a constitutional monarch who reigns but does not rule. Yet no one, including four decades of British prime ministers, trifles with the prim-looking 64-year-old known at Buckingham Palace as the Boss.

This is the monarch who at 27 overrode the objections of advisers and ordered her coronation to be televised because, she said, "I have to be seen to be believed." Who continued to appear in public and ride in open cars after her husband's favorite uncle, Lord Mountbatten, was assassinated by an IRA bomb in 1979. Who, riding sidesaddle, expertly calmed her mount and smiled with a reassuring wave of her hand after a disturbed 17-year-old fired blanks at her at close range during the Trooping the Colour ceremony in 1981. And who in 1982 coolly kept a disturbed intruder talking on the edge of her bed until she could summon help.

She grew up during the London blitz and matured in the ensuing period of austerity. The world's wealthiest woman still wanders around Buckingham Palace turning off lights. The heat is kept low. The Queen saves string. She has palace bed linen turned daily to reduce laundry bills, and instead of nudging up the heat she advises anyone who feels a bit chilly to put on another sweater. She allows nothing to go to waste: When she needs names for her new puppies, she borrows them from the day's obituary columns.

By FORTUNE's calculation, the Queen is the richest woman in the world—number four overall, behind only the Sultan of Brunei, Saudi Arabia's King Fahd and his family and America's Mars candy-bar clan. FORTUNE estimates Elizabeth's worth at $11.7 billion, but other appraisers believe it to be much higher. Her family is worth more than its weight in gold.

This Queen is British to her bones. That means a love of silver service and afternoon tea, bland food, sweetish white wine, jigsaw puzzles, Dick Francis

*Queen Elizabeth.*

mysteries and, most of all, tramps in the country amid her thoroughbreds and her dogs. The Queen feeds her six corgis and two dorgis (the result of an accidental mating between one of Her Majesty's corgis and Princess Margaret's daschund) herself, cutting up their meat and mixing it with biscuits in their separate bowls set out every afternoon by a footman. It is reported that Her Majesty will take a call any time of day or night from her kennel mistress.

---

Sports-loving Prince Charles was out of action for several months after he broke his arm in two places June 28 while playing polo. One of the fractures failed to heal, and doctors at the Queen's Medical Centre in Nottingham removed bone from the Prince's hip and grafted it onto the fracture site in his arm. A metal plate and screws hold the splice together. His critics were predictably unsympathetic: Wasn't it just like Charles, off playing polo again, always thinking of himself?

Pity the Prince of Wales. Adored, honored, saluted and pampered from birth, he must spend his life waiting to become King of England and he isn't even left in peace to do what he wants in the meantime.

Charles, 42, has tried to please. Until he was 32, he lived at home with his parents. Then he found a lovely bride and promptly fulfilled his duty to beget heirs. Now all he can do is try not to go mad with boredom waiting for his hardy mother, Queen Elizabeth II, to pass him the scepter.

In the meantime Charles has been a superior Prince of Wales, maybe the best ever. An archcritic of modern architecture, he wrote and helped to prepare a BBC documentary (and later a prizewinning book) called *A Vision of Britain*. (In 1987 Charles compared his nation's architectural establishment to the World War II German bombers that devastated London. "You have to give this much to the Luftwaffe," he announced drily to an audience of stunned architects. "When it knocked down our buildings, it didn't replace them with anything more offensive than rubble. We did that.")

Charles is working on another documentary on the environment. At his orders, recycling and organic food were introduced at Kensington Palace in London and at Highgrove, the Waleses' posh country estate in Gloucestershire. Lately Charles has become the champion of the Queen's English, battling bad grammar and limp language.

The Prince has also become a tad eccentric. He awakens to farming programs on the radio. He eats odd vegetable dishes like nettle soup and sells organic bread stone-ground from whole meal grown on his own farm. He believes in homeopathic medicine, frets about disappearing peat bogs and collects antique

*Prince Charles.*

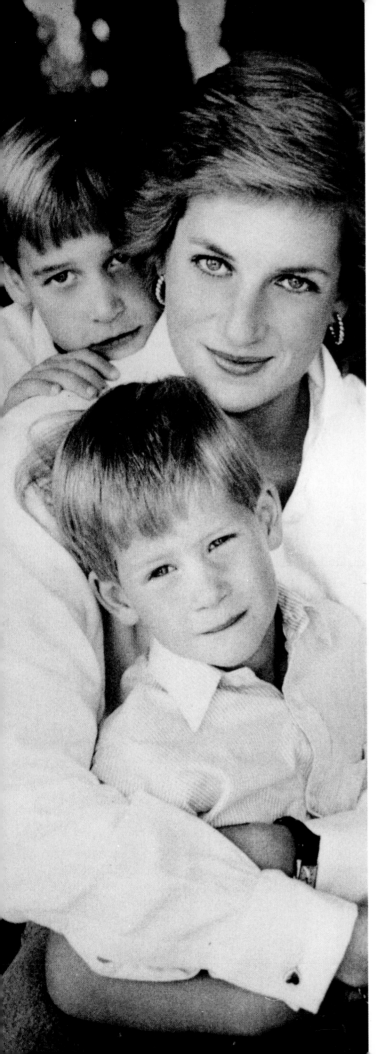

lavatory seats. In his bathroom, Charles, who is believed to be worth about $536 million, keeps a silver keylike device, stamped with the official three feathers of the Prince of Wales, to squeeze the last drop of toothpaste out of the tube.

In recent years Charles's disenchantment with the wife all others adore became painfully apparent. He and Diana weren't getting on. The problems in the marriage seemed to stem not so much from the 12-year age gap but from their different interests, social incompatibility and Charles's refusal to accommodate anyone beyond himself.

The strain first began to show after the birth of Prince Harry in 1984 but grew to embarrassing proportions in the fall of 1987 when the British tabloids started marking the days the couple spent apart. The publicity became so overwhelmingly negative that the Queen reportedly summoned the couple to her quarters one evening to address the problem. After the meeting Charles and Di did appear more civil in public.

Intimates, however, said that the state of the marriage remains unchanged, and these sources further hinted that Charles follows the royal tradition of seeking companionship with discreet women within the royal circle.

———

Our first glimpse of her will remain forever: a gawky 19-year-old kindergarten teacher balancing one child on a hip, holding the hand of another, gazing shyly at the camera. Pure innocence—she didn't even realize the sun was shining through her diaphanous skirt, giving the world an unexpectedly leggy view of the woman who would someday be Queen of England.

That September 1980 photo helped fire an intense

*Diana with Wills (left) and Harry; Fergie, above, with Eugenie.*

fascination with Lady Diana Spencer, now the Princess of Wales, that has continued unabated. She remains the most closely watched public beauty since Jacqueline Onassis.

Diana has taken an ill-defined job and given it a modern twist. This is a princess brave enough to visit victims of an IRA bombing at Enniskillen in Northern Ireland and sufficiently assured to dance onstage at both the Royal Albert Hall and the Royal Opera House.

Married to Prince Charles for ten years now, she has struggled to make a difficult marriage work. As one observer remarked, "Charles must be the only man in London not in love with her." Some renewed warmth, however, is expected in the future—if only for the sake of the succession. "I want three more babies, but I haven't told my husband yet," Diana was overheard confiding to dinner companions some time ago. When a rash of unfounded pregnancy rumors followed, one palace wag quickly quipped, "The biggest news would be that they are actually sleeping together."

Charles may not often share a bed with Diana, but according to a friend of the Princess's, "Diana knows no different. Certainly, she and Charles sleep in different rooms, let alone different beds. But so does everyone else she knows. The Queen sleeps in a different room from Philip. Diana's father has a different bed from Raine," she said, referring to Diana's stepmother, novelist Barbara Cartland's daughter. "Prince Andrew and Sarah have different bedrooms at Sunninghill."

Diana's own mother was a "bolter"—Frances Spencer ran off with wallpaper tycoon Peter Shand Kydd and lost custody of her children in the bitter fight that followed. Diana is all too aware of the price her mother paid. She would not want to risk losing her children, as surely she would. It would also go against all her breeding. "The Spencers support the Crown," said a palace source. "They don't undermine it."

And Diana is first and foremost a Spencer. That makes her more English than half the royal family, according to a recent genealogical study. When her son Prince William accedes to the throne, he will have more English blood in him than any monarch since James I, who, though mostly Scottish, was 25 percent English.

When Charles fell off his pony in June, Di didn't rush to his bedside—but she did retrieve him from the hospital. And at the enthronement of Emperor Akihito of Japan, their second public outing together since a holiday in Majorca, the two enjoyed themselves, or so it seemed. Diana was even able to coax a smile out of her husband.

———

A future queen has one overriding duty—to produce an heir, preferably a male. Diana was fortunate. Within two years she had produced the two towheads known as the heir and the spare.

In June the *Daily Mirror* made note of the "future King of England being tanned on the backside by his mother." Diana's reputation as a concerned parent—

which extends to a hands-on approach—caused some controversy at the school sports day she attended with Prince William, eight. When Wills ignored Di's summons to leave, recalled photographer Jim Bennett, "She followed him onto the field, caught up with him and gave him a smart slap to his backside. William just started crying. The Princess was clearly angry."

The paddling was not William's first. While Harry is a loving, often clinging child, Wills has the reputation of a hellion. At nursery school such pranks as pretending to grab his teacher's bottom earned him the nickname Billy the Basher.

Charles would seldom engage in such a public display of parental pique—or affection. The dignified and distant relationship he has with his sons reflects the Prince's own relationship with his father, Prince Philip, a notoriously stern parent whose main interest in Charles was to toughen him up. There have been, however, small indications that Charles is taking more of an interest in his sons as they grow older. Diana taught the boys to swim and play tennis, but it was Charles who taught them to ride.

At summer's end Diana packed off her firstborn to his first boarding school. With his arrival, Prince William took, at the tender age of eight, the second critical step down the well-trod road to royal manhood. Sandwiched between his parents in the back of a Bentley, Wills got out at the entrance to Ludgrove Preparatory School in Berkshire and shook the hands of the headmasters, Gerald Barber and Nichol Marston. Charles, walking with a cane after his bone-graft surgery, accompanied Diana and their son to the dorm room Wills will share with five other boys, but they didn't linger.

By all accounts it would be school business almost as usual at the 186-student Ludgrove, with no royal treatment for willful young Wills. "We shall treat Prince William in exactly the same way as the other pupils," said Barber. He will rise and shine at 7:15 A.M., visit the communal bathroom and begin classes after prayers and breakfast in the oak-paneled dining room. Bedtime for first-year students is 6:30 P.M., with a compulsory quiet period until lights out at 8 P.M.

Much as they'd like to, the Wales won't be able to make their son's schooling completely normal. It was decided that a detective would stand guard outside William's classroom and sleep nearby at night. (Beefed-up security now surrounding Ludgrove is "an awful lot of fuss for one small boy," groused a local.) The other notable difference is in address: Most boys go by their surnames, but Windsor or Wales was thought to be a bit much for Wills. The young heir will be William to his peers, Prince William to his masters.

Phone calls home are forbidden, and Wills is allowed to leave the secluded 130-acre campus only three weekends a term. As for Diana, she'll have to fill her time by mothering Harry, six, who returned to the days-only Wetherby School to begin his second year.

———

The headlines blared ATTAGIRL! A notice posted on the gate of Buckingham Palace read: "Her Royal

Highness The Duchess of York was safely delivered of a daughter at 7:58 P.M. March 23, 1990. Her Royal Highness and her child are both well."

Fergie delivered the seven-and-a-half-pound infant by her first emergency cesarean section, with Prince Andrew at her side.

On the morning of March 30, the proud Prince, together with the Duchess of York, walked into the spring sunshine carrying a little princess with a big name—Her Royal Highness Eugenie Victoria Helena. (Buckingham Palace requested the name be pronounced "U-jay-nay." The *Sun* set up a hotline offering the Palace pronunciation and received 40,000 calls in two days.)

"Nice one, Fergie," shouted an onlooker. "Well done the Duchess," called another. Her tranquil highness Eugenie, who follows the Yorks' two-year-old daughter Beatrice as sixth in line to the British throne, never opened her birth-blue eyes.

Rapture over Eugenie and its byproduct—approval for Fergie—was short-lived. Sarah, as she is seldom called, once appeared to be the perfect way to legitimately unload the Queen's rowdy second son. Helicopter pilot Andy, 30, seemed interested mainly in oat-sowing and club-crawling with a string of steamy ladies culminating in former soft-porn star Koo Stark. Then the Prince's wandering eye fell upon Sarah Ferguson in 1985. Though a strapping, worldly wench who loved a good time, Sarah was also a well-connected satellite of the royal set and a childhood playmate of Andy's at the fields where her father is Prince Charles's polo manager. True, she had a past, particularly a three-year relationship with semisavory race car manager Paddy McNally. Fergie's past, however, has been vastly overshadowed by her present. If the Yorks often struck the British public as a pair of heedless hedonists, at least they seemed besotted with each other—a touching assumption not applicable to all Windsor marriages. Fergie's erratic behavior in the summer put even that supposition in doubt. Soon after Eugenie's birth, the Duchess resumed her prenuptial fast life, partying with an international set possessing more cash than cachet. Where once she drew fire for leaving baby Beatrice with nannies while she jetted to meet Andrew in foreign ports, now she left her husband at home on shore leave to fly off on a sun-drenched holiday. Reportedly, she flew in the private jet of 30ish Steve Wyatt, unmarried, fun-loving scion of the Texas Wyatts, natural-gas zillionaires. While the British tabloids labeled the relationship with Wyatt "platonic," jet-setting seemed a dubious pastime for a mother of two small children who happens to belong to one of the world's most publicly fusty families.

While Fergie's role is to promote all things British, she bought and borrowed French clothes and tried to hire an American firm to decorate Sunninghill Park (a move vetoed by the Queen). Fergie also seemed to be, if not a gold digger, at least on the financial make. She wrote two children's books and suggested the proceeds were going to charity, not mentioning she was pocketing the lion's share herself. Fergie sold an interview to a British paper for $201,600, but part of the fee was withheld when she "forgot" the all-important scoop that she was pregnant with a second child. One source said the Queen stepped in when Fergie threatened to sue for the balance.

"I'm too spontaneous," she admitted in *Hello!*'s photo spectacular, "and I don't think before I act."

---

Prince Philip, 69, went on a tear about the habits of some of his adopted countrymen in a speech this year. (Philip, who became a British citizen just before he married Queen Elizabeth in 1947, was born in Corfu and raised as a member of the Greek royal family.) He said living in Britain "could be much improved if we all resolved to be clean, honest and polite.... I find it difficult to believe anyone enjoys the smell of dirty bodies or the sight of filthy clothes, matted hair and seven o'clock shadows." All of which prompted the *Daily Express*'s Jean Rook to respond with a column calling the Queen's husband "an ill-mannered Greek immigrant who's been well paid by Britain for 42 years for doing nothing but put it down."

It was hardly the first time the Prince had failed to endear himself. Unhappy with the preponderance of gay servants at Buckingham Palace, Philip sympathized with a footman who had been caught flagrante delicto with a housemaid. "They sacked him," complained the Duke. "He should have been given a medal." During a Middle Eastern tour, the Queen was kept waiting by a potentate. Within earshot of his host, Philip furiously muttered, "The trouble with Arabs is, they breed." And on a tour of Peking he warned a British student that he would "go back with slitty eyes" if he stayed in China much longer.

Philip, who came to the altar to marry Elizabeth in darned socks, was a penniless son of exiled Greek royalty, with two suits to his name. (Actually his ancestry is German and Danish, his family having been invited to fill the vacant Greek throne.) When Princess Elizabeth ascended the throne of the United Kingdom, Philip, the former naval commander, abruptly became an unemployed shadow. "Constitutionally, I don't exist," he once joked. He grew restive and soon took to hanging out with a group of raucous cronies. His piercing blue eyes customarily roved in the direction of attractive women, and when he went solo to Australia in 1956 to open the Commonwealth Games, rumors ran rife.

Elizabeth was too shrewd to stage tantrums or highly publicized reconciliations. When her husband returned four months later, she named him manager of the royal estates. It was an ideal outlet for his ego and energies; he stayed close to home, applied himself, and within a few years the properties were turning a handsome profit. Philip's passion for efficiency later brought time and motion studies to Buckingham Palace.

Philip seemed to enjoy his new lease on life. He became a controversial missionary for the World Wildlife Fund and plumped for population control and other causes. And if at parties he continued to home in on the prettiest lady, gossip was confined to a whisper.

Elizabeth fostered the image of her husband as an

amiable curmudgeon—"It's a waste of time trying to change a man's character," she once declared. "You have to accept your husband as he is." Translation: You have to accept my husband as he is. Everyone did.

———

Saturday, August 4, it seemed as if everyone in Britain had taken leave of his senses. Actor Sir John Gielgud dithered on about fairy godmothers. Fleet Street filled its editorial pages with maudlin treacle. The cause of this nationwide overdose of sentimentality? The 90th birthday of the realm's most adored grandmother—the Queen Mum.

Beaming beneath her powder-blue hat, the good Queen Mother didn't disappoint the 10,000 devotees who gathered outside her residence, Clarence House, to sing "Happy Birthday to You"—although she did keep them waiting. Well-wishers were shooed away from the street under the Queen Mum's balcony until eight A.M. because, as one staff member put it, "we think she deserves a lie-in."

The festivities capped four months of birthday celebrations. Elizabeth, after all, is a national institution, famed for her quaintly appalling hats.

But beneath the millinery lies one of the cleverest public-relations minds of the century. Lady Elizabeth Bowes-Lyon, a determined and serenely beautiful outsider unhampered by royal stodginess, was the Princess Di of her day. She twice rejected the marriage proposals of the painfully shy, stammering Prince Albert, who called her "the most wonderful person in the world." She finally assented and won the nation's heart when she impulsively placed her bridal bouquet on the tomb of Britain's Unknown Soldier in Westminster Abbey.

After Edward VIII tarnished the crown by abdicating in 1936 to marry Wallis Simpson, Elizabeth helped polish it to new luster as Queen Consort to her husband, who took the name George VI. When George, never strong physically, died of cancer at age 56 in 1952, some friends said that the Queen Mother blamed his early demise on the abdication and that she never forgave Simpson. "You think that I am a nice person," Elizabeth once said. "But I am not a nice person."

This 5-foot-tall aristocrat, the last Empress of India and honorary colonel of 18 regiments, is a multimillionaire and noted bon vivant, the only Windsor exempt from the Queen's ethic of total thrift. London couturiers quake when they see her coming. It's not her taste in tulle, it's that she reportedly rarely pays her accounts. And she's still keen as a tack. Said one old friend of her wicked wit: "She doesn't take prisoners."

Nor much time off. Although she dropped out of public life for a while after her husband's death, the Queen Mother is patron to some 300 organizations and puts in more than 100 appearances each year.

*The Queen Mother with the Irish Guards, 1984.*

# THE MONACO ROYALS

Once again, mourning bells tolled in Monaco, this time for Stefano Casiraghi, the 30-year-old husband of its beloved Princess Caroline, who died in a speedboat accident on October 3. In 1982, at Princess Grace's funeral, Prince Rainier faltered and Caroline supported him. On this day the roles were reversed. As Caroline descended from a dark-blue Mercedes to climb the 15 flower-bedecked steps of Monaco's Saint-Pierre Cathedral, it was the Prince who steadied his daughter.

Before she entered the 19th-century Roman Catholic cathedral, Caroline, clutching a white handkerchief against her black dress, stared numbly at Stefano's mahogany coffin, her face gaunt under sunglasses and a black mantilla. Inside, the four members of Monaco's ruling Grimaldi family—Rainier, Caroline, Prince Albert and Princess Stephanie—took their places together in the front row. Across the aisle sat Casiraghi's Milanese family.

After the Requiem Mass, members of the immediate family followed the coffin through a solemn honor guard to a private chapel where Stefano was buried in his red-and-white racing suit. Later, several of Stefano's competitors took a boat to the spot where he was killed and dropped a wreath and flowers into the sea.

"I'm what they call a throttle man," Stefano Casiraghi once said of his consuming passion for the dangerous sport of powerboat racing. "You must not be scared of going too fast." On an overcast morning off Monaco, the tall, windburned Stefano was the victim of his philosophy. A world offshore powerboat champion, he was running hot and true in his 42-foot catamaran, *Pinot di Pinot*. But 30 minutes into the contest, doing an estimated 108 miles per hour, Stefano's craft became airborne, smashed into a rising wave and flipped over. His co-pilot, Patrice Innocenti, was thrown from his seat and survived the accident. Stefano took the full impact of the crash. He was dead before rescuers could free him from the wreckage.

The House of Grimaldi was plunged into mourning. "Monaco," announced the national media, "is in a state of shock. It has lost its Prince Charming."

On a visit to Paris when she received the tragic news, Caroline returned to Monaco, her features drawn, dressed in black mourning. Happily married to Stefano despite rumors to the contrary, she faced widowhood at age 33 with three young children.

Stefano's death capped a lifelong infatuation with speed. After studying economics, Stefano, the son of a Milanese millionaire, built a real estate and construction business but devoted much of his time to racing. He set a speed record on Lake Como of 172 miles per hour in 1984 (which has since been broken), and in a grueling 1984 race, he drove from Lyons to Morocco with Caroline as co-driver. To relax, Stefano liked to put his Ferrari through its paces on mountain roads. He turned to offshore racing in the mid-'80s.

Caroline and Stefano met in 1983 at a Monaco disco. Although no match for little sister Stephanie, Caroline had had her share of scandalous headlines. She petitioned the Vatican to annul her two-year marriage to philandering Frenchman Philippe Junot, 17 years her senior. (Because the annulment has not been granted, her children are considered illegitimate by the Roman Catholic Church.) Caroline won a civil divorce in 1980. She apparently sought solace in an intense affair with Ingrid Bergman's son, Roberto Rossellini. But after he was pictured in the tabloids cavorting with a starlet in the Greek isles, Caroline, friends said, linked up with Stefano out of revenge. Stefano broke an engagement in order to marry Caroline, by then pregnant with their first child. He was warily welcomed into the family by Rainier, who worried that Stefano was an Italian nouveau riche sportsman.

Beneath Stefano's sophisticated veneer was a well-balanced person with strong family values. He and Caroline lived a regal but domestic life, dividing their time between Monaco and Milan, with frequent trips to Saint Moritz, where his family has a home. Both were devoted to the children: Andrea, six, Charlotte, four,

*Caroline and Prince Rainier.*

and Pierre, three. Throughout the marriage, Stefano seemed happy remaining in the background and assisting Caroline with her royal duties. She, in turn, often showed up with the children to watch her husband race, an activity that frequently left her fearful. "This," said a friend about the accident, "is her greatest nightmare come to life."

A private and quiet soul, Stefano seemed almost to lose his energy when not at the wheel of a power-boat. The taciturn sportsman's favorite recreation was to gather a group of buddies and go to discos, where he quietly watched the action. He did not, said friends and intimates, have a roving eye. At his death, he co-owned a Monaco construction company and was involved in major real estate dealings. The nearest thing to a scandal he endured was the revelation that he had avoided Italian military service by falsely claiming he had a genital tumor.

Stefano's sudden death was tragically reminiscent of the freak auto accident that killed Caroline's mother, Princess Grace, on the twisting roads in the

French mountains above Monaco in 1982. Grace reportedly suffered a stroke-like attack and lost control of her sedan, which tumbled down a ravine. Her daughter Stephanie, 17 at the time, a passenger in the car, sustained a fractured vertebra and was unable to leave her bed to attend Grace's funeral. Questions arose about whether Stephanie, who was below the legal driving age, might have been at the wheel, but nothing was ever proved.

The Grimaldis were devastated, and it was a blow from which they never fully recovered. Grace, only 52 when she was killed, was one of the century's most admired and magnetic princesses. She became something of a European version of Eva Perón, revered in death by people of every station. Prince Rainier, jealously guarding his wife's memory and image, in other ways seemed to drift like a rudderless ship, with little of his former fire and sense of purpose. Rebellious Princess Stephanie ricocheted from one career to another and one beau to another. Middle child Prince Albert, the quiet and unassuming heir to the

55

throne, was an unsettled young man, though lately he seemed to be showing some interest in his future position.

After her mother's death, Caroline assumed leadership of the dispirited family, becoming a stable force for the others. The death of Stefano left Caroline consumed with her private grief, and questions arose concerning what would become of her siblings, her father and the already strained family ties.

Although she was a fun-loving teenager, fond of nightlife and multiple boyfriends, marriage and motherhood turned Rainier and Grace's eldest child into an assured adult who carried out official duties with style and energy. Still, she once confided, "It wouldn't bother me at all if I weren't Princess Caroline of Monaco. I would prefer to be at home with my husband and children than attacked by photographers. I'm just the sister of the future Prince, and my children come first. I work my schedule around them."

No one could predict how Albert and Stephanie, for whom Caroline was such a steadying influence, would cope. Amherst-educated Albert, 32, an Olympic bobsled racer and yachtsman, seemed to need an infusion of Caroline's businesslike approach to royal life.

For Stephanie, 25, Caroline was a sorely needed brake to youthful passions. For years Monaco's 30,000 residents found tracking the beaux of playgirl Princess Stephanie as amusing a numbers game as anything inside the casino. Stephanie's accustomed dating logic seemed to consist of passionate flitting between the bad and the beautiful. The youngest Grimaldi dallied with actors Rob Lowe, 26, and Christopher Lambert, 33, as well as the progeny of two French film idols: Jean-Paul Belmondo's son, Paul, 27, and Alain Delon's son, Anthony, 25. At one point, she was thought to be almost engaged to American record producer Ron Bloom, 39, her Los Angeles love since mid-1988. Bloom was an improvement over Stephanie's earlier escort, Los Angeles nightclub owner and sex offender Mario Oliver, 37, whom Prince Rainier banned from his not-quite-square-mile principality.

During the past year, Stephanie fed a tabloid frenzy by breaking off her engagement to French businessman Jean-Yves Le Fur and vamping topless on the beach in a faux erotic embrace with a girlfriend.

Caroline, who by year's end had not been to her office at the palace since Stefano's death, regularly walked the few hundred yards from her pale pink villa, Clos Saint-Pierre, to the Chapelle de la Paix, where Stefano is entombed under an as yet unmarked marble slab. On October 27 she went to Fino Mornasco, Stefano's hometown in Italy, where she joined her in-laws at a Mass at Sanctus Stephanus Church and witnessed the unveiling of a plaque that read: TO STEFANO, ILL-FATED CHAMPION IN SPORT AND LIFE.

# ELIZABETH TAYLOR

**I**t started, as so many of her illnesses did, with something quite ordinary—in this case, a mild sinus infection. But soon she had developed a 104-degree fever, signaling virulent pneumonia. Within two weeks, Elizabeth Taylor was fighting for her life in the intensive care unit of St. John's Hospital in Santa Monica.

It was only the latest scare in years of health crises for the 58-year-old Oscar-winning actress, but it was by far her gravest illness since she suffered a near-fatal bout of pneumonia while filming *Cleopatra* in 1961. (At the time, she was saved by a tracheotomy.) Coming after more than 30 years of drug and alcohol abuse and aggravated by persistent, if apparently unfounded, rumors of AIDS, the illness seemed alarmingly mysterious.

The new decade did not begin happily for Taylor, who lost two close friends in rapid succession. On February 24, billionaire Malcolm Forbes, her frequent escort since his divorce in 1985, died of a reported heart attack. Then, on March 26, designer Halston, a Taylor buddy for nearly two decades, died in San Francisco of AIDS.

Taylor settled in with her grief. As so often in the past, sad news seemed to trigger ill health. On April 9 she entered Los Angeles's Daniel Freeman Marina Hospital in Marina del Rey. Seven days later the deteriorating Taylor was transferred to St. John's, where she registered under the alias of Beth Warner, the last name that of her sixth and most recent husband, Virginia Senator John Warner. There, breathing with the aid of a respirator, fed intravenously and hooked up to a heart monitor, she was put under 24-hour watch.

Finally, on April 28, Taylor was taken off the ventilator and moved to a private luxury suite. A lung biopsy, CAT-scan, bronchial washing and renal and liver tests proved reassuring. There was no sign of irreparable damage, said pulmonary specialist Bernard Weintraub, and "absolutely no evidence" of cancer or AIDS.

That the question of AIDS should arise at all in the case of a much-married, middle-aged superstar might seem odd. A series of coincidences fueled speculation that Taylor might have the disease: Her personal doctor, Michael Roth, happens to be an AIDS specialist; she helped form the American Foundation for AIDS Research (AmFAR); her close

friends Rock Hudson and Halston died of the disease; and, following his sudden death, it was alleged that Forbes had been involved in homosexual activities. The ailing Taylor issued a statement firmly denying that she had had an AIDS-related condition.

Other conjectures focused on the role of alcohol and drug abuse in Taylor's latest illness. Though Weintraub denied that Taylor was addicted at the time of this hospitalization, the extent of her previous dependency was apparent in a report issued April 20 by the Los Angeles County District Attorney's Office. That document, which followed a more than yearlong investigation of three Taylor doctors, did not clear them of charges of overprescribing during 1987 and 1988, but because the inquiry found that they had acted to end her addictions, the matter was referred to a state medical board. According to Dr. David Smith, the San Francisco drug addiction expert who reviewed the investigation, "the drug and alcohol addiction could have been contributing factors" to Taylor's three decades of medical problems.

Yet after two stints at Betty Ford, as well as 20 operations and more than 30 hospitalizations over the years, Taylor refused to succumb to substance abuse—or any other malady. The star of the 1958 movie *Cat on a Hot Tin Roof* hung on to her nine lives, repeatedly seeking medical help.

Even with the height of her film career past, fans rallied around Taylor in staggering numbers, sending her as many as 400 get-well cards each day and floral arrangements so numerous that they outgrew her room and were passed on to other patients. By early May, she was said to be steadily improving.

In June, defying doctors' orders, a shaky but radiant Taylor opened the International Conference on AIDS in San Francisco. Despite daunting odds, Taylor had managed to keep a promise made months before to attend the conference's opening reception. Still recuperating, Taylor had been advised by her doctors not to travel. Yet there she was.

Worried friends and fans were relieved to see that although Taylor was clearly weak, her manner was still as gracious and her beauty as luminous as before she fell ill. She announced a new international fund sponsored by AmFAR, which, she said, would finance AIDS education and prevention projects in Africa, Latin America and Southeast Asia. After her brief remarks, Taylor rested for several hours in a hotel room before flying home to Los Angeles in Merv Griffin's private jet.

In December, sitting in the airy living room of her brick-and-shingle house tucked into a hillside in Los Angeles's Bel-Air enclave, sunlight streamed through fingertip-high windows into a room that is as informal as one can be that has a Frans Hals portrait over the fireplace. Elsewhere the walls glowed with fine oils— a Rouault, a Pissarro—a collection that reflected Elizabeth's upbringing as the daughter of an art dealer.

Taylor talked about her illness last spring, when doctors told her that she was dying. "They all thought at first it was just a bad flu and sinusitis," she said. She'd been fighting a low-grade fever all spring, she explained, "But when I was in the hospital it developed into a viral pneumonia, a rare kind. They wanted to do an open-lung biopsy.... I just didn't want any more surgery in my life. But then they came in and told me that I was lying there a dying woman, and if I procrastinated any longer, it would no longer be my decision. They'd have to put me on life support, and perhaps I'd be there for the rest of my life. Which might not be very long."

At her side in the hospital along with her children—Michael Wilding, 37, Christopher Wilding, 35, Liza Todd-Tivey, 33, and Maria Burton Carson, 29—was her elder brother, Howard, 61. "I thought about it, and I thought about it," she recalled. "And my two boys came into the room, and I realized then that I was dying, but that I wanted to live very much. I wanted to be around the people I loved and to be out of intensive care. So I let them do the open-lung biopsy, and I went on life support, which helped me recover my strength. I remember passing the crucial time. I was still in intensive care and still had a fever of 105 and was slightly out of my mind. But I remember saying, 'Thank you, God.'"

Eight months later, Taylor, newly fit (she lost 30 pounds in the hospital), was busy. She attended the Manhattan gala for AmFAR on World AIDS Day.

At the same time, she was getting ready to launch a new round of skin care and other cosmetic products under her Elizabeth Taylor's Passion imprimatur, enlarging a business that has grown to $100 million in retail sales since its debut in 1987.

At home, the woman who rode a horse to fame 46 years ago in National Velvet was still surrounded by animals. There was Nellie, the collie that Charles Bronson presented to her last year for her charitable work, and Max, a baby parrot she was hand-feeding. Max's predecessor in parrothood, Alvin, lived with Elizabeth for 10 years before he died in the fall. In her store-appearance promotions for Passion, Elizabeth delighted customers by turning on her Maggie the Cat Southern accent and describing Alvin as "my main man, my little green man, and for three years the only man who has been privy to my bedroom."

In his last two years, Alvin was sharing at least some space with Larry Fortensky, the 38-year-old construction worker Taylor met at the Betty Ford Center in 1988. It was Larry who gave Elizabeth her most improbable get-well pet, Marina, a miniature

goat who roamed the yard and greeted visitors with little watchgoat noises.

Fortensky has supported Elizabeth faithfully in her efforts to cleanse herself of pills and alcohol. He attends AA meetings with her. Marriage, though, is out. "I think I've outgrown that," she said. "In today's society you don't need to be married. You don't need to tidy up. Not at my age, anyway."

Her pride in her sobriety explains the $20 million lawsuit she directed at the National Enquirer after it claimed during the summer that she was drinking in the hospital. "They went a little too far, and I finally got sick of it," she said. "They went into long, laborious detail about how I'd been drunk in the hospital, and the doctors had me on a suicide watch, and all this rubbish. This was completely untrue. It hurt me, and it has hurt others who believed in me. I've received thousands of letters from people who said, 'We've looked up to you. How could you?' I felt betrayed, and I felt I was betraying others. People kept saying, 'Well, why don't you sue?' So finally I did—not for the money, but really for the principle of it."

The same sense of indignation has made Taylor a genuine heroine in the battle against AIDS. Her involvement with AmFAR began in 1984 when she was asked to host the first AIDS fund-raising dinner ever. She then ran into "seven months of absolute and abject rejection" before finding supporters. When her friend Rock Hudson later became sick, she said, "I was already involved in it before any of us knew what was the matter with Rock. When I spoke with his doctors, I learned more and more about the disease. And that just made me angry. . . . Nobody asks for this disease. Nobody deserves it. We're all as innocent as babies in the eyes of God."

Dr. Mathilde Krim, the biologist and with Elizabeth the founding co-chairwoman of AmFAR, credited Taylor with helping bring AIDS awareness into the mainstream. "At the time, very few people were willing to speak up publicly for this cause," she said. "Elizabeth said she wanted to be head of it. Elizabeth is a smart, sincere, compassionate woman who commands enormous respect and prestige with the public. No one can match her." Taylor has traveled around the world raising money for AmFAR. Her strongest interest now is expanding the organization internationally.

Taylor's escort to last year's World AIDS Day fund-raiser was her friend Malcolm Forbes, who had already given her a $1 million check for AmFAR. "I miss him enormously," she said. "He knew how to give joy, and he loved to share. He was the least stingy soul I've ever met." Elizabeth bristled at speculation that Forbes was bisexual. "It's nobody's business what Malcolm's sexual preferences were," she said. "It's nobody's concern. I respected him, which means I respected his choices, all the way around. We knew each other very well."

She felt a very different sadness about the death of Halston this year from AIDS. "I didn't know until the last year," she said. "We all thought it was

something else. So many people with AIDS don't want people to know because of the stigma involved."

Taylor broke into self-deprecating laughter at the notion that she performed good works. The only credit she would give herself was her ability to stick with the problem. "You really have to focus yourself," she said. "It doesn't mean that I don't believe in a lot of things or think that they're not right. I can just focus on one thing at at time."

For a person who has been in show business nearly a half century, Taylor remains steadfastly close to her family and her friends. Her mother, Sara, now 94, lives in Palm Springs. Sons Michael and Christopher live in

Los Angeles with their families; daughters Liza and Maria are back East.

Her oldest friend, actor Roddie McDowall, met her when they were both child stars in 1943's *Lassie Come Home*. "I give her enormous credit, " he said. "She is compassionate and empathetic. And she has a wonderful sense of humor." McDowell paused, then added, "She can be tough with people, but she is honest with herself and true to what she is. She never cops a plea."

Her life has been an endless series of tragedies and triumphs. Close calls notwithstanding, Taylor felt no regrets. "I think regrets are a waste of time."

# trans·gres·sions
n., breaking laws or commandments: murder, mayhem, drug abuse, fraud, general degradation and all things unspeakable.

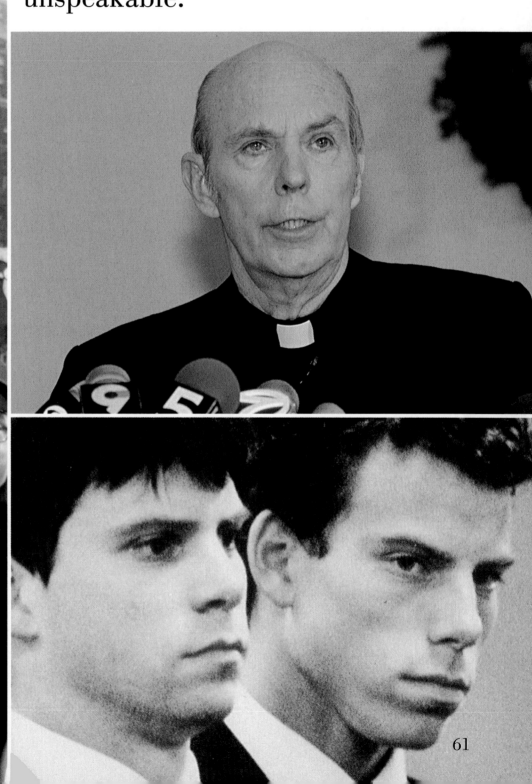

# TRANSGRESSIONS

# FATHER RITTER

**F**or more than 20 years, Covenant House was virtually synonymous with the Reverend Bruce Ritter, the Franciscan friar and onetime theology professor who founded the shelter for homeless youths on New York City's crime-ridden Lower East Side. The organization today serves 25,000 young people in the United States, Canada and Latin America. Did the patron saint of runaways use his position to persuade vulnerable young men to have sex with him? Evidence suggests that he did.

The first allegations were made in December 1989 by Kevin Kite, a 26-year-old former prostitute who not only claimed to have just concluded an eight-month-long sexual relationship with Ritter but also accused him of diverting thousands of dollars to finance their affair.

Ritter vehemently denied the charges and seemed to have survived the assault on his good name until three more men came forward. In January 1990, accusations surfaced from John Melican, 34, of Seattle; the following month both Darryl Bassile, 31, and Paul Johnson, 33, also publicly charged they had had sex with Ritter.

The Manhattan district attorney's office and Franciscan officials announced they were investigating the allegations, and in February Ritter was forced to step down as president of Covenant House. The next day Manhattan District Attorney Robert Morgenthau announced that no criminal charges would be filed against Ritter because there was "insufficient evidence" to warrant any. Morgenthau's three-and-a-half-month probe focused only on what he described as "some questionable financial transactions," by the

priest. Prosecutors had no authority to investigate allegations of sexual relations since the young men were either over the age of consent or because the statute of limitations had expired.

Ritter's religious order did not disclose the findings of its own investigation. It merely instructed the Covenant House founder to return to "daily living" in a Franciscan community instead of engaging in an outside ministry.

In August, a four-month investigation ordered by the Covenant House board of directors and headed by Robert J. McGuire, a former New York City police commissioner, concluded that Father Ritter had engaged in sexual misconduct with young men living at Covenant House shelters. The investigation report said that complaints about sexual contacts between Father Ritter and Covenant House residents had been circulating for almost 20 years and had been referred on at least two occasions to senior staff members and the priest's Franciscan superiors.

According to the report, prepared by Kroll Associates, an investigation agency, and the law firm of Cravath, Swaine & Moore, no single allegation could be proven beyond question, but the "cumulative evidence" was such "that if Father Ritter had not resigned, the termination of the relationship between him and Covenant House would have been required."

Father Ritter declined to be interviewed for the inquiry and has refused to respond to allegations after his initial denial. He maintained he was just being a mentor to troubled runaways. Even if his explanations were accepted, the report said, the conclusion would have been the same: that "Father Ritter exercised unacceptably poor judgment in his relations with certain residents."

# DEATH IN THE HOUSE OF BRANDO

**T**he 911 call came from America's most celebrated actor. His daughter's lover had been shot in the family's Los Angeles mansion. An hour later, the actor's son Christian was arrested and charged with murder.

The frantic voice on the line at 10:45 P.M. on May 16 was Marlon Brando's. When Los Angeles Fire Department Captain Tom Jefferson arrived minutes later and rushed to the den of Brando's sprawling 12-room home, he found an eerie scene. A man was lying back on the couch. The television was on, and channels were flipping continuously, as though the man were scanning the dial. According to police who arrived soon after, the man held a cigarette lighter in one hand and a remote control in the other. He was dead, shot once in the face.

Brando's 32-year-old son, Christian, told police he had accidentally killed the man, the lover of his 20-year-old half-sister, Cheyenne. The pregnant Cheyenne, Christian said, had complained to him at dinner that evening of being slapped around by her six-foot-three-inch, 270-pound boyfriend, a Tahitian named Dag Drollet. Christian, his attorneys later maintained, confronted Drollet with a .45 caliber handgun that went off when Drollet tried to wrest it away from him. There were reportedly no witnesses: Marlon Brando, his Tahitian common-law wife, Tarita Teriipia, and Cheyenne were in other parts of the mountaintop house when they heard a shot. The 66-year-old Brando, defense attorneys said, rushed to the den and attempted mouth-to-mouth resuscitation before and after phoning 911 for assistance. But the bullet had exited through Drollet's neck, and he was beyond help.

Besides the gun that killed 26-year-old Drollet, police confiscated from Christian a .44 caliber carbine, a shotgun, a MAC-10 machine-pistol, an M-14 assault rifle and what they said was a silencer. According to police, Cheyenne showed no signs of injury. The cops arrested Christian on the spot, and two days later he was arraigned on first-degree murder and lesser charges. He pleaded innocent.

Whether or not Christian proves to be criminally responsible for Drollet's death, the shooting was only the latest chapter in a troubled history. From infancy, Marlon Brando's firstborn was at the center of a lurid spectacle of recrimination and brawling between his parents.

Christian's mother, the Calcutta-born and convent-bred actress Anna Kashfi, was a 21-year-old London University economics student when she was discovered by a Paramount talent scout who delivered her to Hollywood in 1955 to play opposite Spencer Tracy in *The Mountain*. She met Brando, then 31, in the Paramount commissary; he was about to start filming *The Teahouse of the August Moon*. In 1957 Kashfi was pregnant and became the first of Brando's three wives. But the wedding bouquets had scarcely wilted when she told a reporter, "Living with Marlon is like an afternoon at the races—short periods of orgiastic activity followed by long periods of boredom and anticipation. He's almost never home." She added, "He attracts women like feces attract flies." After a year of matrimony, she left—taking five-month-old Christian with her. Thus began a brutal 16-year custody war in which Christian was both prize and pawn. Custody was first awarded to Kashfi, but she proved to be less than a model mother. Actress Delores Taylor, then headmistress of the Montessori

*Marlon and Christian Brando at the hearing.*

preschool that Christian attended, remembered rushing to Kashfi's house one day after receiving a call from a neighbor. Taylor discovered the little boy standing alone at the edge of the swimming pool. Inside the house she found Kashfi "passed out, lying in her own vomit."

In 1965, citing Kashfi's dependence on prescription drugs and alcohol, a Santa Monica Superior Court judge placed Christian temporarily with Brando's older sister Frances. Later, the judge returned him to Kashfi. In 1970 the boy was placed in the custody of both parents. In 1972 Christian was a boarding student at the Ojai Valley Military Academy near Santa Barbara. According to Kashfi, he had adjustment problems and was reported by the headmaster to have set a fire in a dormitory. While Brando was away filming *Last Tango in Paris*, Kashfi had Christian taken to Mexico, where an investigator whom Brando hired found him in the care of a group of American hippies. They claimed Kashfi had promised them payment for hiding the boy.

Christian's life was never settled. An 11th-grade dropout, he worked at various trades. For a while he had a tree-trimming business, until he was injured in a fall. A sometime construction worker, he also tried his hand at welding iron sculpture. His six-year marriage to a childhood friend, makeup artist Mary McKenna, ended in an acrimonious divorce in 1987. Two years ago film producer Carmine De Benedittis persuaded him to play the lead, a hired assassin, in the Italian film *What's at Stake*.

Christian's house is a small gray ranch with a junk-strewn yard on Wonderland Avenue, high atop Laurel Canyon in the Hollywood Hills. Reportedly, Marlon bought it and rented it to his son. It apparently had not been lived in for a few months, but whoever had been there last left dirty dishes in the sink, an Alcoholics Anonymous handbook on the floor and a *Soldier of Fortune* magazine on the rumpled bed.

According to the *Los Angeles Times*, police quoted Marlon Brando as saying Christian "always had a very bad temper and could be explosively violent when angry." Marlon reportedly went on to say that he did not believe Drollet had abused Cheyenne, but that his

*Christian and his mother Anna Kashfi in 1965, left. The Brando clan, right: son Miko, daughter Rebecca (the children of his second marriage to Mexican actress Movita), Brando, his third wife Tarita, son Teihotu and Christian's ex-girlfriend Jocelyne Lew.*

daughter had "psychological problems" and made false allegations against family members.

Christian's ex-wife, who once testified in her divorce that Christian had roughed her up and threatened to kill her, now swore by him. She was one of the first to visit him in jail. "He was very protective of his sister," she said, "but not the sort who would kill someone."

Cheyenne's three-year affair with Drollet, the son of a prominent Tahitian politician, had been touched by tragedy before. In March 1989, Drollet, driving in Tahiti with Cheyenne, struck and killed a pedestrian. (Criminal charges were dropped because the victim was drunk.) In August, Cheyenne—the daughter of Brando's 48-year-old wife, Tarita, his co-star in *Mutiny on the Bounty*—swerved off a Tahitian road and suffered disfiguring injuries to her face. For a time after the accident, she was severely depressed, once mentioning suicide.

Some friends think Cheyenne was upset by the fatherly attention Marlon paid to her teenage half-sister, Maimiti, Tarita's daughter by another man.

Sibling rivalry may have been further stoked when Marlon's maid, Christina Ruiz, gave birth last year to the youngest of his nine children, Ninna, while Brando was filming *The Freshman*. This year Cheyenne quit high school—her third—and moved out of Drollet's house in Tahiti. After Marlon failed to convince her to join him in Los Angeles, Drollet prevailed upon her to go. She asked him to accompany her, and he did, but he phoned his mother on May 13 to say that he and Cheyenne were still having problems. Just how serious those problems were will be an issue at Christian's trial. No one in the Brando house told police they heard any fighting or shouting on May 16. Just a shot.

New York civil rights attorney William Kunstler —a friend of Marlon's whom the actor called within minutes of the shooting—pleaded for Christian's release on bail at a May 21 hearing, citing letters from supporters including Jack Nicholson, Brando's next-door neighbor. Kunstler stressed that Christian had a blood-alcohol level of .19 percent (more than twice what constitutes drunkenness for California drivers) two hours after the shooting. "He has had an alcohol problem in the past," said the lawyer, speculating that "one thing led to another" and Christian may have confronted Drollet with the gun to scare him. "I don't know. But he was drunk, and there was a struggle over the gun, and it went off." In support of that contention, Kunstler said that Drollet was *not* originally found with a remote control in his hands and that evidence suggested the gun was fired only an inch or so from Drollet's head. But Deputy District Attorney Steven Barshop argued that Drollet's killing was a premeditated murder. The angle of the wound, the prosecutor said, suggested that Drollet had been shot from above while sitting, not in a struggle.

As a haggard, ashen-faced Marlon looked on, Los Angeles Municipal Court Judge Rosemary Shumsky denied bail. After the hearing, the elder Brando, his enormous girth straining at the belt on his gray slacks, was swarmed by reporters asking how he felt. "It's impossible to describe," he said.

On August 15, after nearly three months in jail, Christian Brando was released when Judge David Perez agreed to accept Marlon Brando's $4 million estate as bond.

Nearly 25 years ago, when Brando built a private retreat along Tahiti's western coast and took Tahitian actress Tarita Teriipia as his lover, he enveloped their family in the island's peaceful beauty. But the majestic paradise wasn't proof against the ugliness that eventually intruded on their lives. While Marlon awaited the start of Christian's murder trial in Los Angeles, Tarita—who sees Marlon infrequently these days—kept vigil outside a concrete-walled hospital room where Cheyenne was recovering from an apparently suicidal drug overdose that slipped her into a coma for a day.

Cheyenne had left for Tahiti soon after Christian shot her lover. In late June, she gave birth to son Tuki, presumed to be Drollet's child.

By phone from Los Angeles, Marlon told the Tahitian daily *La Dépêche* that Cheyenne "simply took too much of the medications that were prescribed by her doctor." But the editor-in-chief of the paper, Daniel Pardon, a family friend who was serving as the Brandos' spokesman, claimed, "She tried to commit suicide. It was not accidental. It was not two or three pills. It was a lot. Cheyenne took a cocktail of pills, antidepressants and such."

Cheyenne was found by Tarita on the morning of November 1 in the Brando compound in the affluent section of Tahiti referred to as the Gold Coast or Mini Beverly Hills. Tarita immediately took her to a local doctor, who called an ambulance to race Cheyenne to Mamao Hospital. According to Pardon, "Her heart was fibrillating. We thought she would die." But her condition stabilized later that day, and the next morning she opened her eyes briefly and squeezed a nurse's finger on request, signaling that she was out of the coma. Several days later, Cheyenne was alert and chatting with family members, but partial memory loss or other neurological impairment would take weeks to assess.

Unlike Christian, whose childhood was torn apart by high-pitched and highly publicized custody battles, Cheyenne grew up in the relative calm and simplicity of Tahiti. "I don't think I will let them go to the States," Marlon said in 1976 of Cheyenne and her brother, Teihotu. "As Tahitians, they are too trusting. They would be destroyed by the pace of life in the States." Indeed, when Cheyenne finally visited the United States as a teen, she experienced a difficult cultural adjustment.

Family friends traced Cheyenne's collapse back to her 1989 car accident. To repair the injuries to her face, she underwent extensive and painful reconstructive surgery in Los Angeles. Though she was still quite striking, friends speculated that she felt flawed. "Inside her flesh, there is plastic and metal," Pardon explained. "In Tahiti, physical appearance is very important for a woman. We elect a Miss This or a Miss That every week."

The shooting in May deepened her despair. It was rumored that Cheyenne had been using drugs, including cocaine. Pardon denied all charges of drug abuse but confirmed that after Tuki's birth, Cheyenne was sent to Vaiame, a local psychiatric hospital, where she was given medication to treat her depression.

After Cheyenne's intermittent visits to Vaiame over a period of two months, Pardon said, "Her problems were beginning to decrease," and she began working as a booking agent for the resort on the nearby island of Tetiaroa, which her father owns. Ironically, it might have been her increased happiness that sent her to the emergency room. According to Pardon, she stopped taking her medication, probably thinking because she felt better, she didn't need the pills. Having stopped abruptly, he believed she became "so anxious" that she attempted to take her own life.

Marlon, said Pardon, was ready to rush to his daughter's side but was afraid to leave Los Angeles just as Christian's trial was set to begin. Because Cheyenne is herself a key element in the trial—in one statement given to Los Angeles police before she left, she said that the shooting was intentional—her continued absence from the country could hamper the prosecution. The Los Angeles district attorney's office managed to delay the trial while trying to bring her back to the United States.

On November 11, Cheyenne made what was apparently her second attempt at suicide, in the family compound in Papeete. In an interview Marlon gave to the *Los Angeles Times*, he said, "Cheyenne hung herself. We don't know if there's been brain damage or not." He said she had been placed on a respirator. At last report, according to sources in Tahiti, Cheyenne appeared to be recovering. After reviewing psychiatric reports, Judge Joel Rudof of Santa Monica Superior Court ruled that prosecutors had not provided sufficient evidence that Cheyenne should be forced to return to Los Angeles to testify. As a result, prosecutors allowed Christian to plead guilty to a single charge of voluntary manslaughter.

# THE MENENDEZ BROTHERS

**T**he screenplay about an 18-year-old who murders his parents for their money was amateurish and banal. But the story line was not without interest, particularly to investigators looking into the brutal murder of a Cuban-born Hollywood millionaire and his wife. It was written by the couple's younger son, Erik.

On August 20, 1989, when the blood-spattered corpses of Jose Menendez and his wife, Mary Louise ("Kitty"), were found in the den of their five-million-dollar Beverly Hills mansion, the evidence pointed to a Mob hit. Jose, 45, chief executive of Live Entertainment, a prominent music-and-video distribution company, had been struck by eight shotgun blasts. In what had the look of a gangland-style coup de grace, the barrel of a gun had been thrust into his mouth, and the explosion had blown off the back of his head. Kitty, 44, had been shot five times. The bodies were found by the couple's sons, Lyle, 22, and Erik, 19, who told police they had returned from a night on the

town to find the front door of the family's Italianate mansion open and their parents' lifeless bodies within.

At first police looked for clues in Jose Menendez's complicated business affairs. But the two handsome sons were never totally beyond suspicion; they were the sole beneficiaries of their parents' estimated $14 million estate, and there was the matter of that curious screenplay. Erik Menendez had written it with a friend two years previously, and his proud mother had even helped type it. Though the two weapons police believe were used in the killings were never recovered, a shotgun shell casing was discovered by Lyle's friend in a pocket of one of Lyle's jackets. A relative found a reference to a will on Jose's home computer but did not know how to gain access to the document. Before a computer expert could be summoned to locate the file containing the will, it was erased. Marta Cano, Jose's sister, said Lyle did it by mistake.

Later, in a highly unusual move, investigators obtained cassette tapes of therapy sessions conducted

*Lyle and Erik Menendez.*

with Erik and Lyle by a Beverly Hills psychologist, L. Jerome Oziel. The tapes were said to contain crucial evidence against the brothers. Although California law protects the confidentiality of most patient-therapist relationships, it makes an exception when there is a threat of violence. According to Los Angeles Deputy District Attorney Elliott Alhadeff, the brothers had threatened Oziel.

Early in March the police moved. Lyle Menendez was arrested by police who stopped him and two friends shortly after they left the family's Beverly Hills home. Three days later his brother was arrested at the Los Angeles airport. Erik had flown home from Israel, where he had been playing in a tennis tournament, to surrender himself voluntarily. The two of them were charged with killing their parents. Their motive, said the police, was greed. Because of the brutal nature of the murders, and evidence of careful planning beforehand, authorities may ask for the death penalty if the brothers are convicted.

Jose Menendez's immigrant odyssey began in 1960, when at the age of 16 he was sent to the United States by his father, a onetime soccer star who stayed behind in Cuba until his last investment property was seized by Fidel Castro. Jose won a swimming scholarship to Southern Illinois University at Carbondale. His mother, Maria, had been a champion swimmer in her youth but gave it up because of the exhausting training schedule. Before graduating, Jose left Illinois for New York City, taking with him Kitty Andersen, a strong-minded young woman who had first attracted his attention in debating class.

After earning a degree in accounting at Queens College in New York, he took a job with the Manhattan firm of Coopers & Lybrand. At 23, he was hired away by one of his clients, a Chicago-based shipping company, as its comptroller. His next stop was Hertz, where he was put in charge of commercial leasing. After Hertz was bought out by RCA, Menendez switched to the parent company's record division and was soon involved in signing pop groups, including Duran Duran and the Eurythmics. Not long after he persuaded RCA to open a Miami office, he was responsible for signing Menudo and Jose Feliciano. Passed over for an executive vice presidency in 1986, Menendez jumped to International Video Entertainment, a California video distributor that eventually became Live Entertainment.

During the 16 years the Menendezes were in New Jersey, the family lived for a time in a Princeton country estate overlooking a lake. Jose, who was as demanding with his sons as with himself, insisted on excellence. When the boys were 12 and nine, he told them to concentrate on either tennis or soccer. When they chose tennis, he signed them up with coaches for private lessons three times a week. On weekends he would drill them for hours.

Erik and Lyle both attended private Princeton Day School, and in 1987 Lyle entered Princeton University, where he earned a spot on the varsity tennis team. He was popular with his classmates but left school after one semester. Though Princeton officials said only that he withdrew, the student newspaper reported that Lyle was suspended for copying another student's psychology lab report.

Lyle returned to Princeton for the 1989 spring semester, then dropped out of the university again after the murders. That fall he took an apartment nearby and showed up, students reported, driving a gray Porsche Carrera. In January, Lyle, who shared with Erik in a $400,000 insurance payout after his parents' deaths, bought Chuck's Spring Street Cafe, a popular student hangout, for a reported $550,000. Shortly after the purchase, Lyle changed the name of

the restaurant and was planning to open other locations in New Jersey and California. But he wanted to do much more than serve food; he planned to make his fortune in, among other things, show business and real estate. Lyle began traveling frequently—he flew to California early in March in an unsuccessful attempt to be named promoter of a Soul II Soul rock concert—and hired a 20-year-old Princeton sophomore as a $125-a-week consultant to Menendez Investment Enterprises, a corporate shell awaiting an infusion of cash that the consultant understood would come from Lyle's inheritance. Lyle's arrest put the investment operation on hold.

As for Erik Menendez, a 1989 graduate of Beverly Hills High School, his goals were even more expansive than Lyle's. In an interview two years ago, he spoke of fulfilling his father's ambition to become the first Cuban-born United States senator and to make Cuba a U.S. territory. According to Erik, he and Lyle planned to move to Florida, where they would establish a political base. "My brother wants to become President of the United States," said Erik. "I want to be senator and be with the people of Cuba. I'm not going to live my life for my father, but I think his dreams are what I want to achieve. I feel he's in me, pushing me."

Before saving Cuba, though, Erik decided to try his luck as a professional tennis player. He had been planning to enroll at UCLA, but after the murders, he hired a full-time tennis coach and set to work improving his game.

Certainly, equaling Jose's successes would have proved a challenge for the most driven of sons. International Video Entertainment (IVE) and its successor, Live, profited handsomely under Menendez's leadership. After losing $20 million in 1986, the company posted earnings of $8 million the following year and $16 million in 1988. (Ironically, its largest source of income last year was the millions it realized on a key-man insurance policy the company had taken out on its chairman.) All the while, Jose was making important connections in the entertain-

ment world. But Jose also had to negotiate with some less savory business associates along the way. The possibility existed that the two deaths had been an underworld hit.

The grisly and calculated nature of the crime made it hard to imagine that Jose and Kitty had been victims of an explosion of family rage, and Erik and Lyle didn't cave in under questioning. They told police they had left home on the evening of August 20 to see a movie. Arriving back shortly before midnight, they said they found the driveway gate unlocked and the front door open. In the den, next to a coffee table holding half-eaten bowls of fresh berries and cream, lay the bodies of their parents.

In the days following the brothers' arrest, members of the Menendez family gathered in the eight-bedroom Beverly Hills house. On hand were Jose's mother, Maria, 72, and his sisters, Marta Cano, 49, a divorcée from West Palm Beach, and Terry Baralt, 51, of West Windsor, New Jersey, whose husband, Carlos, is executor of the estate.

The family's greatest concern now is for the fate of Lyle and Erik, whom all of them believe to be innocent. The brothers remain in custody awaiting a California State Superior Court ruling as to whether the statements they allegedly made to their psychiatrist may be used against them.

*Lyle, Kitty, Jose and Erik in 1987.*

# IKE TURNER

Ike Turner, who was once half of the legendary soul superduo Ike and Tina Turner, sat in the visiting room of a California prison, debating semantics. The question at hand was whether Turner, who had served 13 months of a four-year sentence for cocaine possession, was ever actually addicted to the drug. Sure, he used the stuff for 20 years. And yes, he claimed to have spent more than $100,000 on coke in a two-month period in 1989....

Turner's apparent ability to deny what others might consider obvious goes a long way toward explaining his metamorphosis from pop star to prison inmate, as well as the breakup, in 1978, of his 14-year marriage to Tina Turner. He blamed his drug problems for the divorce. Tina suggested, in her 1986 autobiography, *I, Tina*, that drugs magnified her mate's worst traits. "He was always violent," wrote Tina, who claimed that Ike beat her frequently, "but cocaine made him worse."

Hooked on freebase cocaine since 1974, Turner, now 58, was unable to kick the habit until July, 1989, when he began serving his current sentence after being picked up for drug possession. He had been arrested 10 times previously for drugs and convicted twice. "I was on a 15-year party," he said.

Until he is eligible for parole late in 1991, home is a minimum-security, converted military barracks at the California Men's Colony, San Luis Obispo, where inmates are free to roam manicured lawns and flower gardens, play basketball, pump iron and observe the outside world through barbed wire fences. Among hostile groups, Turner is nonpartisan. "I get along with the Crips, the Bloods, the Klan and the skinheads," he said.

"The first thing he did when he arrived was announce to everybody, 'Hey, I'm Ike Turner,'" said prison guard David Shearer. "The youngsters here tend to look up to him."

The legend in their midst was raised in Clarksdale, Mississippi, by his seamstress mother, Beatrice Turner, after his father, Izear Luster Turner Sr., a Baptist minister, died in a fight. His mother remarried, but life didn't get less violent.

An eighth-grade dropout, Turner began to haunt local honky-tonks and started his own group, the Kings of Rhythm, in 1948. In East St. Louis in the early '50s, Turner met Tina, nee Anna Mae Bullock, 16, a high school junior from Brownsville, Tennessee, who within a year became the band's star attraction. The pair scored their first hit, "A Fool in Love," in 1960 and married in Tijuana in 1962. By 1965, thanks to "River Deep, Mountain High," produced by Phil Spector, they were the First Couple of soul; in 1969 they rocked Woodstock with their cover version of "Proud Mary."

Their marriage, however, was in trouble. His womanizing was one problem. "I was whorish all my life," said Ike, who once claimed to have bedded more than 100 women while wed to Tina. His temper was another danger zone. "All the fights Tina and I had were about her being sad about something. I get real emotional if you're worrying and don't tell me what it is. Then I can't think about nothing else. So I'd slap her or something like that."

After the divorce, Tina remained afraid of her ex. She once claimed to have signed over everything, "property, masters, rights, royalties" to free herself from Ike. He claimed that what he got were debts, problems and a measly $6,000 a year in royalties, and that, even now, Tina owes him. After his release, he said, "I'm going to reopen our divorce and file suit for slander. I still love her, but I don't like her, because she forgot where she came from. Last year I read Tina made $35 million. That name isn't really her name. The name 'Tina Turner' belongs to me. I won't settle for less than $70 million."

"I don't think that would fly," said Hy Mizrahi, Ike's loyal friend and agent for 20 years. "It's his own foolishness. If anything, Tina pulled him up." According to Mizrahi, Tina and her manager Roger Davies "have been swell to us. Ike will realize this and come out of prison a better man."

Perhaps. In the meantime, he rises at 6 A.M., works six hours a day in the prison library and lays plans to form a band upon his release. "I got good songs, good musicians, everything I need to get out of here and go No. 1," he said. "Drugs are the furthest thing from my life."

*Ike Turner at the Men's Colony in San Luis Obispo, California.*

# CHARLES STUART

**C**harles Stuart's claim that a black assailant killed his pregnant wife, Carol, shocked the nation; the deadly truth was even more terrible. This is the story of a husband's treachery, a dark family secret and the inescapable guilt that led to suicide.

In the end, the unfathomable question was "Why?" and Charles Stuart, the only person who knew, chose to go to his grave without providing an answer. He had told an appalling tale of urban violence: On the night of October 23, 1989, as he and his wife, Carol, left a birthing class at Boston's Brigham and Women's Hospital, Stuart said a black gunman forced his way into their car and made him drive to the vicinity of the Mission Hill district. After demanding the couple's cash and jewelry, said Stuart, the intruder shot Carol, who was seven months pregnant, through the back of the head, then seriously wounded Charles in the abdomen, leaving him to call state police for help on his car phone as his wife lay dying beside him. The whole gruesome scene, including the dramatic tape of rescue efforts by police and paramedics, stirred a volatile mixture of grief, fear and outrage.

Then it all began to unravel. By the morning of January 4, Stuart found himself under suspicion, recast as villain and murderer by the testimony of his own brother. With authorities closing in to arrest him, he parked his new Nissan Maxima on the Tobin Bridge leading from Boston to neighboring Chelsea. On the passenger's seat he left his driver's license and a terse note declaring that "the allegations have taken all my strength." Then he jumped 145 feet to his death in the muddy Mystic River below.

No longer were the Stuarts—Carol, 30, an attorney for a publishing house, Charles, also 30, a handsome businessman known as Chuck, and their son, Christopher, who died 17 days after an emergency cesarean—seen as the victims of a random interracial assault. The story that emerged to replace Chuck Stuart's fiction was more sinister—a scheme of murder and deceit concocted by a cold-blooded psychopath. According to investigators, Stuart not only killed his wife, but apparently used his brother Matthew, 23, to help hide the evidence.

Nowhere was outrage more palpable than in Boston's besieged black community. Immediately after the Mission Hill murder, Mayor Raymond Flynn had ordered "every available detective" onto the case. Police poured into the area and carried out "stop and frisk" searches of scores of young black males.

Nineteen days later the dragnet snared one William "Willie" Bennett, 39, who had been charged with burglarizing a video store. In a police lineup, Stuart would only identify him as looking "most like" the assailant. Still, Bennett became the prime suspect, and only hours before Stuart's suicide, prosecutors were presenting evidence to a grand jury to indict him.

To many blacks, the whole affair smacked of racism. Certainly some of the anger was justified. As early as the first week of December 1989, Boston was swirling with vague but persistent rumors that Stuart had murdered his wife.

Soon after the killing, Matthew flew to California, where he remained for six weeks while Chuck was recuperating. But on the evening of January 3, Matthew went to Boston Police Headquarters and for the next six hours told his extraordinary story—that on the night of the murder he rendezvoused on a deserted street in Mission Hill with Chuck, who passed him Carol's Gucci purse and a nickel-plated, snub-nosed .38 revolver. Matthew said that he and a friend, John McMahon, then dumped the incriminating evidence from a railroad trestle over the Pines River in Revere—everything except Carol's supposedly stolen engagement ring, which he kept for 72 days before turning it over to authorities. Matthew reportedly denied he had known that Chuck intended to murder Carol.

With Matthew's admission, authorities began to move in on Chuck. Stuart had apparently been tipped off that the police were after him, and spent the night at a motel. Early the next morning he drove to the Tobin Bridge.

*Police pull Stuart's body from the Mystic River.*

After Stuart's death, authorities pursued a host of possible motives for Carol's murder. According to one source, police believe he may have taken out some $600,000 in insurance policies on Carol's life, though he cashed only $82,000 worth. Investigators believe that Chuck, an accomplished chef, wanted the money to open his own restaurant. A Lowell man, reportedly approached by Chuck about killing his wife, publicly confirmed that the conversation had taken place. He also said Chuck told him that he wanted Carol killed because she had refused to have an abortion and he feared that with a child she might give up her job—and income—thus foiling his dreams of opening a restaurant.

How was Stuart able to avoid suspicion for so long? Partly because he realized the usefulness of playing on whites' racial fears. Stuart's credibility was also enhanced by the seriousness of his wound, which required seven hours of life-threatening surgery.

Before the crime, Stuart went about his business as if nothing were amiss. Nor did Chuck's performance waver after the killing. In a much-publicized gesture, hours before his son, Christopher, died, he asked to be wheeled beside the incubator to say goodbye.

Boyhood friends remembered Chuck as intensely ambitious. After his death it turned out he had for years been lying to some people about his education.

He claimed to have gone to Brown on a football scholarship when in fact he had attended Salem State College, and only for a few months. Like Chuck, Carol came from a middle-class background, the second child of Evelyn and Giusto DiMaiti. A native of Medford, she was an excellent student who graduated from Boston College and cum laude from Suffolk Law School. Chuck and Carol married in 1985. There were some signs of discord in their relationship, but nothing remarkable and certainly nothing to suggest murderous hatred. The news of Chuck's guilt and his suicide devastated his parents, yet investigators say all but one of his siblings may have known of Chuck's involvement before Matthew came forward.

Though Willie Bennett was cleared of any involvement in the Stuart case, he and his family angrily maintained that no words of apology would undo their suffering.

It seemed for a time as if the legacy of Carol DiMaiti Stuart could only be one of pain—both to the family bereaved by her murder and to the city riven by her husband's unconscionable lie. Hoping in some small way to set right the insult upon the neighborhood, the DiMaitis decided to establish a scholarship foundation and to devote the proceeds to the residents of Mission Hill.

# JUSTICE FOR THE CENTRAL PARK JOGGER

**T**hirty-three witnesses had appeared for the prosecution in the trial of three New York teenagers accused of the gang rape and attempted murder of the woman known as the Central Park Jogger. After a three-week procession of cops, forensic experts and seven less seriously injured victims of the infamous April 1989 rampage, the victim, known simply as the Jogger—because the press traditionally protects the privacy of rape victims—was called to the stand by Manhattan Assistant District Attorney Elizabeth Lederer.

Through the side door of the court came a woman who was all but back from the dead. The frenzied mob of some dozen young men that allegedly attacked her as she ran alone on a deserted road at about 9:30 one pleasant spring night had silenced her screams and stilled her desperate struggles by smashing her face and skull over and over again with a brick, a rock and a lead pipe. After being raped and sodomized, she was left naked in a mud puddle, bound and gagged with her own bloody shirt. Two men walking home through the park discovered her at 1:30 A.M. and summoned help. By the time an ambulance arrived 25 minutes later, she had lost two-thirds of her blood. Her pulse rate had fallen to 40, her body temperature down to 80 degrees Fahrenheit. Doctors were doubtful she would live. But during the next 15 months, she fought her way out of a coma and back to work as an investment banker. Every step of the way she had to contend with the fact that her private pain had become an international drama. The Jogger became a symbol of urban crime, of violence against women, of racial antipathy.

A young woman carrying only 90 pounds on her five-foot-five-inch frame, her blond hair cut in a pixieish wedge, hobbled up the steps to the witness chair. After being sworn in, her hand trembling on the Bible, she was asked to state her name. She gave it in a strong, clear voice. In that instant she reclaimed herself from the headlines. She was no longer a symbol, but a woman—somebody's sister, somebody's daughter, a human being who looked in the mirror each morning and saw a scarred face looking back.

It once seemed incredible that that face would ever be seen in the courtroom. Doctors had speculated that the brain damage that left the woman comatose for two weeks might keep her from walking or talking again. A month after the attack, she had trouble recognizing her mother and couldn't remember what year it was. At best, specialists had predicted, she had only a 50-50 chance of ever being able to dress and feed herself. But after seven weeks in the hospital, she was transferred to a rehabilitation center, and seven months later she returned to work at the investment banking house of Salomon Brothers, though she had to take a daily break for rehabilitative therapy. She even resumed jogging, with colleagues alongside to steady her.

A strong-willed woman, she was determined to testify, reportedly over the objections of her family. Intent upon maintaining her anonymity, she obtained a court order barring courtroom artists from sketching her face. But she believed it was her responsibility to aid in the prosecution of the defendants— Yusef Salaam, 16, Antron McCray, 16, and Raymond Santana, 15—who, as youthful offenders, faced maximum prison terms of five to 10 years. Three other teens also charged with her rape were still to be tried.

After eliciting basic information—the woman is 30, single, and came to New York City in 1986— Lederer moved to the heart of the testimony that was

*The Jogger's sneakers, running pants and socks.*

to be presented to the 10-man, two-woman jury. "For what reason did you run at night?"

"Because running was something I enjoyed to do quite a bit and because of my hours at work," said the witness, her nervousness evident only in the tight grip of one manicured hand on the other.

"Can you tell the members of the jury, please, what you remember about April 19 of 1989?" The woman, her right eye sometimes wandering, described her workday, then recalled the tiny decision that changed her life. "I remember a phone conversation I had about five o'clock in the evening with a person I was going to have dinner with that night, but I had to say I couldn't go to dinner because I had some more work to do. And I was going to be at work a few more hours."

That schedule put her in the park at the wrong time, but mercifully her brain injuries blotted out any recollection of the horror that befell her there. "Do you have any memory whatsoever of what happened to you in the park on April 19, 1989?" asked Lederer.

"No, I do not." In fact, the witness explained, she remembered nothing between the five P.M. dinner conversation and awakening in a hospital room more than five weeks later. She could not identify the defendants as her attackers. McCray and Santana had given videotaped confessions, and police claimed they had notes of admissions by Salaam. The defendants' attorneys insisted their clients' statements were coerced.

"Do you recognize People's 33 in evidence?"

"Yes, I do," said the woman, anxiously licking her scarred lower lip.

"What do you recognize this to be?"

"It's the shirt that I used to wear."

"Prior to April 19, what color was this shirt?" the prosecutor then asked her.

"It was white." The shirt in Lederer's hands was a distinctive shade of brown, caked as it was with dried blood.

The witness moved on to tie up a loose end in the prosecution's case. DNA tests had failed to identify any semen on the woman as that of the accused, but traces on her clothing were matched to her boyfriend. She explained that she had had sexual relations with him, and then gone running, three days before the attack. She described the injuries she lives with: Problems with balance cause her to veer right or left when she walks; she needs help with stairs; she has completely lost her sense of smell; she suffers double vision. "Do you have any scarring?" the prosecutor asked.

"Yes, I do," she said.

The trial ended on August 18. Antron McCray, Yusef Salaam and Raymond Santana were convicted and sentenced to five to 10 years in prison. Their convictions are being appealed.

On December 11, Kevin Richardson, 16, was convicted on all eight counts on which he was charged. He will be sentenced on January 9, 1991, and faces five to 10 in a state youth correction center. Kharey Wise, 18, was acquitted of rape and attempted murder charges. He faces eight-and-two-thirds to 26 years in state prison if New York State Supreme Court Justice Thomas B. Galligan orders his convictions of assault, sexual abuse and riot to be served consecutively. Because he was 16 at the time of the attack, he will be sentenced as an adult. Both Richardson and Wise are appealing their convictions.

One more defendant remains. Steven Lopez, 16, is scheduled to go on trial in 1991.

# THE CASE OF HILARY FORETICH

**A**t the age of seven, Hilary Foretich had already seen the world—probably too much of it. As the object of the most desperate custody battle in memory, she spent 30 months on the run with her grandparents, touching down on three continents and traveling 15,000 miles. On the morning after authorities tracked her down, in a motel room in Christchurch, New Zealand, Hilary did what came naturally—she made a tent of blankets and crawled inside, trying to escape the bewildering adult world that had been so unrelenting in its pursuit of her.

The sensational news that Hilary had been found set legal machinery grinding on both sides of the Pacific. In August 1987, Hilary's mother, Dr. Elizabeth Morgan, sent her into hiding after charging in court that her ex-husband, Dr. Eric Foretich, had sexually abused the child. Morgan, 42, a Washington, D.C., plastic surgeon, spent 25 months in jail on contempt charges for refusing to turn over her daughter for unsupervised, court-mandated visits with Foretich.

Meanwhile, Foretich, 47, who launched an international search for Hilary, rejoiced that his daughter had been found—and once again vehemently denied the allegations of sexual abuse, reminding reporters that he had never been charged by police with any improprieties against her. "I am a good father trying to find my child," he told a reporter before flying to New Zealand to shape legal strategy with his attorneys. "I am tired of being portrayed as a latter-day Jack the Ripper." Public accusations were an ugly hallmark of the case from the beginning. One target was William Morgan, 79, who along with his wife, Antonia, 75, was responsible for spiriting away granddaughter Hilary. Following several intemperate outbursts from William while being hounded by the press—at one point he called Foretich "a psycho-

pathic pedophile pervert"—the outside attorney appointed in 1986 by a Washington court to represent the child characterized the elder Morgan as an "extremely unstable" man whose presence could pose "a danger to Hilary's best interests."

With Hilary's whereabouts no longer unknown, both sides had a chance to resolve the case once and for all—though not before what promised to be an acrimonious court fight. A judge in New Zealand granted temporary custody of Hilary to her grandparents and imposed a gag order. The proceedings would be conducted in secrecy.

The long, bizarre flight of Hilary and her grandparents was over. From the day Elizabeth handed over the little girl in the parking lot of a Virginia diner, Antonia and William, both retired psychologists, carried out their mission with determination and cunning. During World War II, William had served as a major in the Office of Strategic Services, the forerunner of the CIA, and that gave him more than a passing familiarity with clandestine methods. While on the run, the couple used only cash, never checks or credit cards, to avoid leaving a paper trail. Yet they always traveled under their own names to avoid later allegations that they had broken the law. (According to her mother and grandparents, Hilary insisted on being called Ellen in an effort to distance herself from the pain they said she was leaving behind.)

Their first months on the run were hectic ones. After remaining briefly in the Washington area, the Morgans flew to Nassau, in the Bahamas, and set up house in a beach cottage. Within three months, the high price of island living sent them packing for Toronto. There they rendezvoused with their son Jim, 44, a New York City investment banker, who drove up one night with $30,000 in money orders to pay their expenses. Their next stop was Vancouver, where they stayed for several days in a downtown hotel. The city

*Hilary, mother Elizabeth Morgan and father Eric Foretich.*

*Hilary with her grandparents William and Antonia Morgan.*

looked inviting, but Antonia worried about being so close to the U.S. border, where publicity about the Morgan case threatened constantly to give them away.

According to the Morgans, those first few months were the most traumatic for Hilary, who suffered from nightmares and screaming fits. Occasionally she seemed almost suicidal—a result, her grandparents insisted, of her alleged molestation, not of her disrupted life.

Hilary appeared to have made a remarkable recovery by the time she and her grandparents reached their next destination, Great Britain. (Antonia, who was born in London, holds both British and U.S. passports.) After stopping over briefly in Glasgow, they settled in a two-bedroom apartment in a suburb of Plymouth in November 1987. Hilary enrolled in the private Beechfield College school. By all accounts she seemed normal and content.

Meanwhile, her mother was serving time at the District of Columbia jail. Elizabeth said she never attempted to contact her daughter directly for fear of unwittingly disclosing Hilary's location. Instead she relied on relatives to bring her news of the child.

Antonia feared Foretich might trace them to her native land and after eight months convinced William that they should head for New Zealand, which she had visited two years earlier. Their two-bedroom apartment at the Diplomat Motel in Christchurch was far from sumptuous, but cozy enough. It was also less than a minute's walk from Selwyn House, the prestigious girls school where Hilary was enrolled in kindergarten. Once again she took root and seemed to flourish.

The motel apartment became a kind of haven dedicated to providing Hilary with a normal childhood. There was a goldfish bowl and a dollhouse, plus piles of toys scattered throughout the five rooms.

Even so, the Morgans never let down their guard. Until last May, only a few people knew their secret. And Hilary never seemed totally secure; she insisted that her grandmother sleep in the same room with her. The Morgans had spent some $200,000, most of it from their own savings, to finance their flight. (Elizabeth's legal bills have put her nearly two million dollars in debt.) One unanticipated result of the ordeal was that it brought William and Antonia closer. The couple had separated in 1980 and divorced in 1986. Thrown together again by the effort to hide their granddaughter, they decided to remarry.

In May 1989 a New Zealand television station broadcast a documentary on celebrated child-custody battles. One of the children featured was Hilary. By that time, the private detectives Foretich had hired to find his daughter were starting to close in. In December they got a break after a British television show aired its own program on custody fights, with a photo of Hilary. Within weeks Foretich's detectives had traced Hilary to Christchurch.

Despite Hilary's U.S. citizenship, the New Zealand family courts had jurisdiction over her case. While returning Hilary to her grandparents, the court immediately appointed a neutral child-abuse expert to examine Hilary and determine the credibility of her accusations. (Elizabeth Morgan had vainly asked the District of Columbia courts to do just that rather than rely on the contradictory testimony of experts hired by her and her ex-husband.) The New Zealand judge also named a lawyer to represent Hilary's legal interests and barred Foretich from even seeing his daughter face-to-face until it could be determined whether she would agree to such a visit and whether it might be psychologically detrimental to her.

Perhaps more critical to Morgan's case was the fact that her lawyers would be able to introduce testimony from Heather Foretich, Eric's nine-year-old daughter by a previous marriage, who claimed, in court documents, that he molested her as well. (Eric had been denied visitation rights with Heather, but he had never been charged by police with sexually abusing her.) The Morgans hoped that they could do in New Zealand what they failed to do in Washington: win an outright victory, depriving Foretich of all visitation rights.

On November 21 a family court judge in Christchurch awarded custody to Morgan and barred Foretich from visiting Hilary "in the immediate future." By court decree, Hilary must remain in New Zealand where Morgan is studying for a degree in clinical psychology. Since Paul Michel, the federal judge Morgan married a year ago, is required by law to live in the Washington area, the two have a commuter marriage. Meanwhile, a Fairfax county court has forbidden Foretich visitation rights with his other daughter until she asks to see him.

# THE KILLING OF YUSUF HAWKINS

**O**n the evening of August 23, 1989, Yusuf Hawkins, 16, and three friends from the East New York section of Brooklyn emerged from the subway in the mostly white, Italian working-class neighborhood of Bensonhurst. The four were on their way to look at a used car they had seen advertised for sale when they were surrounded by about 30 white youths, some wielding baseball bats. Moments later four shots rang out, and Hawkins crumpled to the sidewalk, dying from two bullets to the chest.

Moses Stewart, Hawkins's father, had been home from work for about an hour when there was a knock at the door. The sister of Diane Hawkins, Yusuf's mother, told his parents their son had been hurt in an accident and that they were needed at the hospital.

"Before we left," Stewart recalled, "she pulled me aside and said, 'Your son, Yusuf, he was shot.' My first assumption was uh-oh, they went somewhere and got into it with somebody, and somebody shot him in the arm or his behind or leg or something, and he's lying in the hospital waiting for somebody to come get him and bring him home.

"But when I walked through the door, our nephew walked out of the room with the doctors, and I could see from the expression on his face that something was very, very wrong. I took the doctor off to the side, and he took me into a room. He said something like, 'Your son was shot twice in the heart, and he's dead. Would you like me to tell your wife?' I said, 'No. I don't believe you told me like that. Are you trying to tell me my son is dead?' He said, 'Yes, that's what I'm telling you. Would you like me to tell your wife?' I said, 'No, I don't want you to say anything to her, not if you're going to tell her like you told me.' So I called her into the office, and I told her."

"He got down on his knees and told me," said Diane.

Six days later thousands of mourners flocked to the Lawrence H. Woodward Funeral Home in Bedford-Stuyvesant to file past Yusuf's body. A host of poli-ticians and black leaders, including the Reverend Jesse Jackson, came to pay their respects. Moses was less than flattered by some of the attention. "I had made it known to everybody that I was not going to allow my son to be used for any political game, because I didn't want them bouncing him around between them for votes."

After the burial, neither parent was able to return to work—Stewart, 35, as a driver, 36-year-old Diane as a secretary. Together with their surviving sons, Freddie, 19, and Amir, 15, in high school and junior high school, respectively, they struggled to cope with their loss.

"He was loved. Between Amir and Freddie, he was like the scales of justice. They'd put their weight on him and see which side he would lean to. Freddie being the first and a few years older was more independent, more like myself as I came up. Amir and Yusuf were very, very tight. They were so close, you would think they were twins. They did everything together.

"He was very good at basketball. He was a helluva good checker player too. He used to beat me all the time. He was also academically very good. He maintained an 85 average and received all these awards in elementary school, junior high school, and he was headed to Transit Tech." Yusuf, who wanted to be a technical engineer, had been scheduled to go to the vocational high school in East New York for a three-day orientation the Monday after he was killed. Diane remembered his excitement. "He said to me, 'Mom, I can't wait till Monday comes.' His father had bought him a new outfit of clothes to go in, and he was so much looking forward to it."

"He never got to put the clothes on," said Moses. "In every other case of racial violence, there was always some sort of excuse. But here there were no drugs, there were no women, there were no weapons, there was no confrontation. So often, in the black community particularly, we lose our children to the streets. But we can safely say that our sons don't do drugs, they don't run around and get in any kind of trouble with the law, they're not having children out of wedlock. Yusuf was aware that racism existed, but he had never experienced it. He would hear about it on television, or read about racial incidents, and he would always want to know, 'Why?' It kinds of gets to me every time I think about it. For him to have lived his 16 years within the black community, where we have a higher rate of killing one another than anybody else, and then to venture into a neighborhood that one would call middle-class, and then to lose his life—it's very, very strange when you really sit down and think about it.

"It's the same thing my younger son asks to this day: 'Why are people like that?' To him it's inconceivable that somebody could just dislike somebody because they have a different color skin. Yusuf and his friends didn't know they were walking into the lion's den. They were going into Bensonhurst, another area with another people who had an altogether different set of rules. These people have a deep-rooted hatred for anybody outside them, and they don't feel they've done anything wrong. Yusuf's first experience with racism was fatal."

With the Reverend Al Sharpton, a controversial black activist, and other community leaders, Stewart and Diane and hundreds of supporters went on a series of protest marches through Bensonhurst, where they were met by jeering white residents.

"You would think the community would understand, and it would be a little remorseful," said Stewart. "But instead they pulled their pants down, told us what we could kiss. They walked up and spit in my face."

"It seems like no one there cares about any other human being," said Diane. "I don't see any people trying to go along with us and saying that, okay, we're sorry this happened."

Stewart added: "I've always said that out of this tragic thing, you've got to find some good. I went out there and I was looking to see if just somebody breaks through that line and says, 'Mr. Stewart, Ms. Hawkins, I'm so sorry about what happened.' That would have made me feel 100 percent better.

"They did send us letters, but it was like they were signing a petition, like it was almost an orchestrated thing. I can read between the lines. We got three letters from three white elementary school kids in Boston that were more touching and personal than anything that ever came out of Bensonhurst.

"Instead of protesting, I could say, well, he was shot and he's dead, and the courts are going to handle it. But his death did this to me: I don't ever want to see that again. I feel that it's my job to make some noise. You've got to wake people up to what's happening, because there're thousands of Yusufs out there of all races. Right now, as we talk, some kid is

being murdered simply because of his color. And if the fathers don't take an active role, who will?"

The family visited Yusuf's grave March 19, on what would have been his 17th birthday.

"It was very, very rough, because to go to your child's grave is the final step. Every time you go to that grave it's the same—your loved one is there," said Stewart. "He was just touching the surface of what it was really going to be like to grow up, and he never got that chance. When I go to that cemetery, I say to myself, 'I wish it was me. I wish I could have been the one that took the bullet.'"

The racially charged drama switched to the Brooklyn State Supreme Courthouse in April, when Keith Mondello, 19, charged with organizing the mob and instigating Hawkins's murder, and Joseph Fama, 19, who was accused of firing the shots, went on trial for Yusuf's murder. Diane could not bring herself to sit through much of the testimony, but Stewart went to the proceedings religiously.

"There were 30 guys with bats talking about killing 'niggers' and Puerto Ricans, and nobody sees this? Come on. For the justice system not to pursue it, that killed what faith I had in it. When I get into that courthouse and see Mondello walk up and down that hallway, and I look in this guy's face, I want to become a murderer myself," said Stewart. "Those who I've had around me, Reverend Al Sharpton, my family and everybody, say, 'Let justice be served, let it work itself out.' But personally, it couldn't give me greater pleasure to just snap his neck and get all this over with. You never know what the death of a child will do to you. It's almost like somebody pushing buttons in there that you didn't even know were there.

"I'm going into that courtroom hoping for a guilty verdict, like I was hoping Yusuf was only wounded. But if they come out there and say not guilty, then I've taken the loss again. Yusuf to me would have been killed two times.

"Yusuf died three days before my 35th birthday. We'll be in the house, and we're always looking for him to come out of that room. We walk into his room, and there's his shoes, there's his clothes, his posters on the wall. And you don't want to feel uncaring by going and taking them down. You want the memory to live on, but every time you look at the memory, it brings back that hurt and that regret. His death did this to me: I don't ever want to see that again. You've got to wake people up to what's happening."

In May, Joseph Fama was convicted of second-degree murder. He was sentenced to 32 years and eight months in prison. On the following day, Keith Mondello was acquitted of both murder and manslaughter. The jury found him guilty of 12 lesser charges—ranging from first-degree riot to

*Yusuf's parents, Diane Hawkins and Moses Stewart.*

menacing—but Hawkins family supporters were bitterly disappointed. When the verdict was read, Diane doubled over as if hit in the stomach. Rage spilled into the streets of Brooklyn as angry blacks attacked TV news crews.

But even as the Mondello jury was being dismissed, the Bensonhurst case took on still another twist. *Eyewitness News*, a newscast on ABC's New York City station, interviewed a woman, identified only as Maria, who said she saw the murder. Just before the fatal shots, she claimed she saw Fama hesitate and then heard Mondello say, "Shoot him, he's just a nigger." A prosecutor in the U.S. Attorney's office in Brooklyn said that federal law-enforcement officials were considering pursuing federal civil rights charges in the case.

Moses Stewart, whose sister, according to a source, died the night of the second verdict and whose father fell into a coma two days later, remained in seclusion with his family.

# in·dis·cre·tions

n., injudicious acts: lapses in judgment, criminal screw-ups, major faux pas and tacky celebrity shenanigans.

# BISHOP MARINO

**E**ugene A. Marino seemed to be all one could ask for in a priest. By 37, the Josephite pastor from Biloxi, Mississippi, was vicar-general of his order; by 40, he was an auxiliary bishop in Washington, D.C. Two years ago, at 53, he was elevated to Archbishop of Atlanta and became the highest-ranking black Catholic in the United States. Archbishop Pio Laghi, Pope John Paul II's personal representative, was impressed by the turnout of bishops at Marino's consecration: "That means the selection by the Holy Father . . . is the right one," said Laghi.

Or was it? Church officials admitted early in August that Marino had resigned his office after an internal investigation revealed his two-year affair with Vicki Long, 27, an aspiring singer and Eucharistic minister.

Long has a history of involvement with men of the cloth. Two days after the Marino disclosures, a second priest—the Reverend Michael Woods, 48, pastor of St. Jude the Apostle in the Atlanta suburb of Sandy Springs—confessed in an open letter to his parish that he too had had an affair with her. But through her attorney, Long denied any misconduct with Woods, who served at her church in nearby Hapeville for more than a decade. "Woods is the godfather of her child and a close family friend," said the lawyer, Anthony Fontana. "She's never had anything to do with him sexually."

In a bizarre twist, that child, 4-year-old LaDonna, figured in yet another of Long's alleged sexual relationships with priests. In 1987 Long filed a paternity suit against the Reverend Donal Keohane, formerly of the diocese of Savannah, naming him as LaDonna's father. Although a 1988 court-ordered blood test seemed to clear Keohane, the Church had already reportedly promised to pay Long compensation.

In the Marino case, Long claimed that it was the Archbishop who seduced her and even committed himself to marriage. She said, through her attorney, that she approached Marino because he expressed a desire to help victims of sexual abuse. "That's when the Archbishop reached in to take control of her life," said Fontana, "and to establish a sexual relationship with her."

Long alleged that the entire cycle began when she was molested by a nun at age 19. Marino was said to be receiving counseling and medical care out of state.

*Marino celebrating Mass in 1988; Vicki Long, inset.*

# INDISCRETIONS

# ZSA ZSA GABOR

**Z**sa Zsa Gabor was in trouble again. At a probation hearing in Los Angeles, Judge Charles Rubin ruled that the 73-year-old actress had violated her probation by failing to complete her 120 hours of community service at a homeless shelter. He ordered The Zsa to complete her sentence and tacked on an additional 60-hour penalty, which had to be fulfilled by September 28.

Gabor was first sentenced in December 1989 after being found guilty of slapping a Beverly Hills policeman, driving without a valid license and having an open bottle of liquor in her car.

Then just when it seemed that things on the Zsa Zsa Gabor front had quieted down, the Princess von Chutzpah struck again. According to Beverly Hills Realtor Elaine Young, 55, Gabor contacted her about selling her Bel-Air home. Zsa Zsa wanted Young to list her house for $15 million. The house, once owned by Howard Hughes, was purchased by Gabor in 1973 for $245,000.

Young said Gabor agreed to hold an open house in August for potential buyers. Young estimated she spent $2,500 on newspaper ads, sales brochures and two security guards for the open house.

"The ads were already published," said Young, "when Zsa Zsa called and demanded that I also pay to have her carpets cleaned for the open house. She asked for $1,500, which I knew was outrageous for carpet cleaning, so I sent her a check for $400."

When Young arrived at the Gabor house on August 12, the first thing she noticed, she said, was that the carpets had not been cleaned. Then, 20 minutes before the open house was to begin, Gabor, who had said previously she would not be there, appeared and asked Young what she was doing.

Young reminded her about the open house, to which Young said Gabor replied, "What open house? Everybody out!"

In a letter to Young the following day, Gabor wrote, "Even though you think I have no manners, I am Princess von Anhalt and Zsa Zsa Gabor!!! My jewelry and furs were in the closets. My expensive paintings, silver and antiques were everywhere. Nobody I know has an open house like this where people can tell their friends who tell their friends where everything is—as I really don't need another burglary."

Young, who stood to earn a 4.5 percent commission if she had sold the house, said that "no amount of money" would ever make her go back to Zsa Zsa's.

# ROB LOWE

**T**he setting is a louche Los Angeles club where disaffected young moderns are sipping Stoli, watching an arty sex show and languidly cruising for a night's company. Actor Rob Lowe has his choice of astonishing-looking women; that night, he takes home not one bedmate, but two. After thrashing about with his brunet partner, he hops out of bed, naked, to saunter into the bathroom. The blond, reaching out to caress her companion, pipes, "I'm next."

To those who saw the pornographic home video that set off a fire storm around Lowe in the summer of 1989, this scene from his movie *Bad Influence* may have seemed ironic, if not exploitative. *Bad Influence* was less graphic than the tape of Lowe's real-life ménage, but the parallels were unmistakable: Alex, the character he played, used a video camera to record a sexual encounter that later proved as embarrassing as it was self-destructive.

*Bad Influence*, written several years ago, was shot in Los Angeles during the height of the scandal that broke when a segment of Lowe's low-life video was leaked to the press. He was besieged by reporters and slapped with a civil suit by the mother of one of his playmates (Jan Parsons, a 16-year-old Atlanta-area girl whose performance was not part of the widely seen tape). He kept his silence as yet another segment of the pirated tape, showing Lowe cavorting with an unidentified "Justin" and "Jennifer," was becoming an underground classic. While Lowe was discussing the fine points of his *Bad Influence* character with director Curtis Hanson, *Screw* magazine publisher Al Goldstein was doing a brisk mail-order business with a clip featuring an impressive closeup of a naked, fully aroused Rob.

Lowe's lawyers paid an undisclosed sum to Jan Parsons and her father, John (a retired Air Force major who won custody of Jan after he and his wife divorced in March 1989). After a meeting with Fulton County District Attorney Lewis Slaton—who chose not to prosecute him for taping a sexual encounter with a partner under 18—Rob agreed to do 20 hours of community service, speaking at prisons and halfway houses and in his hometown of Dayton, Ohio.

Lowe did not dispute the fact that he videotaped his guests in bed or that they knew the proceedings were being recorded for posterity. "There was never any question," said Rob. In fact, few of those who knew Lowe were shocked when the videotape surfaced later.

These days Lowe was keeping a relatively low social profile. Inquiries about his private life were met with polite evasions and he was not prepared to discuss the ethics of taping one's intimate encounters. "I don't have time to sit and judge somebody else for what they might do in their bedroom," he said with exasperation.

Lowe's own hot topic was How I Have Become a Better Person Through Adversity. "I've learned the importance of admitting when you have made a mistake, when you have been wrong or made bad judgments," he said. "And I learned that you must accept the consequences of your actions. That's part of being the man that I want to be."

# RICHARD BERENDZEN

**R**ichard Berendzen, the son of a Dallas hardware-store salesman and his wife, earned a doctorate in astronomy and education from Harvard at age 29. Moving on to teaching stints at Harvard, Boston University and American University in Washington, D.C., Berendzen boasted that he worked seven days a week and slept only three or four hours a night. His energy did not go unrewarded. Ten years ago, at age 42, he was named president of American University—a stunning achievement for a man who was the first member of his family to attend college.

With characteristic zeal, Berendzen channeled all his efforts into American, an 11,500-student private university with a lackluster reputation and a paltry endowment. Under his direction, the school became more academically competitive and the endowment quadrupled. His ceaseless fund-raising and networking with the rich and powerful soon turned the lanky, bespectacled Berendzen into a semicelebrity himself. In between wooing high-profile donors like Saudi millionaire Adnan Khashoggi and recruiting a team of advisers that included Walter Cronkite, Carl Sagan and Farrah Fawcett, he even found time to publish a celebratory book about his experiences as a college president. The title: *Is My Armor Straight?*

Obviously it was not. On April 8, Berendzen abruptly stepped down as president of American University, citing "exhaustion." Two weeks later the real reason for his resignation burst over the Northwest Washington campus like a supernova: Authorities in Fairfax County, Virginia, disclosed that Berendzen, who is married and the father of two grown children, was believed responsible for making dozens of obscene telephone calls from his university office.

The calls began in late March after a 33-year-old woman in suburban Fairfax placed a classified ad in the *Washington Post* for the child-care service she ran at home. In response, a man phoned and started asking vague but suggestive questions. At that point, the woman concluded she was dealing with a sick caller and felt a sudden surge of anger. As a girl she had been sexually abused, and the call reopened old wounds. Instead of slamming down the phone in disgust, she stayed on the line for half an hour, listening as the man became increasingly lewd. "I realized I had the capability of getting him—and I was going to," she said. "He called the wrong person."

He had indeed. The woman's husband worked with the Criminal Investigations Bureau of the Fairfax County police. Within two hours after the first call, the couple had a recorder and an electronic tracing device installed on their phone. Over the next two weeks, the family received more than 30 calls from the man, many of them lasting longer than half an hour. According to the woman, he described in graphic detail how he and his wife had sex with their children. He talked about his extensive collection of videotaped child pornography and sometimes even insisted that he kept a four-year-old Filipino girl as a "sex slave" in a basement dog cage. Learning that the woman had two daughters of her own, aged 12 and five, he often suggested—in vain—that they be put on the line so that he could instruct them in performing sexual acts on their mother. The caller also boasted that he exerted "tremendous discipline" over his family and that he employed bizarre sadomasochistic implements. Sometimes, the woman said, the man told her he was masturbating as he talked.

Tracking the source of the calls proved difficult. The police gradually zeroed in on American University, but couldn't determine which extension the calls were coming from. In early April, university security officials agreed to help find the caller by using computers to log every outgoing call. This swiftly led them to Berendzen's private office phone.

Hoping to end the matter quietly, American University lawyers and board chairman Edward R. Carr confronted Berendzen on April 7 and asked for his resignation. On campus and on the Washington social circuit, speculation swirled. Attempting to dispel the rumors, the university issued a cryptic statement declaring that Berendzen's departure had been prompted by accusations about his "personal actions."

*Berendzen at his 1980 inauguration as American University President.*

Two days later, when it became clear that the university was desperately hoping to avoid a scandal, the Fairfax woman began leaking details of the case to reporters.

Police said they had no reason to believe that any of the sexual activities described by the caller ever took place. There was apparently no child in a cage, no bizarre implements, no family orgy; authorities suspect the caller's story was all an elaborate, sick fantasy. After the case became public, at least two dozen other women, all of whom had put child-care ads in the newspaper, contacted police to report receiving calls similar to those described by the Fairfax woman. Under Virginia law, making obscene phone calls is only a misdemeanor, punishable by a $1,000 fine and up to a year in jail.

On May 23, Berendzen pleaded guilty to two misdemeanor charges of making obscene phone calls. He was sentenced to two 30-day suspended jail terms, provided he continued his psychiatric counseling for one year. Following his sentencing, Berendzen's attorney released a report from the psychiatric team at Baltimore's Johns Hopkins University Hospital (which has a nationally known Sexual Disorders Clinic), where Berendzen was undergoing treatment. The report stated that his behavior was a result of severe emotional and sexual abuse as a child.

In August, Susan Allen, the Fairfax homemaker who had received and taped three weeks of Berendzen's obscene phone calls, filed a $15 million lawsuit against Berendzen and American University.

Trustees at American initially offered Berendzen $1 million to buy out his tenure and cut his ties with the university. The offer caused an uproar on campus. Students and faculty members vigorously protested the sum, given the financial needs of the school. Berendzen himself requested that the offer be withdrawn. An agreement was reached whereby he will return to the campus in the 1992 spring semester to teach physics. Until then, Berendzen is to receive a salary comparable with that of a full-time senior physics professor. He will continue at that salary when he begins teaching. In addition, Berendzen will be given a severance package of $380,000 based on two years presidential salary and other benefits, to be paid out over two years.

# SAM KINISON & THE BIG SLEEP

For years, primal-scream comedian Sam Kinison built his act on the elements of psychic terror and sexual violence. On the morning of June 21, his dancer girlfriend of two years, Malika Souiri, 25, claimed she was raped by Kinison's newly hired bodyguard, Unway Carter, 22, while the comic slept off a long, hard night of drink in another part of his spacious Los Angeles home.

Kinison, 35, who had been attending Alcoholics Anonymous meetings, was sober for 88 days. The night before the alleged rape, said Malika, he began drinking again. Angered by his relapse, Souiri left the Sunset Strip restaurant where they had stopped for pasta and returned to Kinison's Nichols Canyon home, where she lived. She said she heard the front door of the house creak open shortly before 8:30 the next morning and went downstairs to find Kinison

passed out in the guest room. "I started crying and yelling at him," said Souiri.

"I went back to my room and sat on the bed, crying. Suddenly, this big guy came in the room. I looked at him and said to myself, 'Who is this?'"

He was Unway Carter, a six-foot-four-inch, 320-pound man whom Kinison had apparently met the night before at a Hollywood club and hired on the spot as a bodyguard. Had Kinison checked his references, he would have discovered that Carter, the son of a Greenville, South Carolina, deputy sheriff, had once been accused of, but never charged with, rape, Greenville police reported.

According to Souiri, Carter said, "'Don't worry, I took care of Sam.'... He put his hand on my back as if he were comforting me. But then he started pressing me close to him, fondling me. The more I struggled, the more excited he became." Souiri said she finally gave up, realizing that at five feet three inches and 115 pounds she was no match for Carter.

Souiri alleged that Carter raped her five times. She said she was able to get away by telling him, "I'm bleeding to death. I have to use the restroom." Once in the bathroom, she ran into an adjoining bedroom, grabbed a .44 Magnum kept near the bed, went back to the bathroom and fired four shots through the locked bathroom door. Souiri then climbed onto the bedroom balcony, jumped to the ground and ran to the house of a neighbor, who called the police.

Minutes later, at 9:15, Hollywood police found Carter, unhurt, walking down Kinison's driveway. Kinison was still at home asleep, as he had been throughout the attack and gunfire. It was only after the police poured Evian water on Kinison, said Souiri, that he mumbled something about hiring a bodyguard, explaining how Carter had gotten into the house.

Carter was charged with three counts of rape and two other related charges. He pleaded not guilty.

As for Kinison, he reportedly went with friends to a local nightclub after the alleged assault.

*Malika Souiri and Kinison.*

# INDISCRETIONS

# JAMES BROWN

**J**ames Brown, the Godfather of Soul, hoped to have a brand-new bag when he was released from State Park Correctional Center to a prison work center. Noting that most inmates have no future when they get out, Brown declared, "My prime program is to educate the black American. I'm one of the lucky ones. I'll make a movie and a documentary. This has been great for my career."

A feeding frenzy by those who could make money at the expense of the jailed singer began.

Brown, 61, an inmate since 1988 at State Park Correctional Center, near Columbia, South Carolina, for aggravated assault and failure to stop for a police officer, was transferred to the minimum-security Lower Savannah Work Center in Aiken, South Carolina, so he could join a work-release program. Brown went to work for the Aiken/Barnwell Counties Community Action Commission, a nonprofit agency that serves the area's poor and elderly.

The agency's status, however, didn't stop its executive director, George Anderson, from asking reporters for money in the form of a contribution to the agency in exchange for arranging an interview with Brown.

Similarly, Thomas Hart, a lawyer whose Washington D.C.–based company is co-producing a TV documentary on Brown, offered up the singer to reporters in return for money that Hart said would go not to Brown or himself, but toward financing his documentary.

Francis X. Archibald, a spokesperson for the South Carolina Department of Corrections, said he was "shocked" by Anderson and Hart's money requests. He called the requests "reprehensible" and said the department was "this close" to ending Brown's work-release. The department had earlier cracked down on Community Action's plan to have Brown perform a fund-raising concert.

# INDISCRETIONS

# MARION BARRY

**D**istrict of Columbia Mayor Marion Barry liked to boast that he was invincible, and for many years it seemed that he was. Throughout the '80s his administration was awash in scandal, and rumors of drugs and womanizing swirled around its imperturbable leader. Yet even as key aides went to prison for taking kickbacks and a former girlfriend was prosecuted for dealing cocaine, the Mayor himself remained unindicted—and apparently unconcerned. He taunted his accusers and carried on as usual. A federal investigation went nowhere, officials say, because Barry's inner circle remained adamantly loyal.

His associates may have feared the Mayor's considerable power or believed, along with his huge black constituency, that he was being singled out for harassment by white federal authorities. Whatever the reason, few would cooperate—until January 18, when a longtime friend lured Barry into the trap that was his undoing.

"The only way to nab the Mayor was with a woman," said one investigator.

Federal agents, assisted by D.C. police, persuaded former model Rasheeda Moore to invite Barry to a room at Washington's Vista International Hotel, where he was filmed asking for, paying for and then smoking crack.

Moore's relationship with Barry dates from the early '80s, sources said. Working for the city with her sister Mertine, Moore ran a program called Project Me teaching young teens to put on fashion shows and skits. She was also listed on city records as a social worker.

In 1984 Moore was convicted of "unauthorized use of a vehicle" in Alexandria, Virginia. Sentenced to three years, she served six months in prison.

How often Moore saw Barry over the years is unclear. But Charles Lewis, a former Barry aide who was arrested for drug dealing in 1989 and eventually began to give evidence against the Mayor, said that in 1988 Moore joined him and the Mayor in the Virgin

Islands, where Lewis claimed to have seen Moore and Barry smoking cocaine. His testimony may have given the FBI the leverage it needed to enlist the 38-year-old Moore in a sting. Moore told a friend that she had had a "religious experience," which might also have influenced her to cooperate.

Whatever the reason, Moore made her date with the Mayor—who turned to her as federal agents came crashing into their hotel room and said accusingly, "You set me up." But when he faced the press three days later, he was past recriminations. "I felt for some time that I could do any and everything," said Barry, who confessed to suffering from the "deepest of human frailties." Resisting pressures to resign, he flew the next day to a rehab clinic in Florida, leaving D.C. government temporarily in the hands of City Administrator Carol Thompson.

Barry's staff and colleagues were more saddened than surprised by the arrest. "He came into office energetic, bright and idealistic," said a woman who worked 12 years for the Mayor. "Women and drugs were his downfall."

Those close to him date Barry's decline from the 1985 conviction of his friend and closest aide, Ivanhoe Donaldson, who pleaded guilty to defrauding the city government of $190,000. A veteran of the civil rights movement, Barry, a Mississippi sharecropper's son, became the district's second elected Mayor in 1979 and soon made good on his promise of a better deal for Washington's black majority—launching an ambitious downtown revitalization that provided hundreds of new jobs. But the conviction of Donaldson tarnished that crusade. More important, "Ivanhoe was the only one who could tell Marion what to do and make him do it," said a former aide. "He would go and pull him out of bed and get him to the event."

Initially hailed for his economic development of downtown D.C., Barry, the onetime stalwart of the civil rights movement, saw two deputy mayors convicted on corruption charges and 11 of his appointees sentenced for political crimes. Karen Johnson, the woman with whom Barry was alleged to

*Effi and Marion Barry.*

have had an affair in 1982 and '83—and who later pleaded guilty to cocaine charges—told federal prosecutors that she had been paid $20,000 not to testify against Barry before a grand jury investigating drug use among city officials. The man the *Washington Post* once glowingly hailed as "A Man for All Stormy Seasons" had become a cynical spectator whose leadership was hopelessly compromised.

Day after day during the summer, 46-year-old Effi Barry sat in the D.C. federal courthouse, listening as a succession of witnesses accused her husband of drug use and recounted stories of his sexual exploits.

Whatever Effi Barry was feeling inside, she seldom let on in public. Through much of the proceedings she patiently and methodically worked away at a small pink, white and green hooked rug, her sharply beautiful features showing scarcely a hint of emotion.

That controlled demeanor characterized Effi's relationship with Barry during the eight years he was Mayor of the nation's capital. The child of an unwed black teenage mother and a part-Italian father she never knew, Effi grew up in Toledo, Ohio. She was a health inspector with the D.C. Department of

Environmental Services when she met Barry. They married in 1978, and son Christopher was born two years later.

Over the years, Effi acknowledged Marion's wayward tendencies. "If my husband is involved with another woman, I don't care," she once declared. It was an aspect of his life, she said, and he had to deal with it. Her son's lack of contact with his father bothered her more. "It's like being a single parent," she told a writer in 1988. "My husband gets upset when I say that, but it's true." Occasionally, Effi conceded, the pressures became too much. At such times she would retreat to the den of the family's four-bedroom home in southeast Washington. "Maybe it's a way of dealing with the garbage around me," she said. "I laugh. I dance. I drink, I party there all by myself. Christopher and Marion know not to go in there."

Effi may have found an even more effective way of dealing with the "garbage" around her. Around Thanksgiving, she moved with Christopher to an apartment in northwest Washington. There has been no talk of a reconciliation with Barry, who was convicted of just one count of cocaine possession. He is appealing the six-month sentence he received.

# out·ra·geous

adj., offensive; insulting; shocking: shameless flaunting, tasteless displays; an exposé of excess.

# MILLI VANILLI

**M**illi Vanilli hoped their Grammy award would put an end to silli vanilli jokes. "Girl You Know It's True" was the title of the 1988 single and album that sent the phenomenally successful Eurodisco duo to the top of the pop charts. But less than a year after Rob Pilatus and Fab Morvan brandished Best New Artist Grammys on national television, the world knew it wasn't true at all—the high-stepping duo never sang a note. Their German record producer, Frank Farian, confessed after Pilatus and Morvan insisted they be allowed to use their actual voices for a change on an upcoming record. Instead, Farian showed them the door, then revealed at a November 14 press conference that he had originally hired the two unemployed male models in 1987 to appear in promotional videos lip-synching songs he'd already recorded with vocals by three studio musicians.

The incident led to the Millis being stripped of their Grammys—and accusations that fraud was perpetrated by Farian and the group's label, Arista, which denied prior knowledge of the deception. For the Millis, however, the announcement was cause for relief. "We were afraid for two years that this day would come," said Pilatus. "We've cried about it sometimes, that the secret might come out."

The Millis admitted early on that they weren't entirely what they appeared to be. After all, their video and stage appeal depended in part on $750 hair extensions, as well as chest and leg waxings.

Don't laugh. Although their brand of flyweight dance pop made critics cringe—*Rolling Stone*'s reviewers awarded Milli Vanilli both Worst Album and Worst Band honors for 1989—their debut LP, *Girl You Know It's True*, sold six million copies in the United States and brought them three American Music Awards, the Best New Artist Grammy and the

respect of industry accountants. Not bad for two guys whose musical credentials were so shaky that the *least* damaging charge made against them was that somebody else sang the lead vocals on their LP.

Milli Vanilli got its start in 1987 when Frank Farian, a German music impresario, decided to create a band. Musicians he could hire; songs he could buy; the tough part was finding front men to provide a dramatic image. Enter longtime friends Pilatus, a German-American, and Fabrice Morvan, a Frenchman, who auditioned for and won the job.

Their personal histories were even more complicated than the band's. Pilatus was abandoned at birth by his mother, a German stripper, and father, a black American GI. He spent five years in an Alpine orphanage before being adopted by a professional couple who were kind but unable to protect him from the trauma of growing up black in Bavaria.

To escape his isolation, Pilatus went dancing. "For 10 years I spent nearly every day in a club," he said. Working as a deejay and sportswear model after graduating from high school, he flew to Los Angeles for a vacation in 1985 and met Morvan, another dance obsessive who had grown up a cultural outsider. Morvan, whose parents are divorced, was raised in Paris by his mother, a Guadaloupe-born research biologist. A champion gymnast as a teen, Morvan broke a vertebra in a 1983 trampoline accident and took up dancing as therapy.

Soul mates virtually since their first encounter, the pair returned to Europe and scratched out a minimal living until their fateful audition for Farian. Said Pilatus: "We told him if he hired one of us, he had to hire both of us." The rest was Milli Vanilli.

Pilatus, 24, and Morvan, 24, who retreated to their home in the Hollywood Hills after the revelation, vowed to find a new producer and record an album "with our own voices on it, which will prove our talent."

*Rob Pilatus and Fab Morvan.*

# SANDRA BERNHARD

**S**andra Bernhard sauntered onstage with a smile menacing enough to send a Doberman whimpering.

"Society is one big screwed-up mess. Nobody knows what they want and where they're going," Bernhard, 35, announced before reading selections from a philosophy book, singing a few Israeli folk songs and launching into a tirade about "polyunsaturated sexuality."

"Oh, there is so much I want to tell you tonight," she told her audience in a motherly tone.

And there was so much her audience wanted to know. For example, they wanted to know—despite the reams of paper already devoted to the subject—about the precise nature of her relationship with Madonna. The pair came on the David Letterman show two years ago dressed in identical jean shorts, T-shirts and cowboy boots, and Sandra warned Dave not to flirt with her girlfriend Madonna. Last year the two appeared at a "Don't Bungle the Jungle!" benefit for the rain forest, cooing "I Got You Babe" to each other while bumping behinds.

Here, briefly stated, is the Sandra Bernhard credo: I provoke, therefore I am. Nowhere was that provocative sentiment more in evidence than in *Without You I'm Nothing*, the movie version of her one-woman show that ran for seven months off-Broadway. During the course of the film, which played around the country, Bernhard sang a little, whined more and received visits from friends like cable-TV porn star Robin Byrd, who stopped by to take a shower on-camera. At the end of the proceedings, Bernhard stripped down to a G-string and danced to "Little Red Corvette," gold tassels dangling wildly from her breasts.

The girl is strange, no doubt about it, but she had an explanation. "My father is a proctologist, and my mother's an abstract artist. That's how I view the world." The youngest child of Dr. Jerome and Jeanette Bernhard (yes, proctologist and artist, respectively),

Sandra and "my three sensitive older brothers" grew up in Flint, Michigan, where she read Nancy Drew but said she preferred Jacqueline Susann. By age three, she'd already made her career plans clear. "She would mimic everybody," remembered her mother. "I would have these friends of foreign extraction come over, and Sandra would just mimic their voices. I was a little embarrassed. I guess she was gathering material even then."

When Bernhard was 10, her family moved to Scottsdale, Arizona. The wonder years were not great for Sandra. After graduating from Saguaro High School, Bernhard spent a year on a kibbutz in Israel, then decided to try her luck in Los Angeles. "I wanted her to be something practical," said her mother. "I tried to encourage her to become a dental hygienist." Her daughter had somewhat grander plans, and in an old, run-down mustard-colored Plymouth Volare, Bernhard headed for Hollywood. She worked as a manicurist by day; at night she tried out her frequently abrasive monologues at clubs like the Improv and the Comedy Store. Fodder for the act was her family, her Midwest upbringing and—once her parents divorced after 38 years of marriage—her father's second wife, whom she called a "blond bimbo with a bubble hairdo and no lips." Her father was not pleased that Sandra was using him as a whipping post. Better received were her "Oh, Rob!" impersonations of Mary Tyler Moore, which led to appearances on Richard Pryor specials in 1977 and to her role as an unstable groupie opposite Robert De Niro and Jerry Lewis in 1983's *The King of Comedy*.

Many still don't understand what gives with her and Madonna. Frankly, Bernhard is pretty sick of the whole subject.

"I'm not a lesbian, and I'm sick of being called one. I'm not, and I want to set the record straight." To prove that claim, Bernhard said she intends to be married and start a family within the next two years. "I'm going to blow everybody's minds," she promised. "I'm going to get married and belong to Hadassah."

# OUTRAGEOUS
# MADONNA

**A**fter routinely violating taboos about sex, sacrilege and the public display of underwear, what was a girl to do for new material? For starters, Madonna kicked off a four-month tour that no doubt delighted fans, fetishists, cross-dressers and topic-starved conservative columnists the world over. Mimed masturbation? Madonna had it during "Like a Virgin." Topless guys in foot-long pointy brassieres? They popped up a third of the way through the show. A hint of discipline? "You may not know the song, but you all know the pleasures of a good spanking," Madonna cooed after "Hanky Panky," an ode to the joy of the slap. The 105-minute hullabaloo was amazing for its breadth of controversy. And that was just the beginning.

"She said, 'Let's break every rule we can,'" said choreographer Vince Paterson. "She wanted to make statements about sexuality, cross-sexuality, the Church and the like."

Despite the contributions by other talents—including avant-garde fashion designer Jean-Paul Gaultier, who created most of the costumes—there's no question that responsibility for the final product, controversy and all, rested with the star. As a no-nonsense Madonna put it to a technician who questioned one of her decisions during a sound check, "Listen. Everyone is entitled to my opinion."

The eight-week, 36-performance U.S. leg of the tour, dubbed Blond Ambition, opened in Houston—just in time to promote a new Madonna album, *I'm Breathless*, comprised of "music from and inspired by the film *Dick Tracy*." The LP, in turn, helped promote the much-talked-about movie, starring Madonna and Warren Beatty.

Just a good Catholic girl with a song in her heart, a crucifix around her neck and a jiggle in her bustier, Madonna, 31, had already exposed most of her body

parts on video and, via unearthed unauthorized photographs, on the pages of *Playboy* and *Penthouse*. She had grappled with the great themes: teen pregnancy, crotch grabbing, spanking (she defended all three); toyed with voyeurism (in *Open Your Heart*), bondage (in *Express Yourself*), masturbation (during the *Blonde Ambition* tour) and stigmata (in *Like a Prayer*); and endured tabloid reports that she once spent nine hours "trussed up like a turkey" after a spat with then hubby Sean Penn. Then there was that oh-so-close relationship with Sandra Bernhard and a fling with the world's friendliest bachelor, Warren Beatty—which, mirabile dictu, began during the filming and lasted barely a nanosecond beyond the launch of Beatty's would-be blockbuster, *Dick Tracy*.

What to do for an encore? Madonna's answer was *Justify My Love*, the video that, in what turned out to be a marketing coup, was banned by MTV, the music video network that Madonna and nameless female models in black lace underwear helped popularize.

How did *Justify My Love* differ from other skin-with-a-beat videos? Let us count the ways. There was Madonna, in black bra, stockings and stiletto heels, putting the moves on her real-life boyfriend Tony Ward. Moments later she was lip-synching with Parisian model Amanda Cazalet, 25, who was dressed like a Nazi hooker with suspenders that barely covered her nipples. Then Madonna, Cazalet and Ward offered free instruction in a certain Kama Sutra technique while two very androgynous gentlemen patted each other affectionately. All of which left fans hot, censors bothered and fearless news programmers lined up to air the forbidden footage. The "video single" was on sale before shopping malls closed for the holidays. Madonna told the *New York Times*, "I think the video is romantic and loving and has humor in it.... Why is it that people are willing to go to a movie and watch someone get blown to bits for no reason and nobody wants to see two girls kissing or two men snuggling?"

# MÖTLEY CRÜE

**S**urveying the damage done to themselves and to the trashed arena of one battle—Milwaukee's Bradley Center, where fans and security guards clashed in the night—the four members of Mötley Crüe stood battered but proud. As lead singer Vince Neil, 28, awaited arrest for inciting a riot (having sounded the charge of the heavy-metal brigade by inviting fans to rush the stage), drummer Tommy Lee, 27, and bassist Nikki Sixx, 31, wiped blood from their hands—battered and bruised by enthusiastic playing—while guitarist Mick Mars, 35, complained that he spent much of the concert dodging exploding projectiles hurled from the audience.

Thanks to a timely $5,000 donation to the arena—which later turned the money over to charity—Neil was not arrested. And the band was allowed to leave town with their reputation as rock's reigning wild men intact, even though the Crüe, once prime exemplars of rock's creed of sex and drugs *über alles*, conducted this year's world tour clean and sober. By outward appearances, the Crüe, sporting some 60 tattoos, one pierced nose and a pierced nipple among them, were the same guys their fans have come to know and love. Record sales—the Crüe's LP *Dr. Feelgood* is the band's fifth consecutive multiplatinum release—and concert performances, powered by 100,000 watts of sound, 11 tons of equipment and 2,000 lights, didn't seem to have suffered during their claimed year of sobriety.

Neither self-discipline nor great musicianship has ever been a requisite for Crüe membership. Neil was asked to join his first band, in Covina, California, "because I had the longest hair in school," he said. Schoolmate Lee kept in touch after Neil got kicked out of high school for drug possession. After recruiting Sixx and Mars (a motorcycle mechanic who ran a want ad in a Los Angeles paper that read, simply, "Loud, rude, aggressive guitarist"), Lee auditioned Neil to round out his group. The Crüe soon embarked on an odyssey of self-destructive excesses and stunning successes, selling 13.5 million albums in the United States and incurring the wrath of Tipper Gore.

It was an offstage performance—Lee's 1986 marriage to former *Dynasty* actress Heather Locklear—that alerted the postadolescent world to the Crüe's existence. Lee has been a featured player in the tabloids ever since, most recently in a lurid report that Locklear had caught him in a hotel room with a model. "Bullshit," said Lee. Added Locklear: "I'm not going to dignify those stories. Honestly, though, Tommy was bummed that he wasn't matched up in the story with someone better-looking."

The 28-year-old actress flies to meet the band most weekends and frets between phone calls. She put in a late-night call of her own after hearing of Lee's arrest for indecent exposure in Cincinnati. "Hey, honey, I heard you were arrested for showing your thang," said Locklear. "Naw, gorgeous," Lee assured her, "I just hung a BA." That signifies a moon, not a diploma.

The other wife in the Crüe's tiny domestic universe is Sharise Neil, a former mud wrestler.

Neil appears to be philosophical about the band's former life-style and its current drug-free status. "Really," he says, "it's amazing that one—or all—of us isn't dead." It wasn't for lack of trying. In 1984 Neil smashed into an oncoming car while driving drunk, killing a friend in his own car and severely injuring a couple in the other vehicle. Even in the aftermath of his punishment—30 days in jail, 200 hours of community service, five years probation and $2.6 million in payments to the couple and to his friend's estate—the Crüe kept boozing and drugging but left the driving to others. It took Sixx's near-fatal heroin overdose in 1987 to scare the perpetually wrecked Crüe straight. The experience sent the entire Crüe into rehab. Today, a drug counselor meets the band on tour to help keep everyone honest. And despite the taunts of one friend of the band, comedian Sam Kinison ("What're you gonna do tonight—go out and wreck a salad bar?"), when temptation appears, it's resisted.

*Tommy Lee, top. Below, Lee, Vince Neil, Nikki Sixx and Mick Mars.*

# OUTRAGEOUS

# ANDREW DICE CLAY

**H**is humor has drawn complaints from women, gays and other groups that have been its targets. In 1988 he was banned for life from MTV for ignoring a pledge to forgo profanity. Some of the offended have retaliated; a West Hollywood billboard with his picture was defaced by a group calling itself Activists Against Sexist Pigs. *Saturday Night Live* cast member Nora Dunn and Irish singer Sinéad O'Connor both refused to appear with him when he was *Saturday Night Live*'s guest host. The pair's protest, however, stirred up so much publicity that the show got a huge ratings boost, and the controversial comic wound up with his biggest audience yet.

With his hair slicked back and a cigarette in one hand, comic Andrew Dice Clay was in his tough-guy greaser pose onstage at Rascal's in West Orange, New Jersey. The "Diceman," whose real name is Andrew Silverstein, was muscling through his act, pummeling the crowd with four-letter punch lines, misogynistic put-downs and enough filthy humor to make a truck driver squirm. Finally, from the back of the room, a woman who had heard enough yelled out, "Monster!" Clay, 33, simply cocked his head, fired back an X-rated insult and continued on.

Thanks to Clay's mostly young, white male fans, he had become a top concert draw off-camera, and his 27-city "Dice Rules" tour reportedly grossed (no pun intended) more than $4 million. "I don't think there's anyone that doesn't have a little bigotry in them," he said, defending his gags. "Italian guys will make Jewish jokes, but they don't hate Jews. So when I do gay jokes, that's like me doing Polish ones."

Clay complained that his critics don't understand the concept of a stage persona and that people take the act too seriously. According to Clay, the Diceman character "is a macho moron. It's juvenile comedy. I just like to make people laugh."

This past summer the comic tested the turf in movies. *The Adventures of Ford Fairlane*, co-starring Priscilla Presley and Wayne Newton,

featured the prototypical Brooklyn roughneck in his first starring role as a rock musician turned detective. Signed to a three-picture deal with Twentieth Century Fox, the comic was confident about his reception, predicting, "It will be the biggest comedy hit of the summer." The box office fell somewhat short of his bravado.

Born in the Sheepshead Bay section of Brooklyn, New York, Clay was a below-mediocre student. In 1978 he made his comedy debut at a local club, mimicking Jerry Lewis's Nutty Professor role, then tearing off his pants and shirt to ape John Travolta's character in *Grease*. From then on, he said, "I felt I was meant to entertain."

Heading for Los Angeles in 1980 to pursue acting, Clay kept working on his street-tough stage character at Los Angeles's Comedy Store. There he met an aspiring actress named Kathy Swanson, then 23, who was in the audience. The couple began living together in 1981 and married three years later. Clay called his two years of wedlock "a complete horror show." Both he and Swanson blamed the other for the marriage's failure, and she's seeking a six-million-dollar settlement with the help of Hollywood divorce lawyer Marvin Mitchelson.

Now the Diceman's love is a woman he calls Trini Benini (her real name is Kathleen Monica), whom he met three years ago while doing a turn on the former NBC series *Crime Story*. Asked what Trini does, Clay replied, "She's with me. She's like a wife would be and takes care of things." For now, though, Clay still lives alone in a three-bedroom Brooklyn apartment, because, he said, that's the only place he feels at home. "Hollywood can demean you. That's why I'm here. Brooklyn is everybody."

With his movie ambitions, Clay hinted that his concert career might soon be ending, and with it, perhaps, the carping about his language and material. His fans would understand, he believed, and simply choose to see him on the big screen instead. Said the Diceman proudly: "I think my audience sees that here's a guy who didn't kiss ass to get where he is."

# ROSEANNE BARR

**F**ans at San Diego's Jack Murphy Stadium couldn't remember anything so tasteless since a horse carrying their chicken-suited mascot as a promotional stunt unceremoniously relieved itself on the baseline between second and third. That turned out to be an easier mess to clean up than the caterwauling version of the national anthem sung by TV star Roseanne Barr as part of the Padres' Working Women's Night.

Within 48 hours of Barr's fingernails-on-the-blackboard performance before a crowd of nearly 30,000—after which she hitched up an imaginary athletic supporter and p'tooied on the field—the comedian drew salvos from the national press, from President Bush ("a disgrace"), from Secretary of State Jim Baker ("disgusting") and from more than 2,000 irate fans who called the stadium to complain.

Later, at a Beverly Hills press conference with her husband, Tom Arnold, an apologetic but unbowed Barr called the flap a misunderstanding. "I figured everybody knew I wasn't the world's greatest singer," she said. "I thought it was going to be very well received." Barr, who sang as an invited guest of Padres co-owner Tom Werner, who also produces the *Roseanne* show, said that when the booing started, "I went into this panic thing, and I thought, 'Can I get out of here? Can I quit?' But I couldn't. It took all the guts in my life to finish that song." The crotch-grabbing gesture, she reported, resulted from some good-natured pregame goading in the players' dugout. "I thought it would be really funny."

Barr's anthem brouhaha capped a series of bizarre antics that puzzled fans and perplexed the press. The news conference itself was delayed for nearly a half hour while Arnold called police to eject free-lance photographer Kip Rano, whose work has appeared in the tabloids. Shortly before, two reporters for the *National Enquirer* had revealed that Arnold, who had done rehab time for drug use, sold quotes to the paper last winter, a charge that Barr acknowledged. Arnold, she said, felt awful about it. "All's he did was buy drugs

with it and try to kill himself.... It was a huge mistake we wish we hadn't made."

At least some of Barr's wrath against the media seemed justified. In 1989, for example, despite her entreaties, the *Enquirer* reported the existence of an illegitimate daughter whom the then teenage Barr had given up for adoption 18 years before. Barr said she and Arnold will be suing the *Enquirer* for libel, slander and possible copyright infringement, all stemming from what they charged were other incidents of harassment.

Some examples of the couple's unbridled conduct seemed harder to fathom. In October 1989, displeased at the score in the first game of the World Series, Barr and Arnold "mooned" the crowd at the Oakland Alameda County Coliseum, revealing his and hers tattoos on their backsides.

Though its ratings—even in reruns—were solid, Barr's *Roseanne* show suffered behind-the-scenes turmoil. Last March, executive producer Jeff Harris resigned, taking a full-page ad in *Daily Variety* to announce that "my wife and I have decided to share a vacation in the relative peace and quiet of Beirut." Within the same four-month period, Barr fired *Roseanne*'s writer-producer, as well as her personal manager and publicity firm.

Barr divorced writer Bill Pentland last January after a 16-year marriage. The couple finally hammered out a temporary financial settlement and custody agreement regarding their three children, ages 12 to 15. Pentland, who hired attorney Marvin Mitchelson to bolster his case, filed a $28 million palimony suit against Barr for the three years they lived together before marrying. Mitchelson also filed a protective order against Arnold for a security guard to be present during depositions because of Arnold's alleged abuse, battery, unwarranted annoyances and "propensity for violence" and "acts of dangerous behavior."

Despite appearances to the contrary, Barr insisted that bad press was something she doesn't seek. "I don't choose the negative attention over and over, despite what people think," she said. "I sometimes get what I think is a good idea, but my judgment is wrong."

*Tom Arnold and Barr.*

108

*Luke Campbell, Brother Marquis, Fresh Kid Ice and Mr. Mixx.*

# AS NASTY AS THEY WANNA BE

**E**ver since Elvis first freed his hips, Jimi Hendrix flashed his guitar and Donna Summer moaned suggestively, outraged parents and ambitious politicians have worried noisily that prolonged exposure to rock and role models could lead to sex, drugs and drive-in movies. Somehow, civilization as we know it survived. Cut to 1990. Rock performers are at it again, but this time somebody's listening.

Thanks to sadomasochistic "slasher" lyrics and sexually graphic messages, eight states considered legislation that would require special warning labels for albums that contain explicit lyrics about sex, drug or alcohol abuse, racism, violence or a host of other taboo topics. Some of the proposed laws would prohibit the selling of certain albums to minors and provide jail time for anyone who did so. The movement ignited a lively debate. "I'm not a bluenose or a prude—I'm a Christian," said Jack Thompson, 38, a Coral Gables, Florida, lawyer who played a leading role in trying to ban obscene lyrics in that state. *New York Times* music critic Jon Pareles called the uproar "the most hysterical reaction to popular music … since just before World War I, when the Pope declared tango dancing a mortal sin."

At the core of the controversy are a new wave of hypergraphic lyrics and the question of whether, and under what circumstances, such lyrics should be consumed by kids. On their album *As Nasty As They Wanna Be*, the Miami-based rap group 2 Live Crew sings loudly—and explicitly—about anal, oral and abusive sex. The Los Angeles–area rappers N.W.A. ("Niggers With Attitude") received an intimidating letter from the FBI after releasing a paean to cop killing. Metal heavyweights Guns N' Roses outraged millions by putting a back beat to bigotry in "One in a Million," a rant against "niggers, immigrants and faggots."

While the pro-labeling or "stickering" movement has its right-wing and religious zealots, not all of its supporters can be so easily pigeonholed. Said a mother of two: "I am not as worried about swear words as about racist words. We bend over backwards to teach our children that we live in a society where people are supposed to be created equal. And then you have lyrics that say it's okay to do drugs, to break the law, to kill Jews or blacks. These messages just keep escalating all the time."

As do the fears of civil libertarians like Danny Goldberg, a rock manager and ACLU activist. "The only alternative to free speech is government-controlled speech," he said. "I'm offended by racism and anti-Semitism in music. But I don't think it's appropriate for any government to decide what is offensive."

Hoping to head off any such intervention, the Recording Industry Association of America, the industry's trade association, initiated a voluntary, nationwide campaign to sticker objectionable albums with the uniform label: PARENTAL ADVISORY—EXPLICIT LYRICS.

Tipper Gore, wife of Tennessee Senator Albert Gore and the 1985 co-founder of the Parent's Music Resource Center, a pro-labeling lobby, said that the RIAA's action "speaks to our solution perfectly. We are firmly opposed to censorship. We don't want legislation. All we have ever wanted was for companies to voluntarily provide consumer information so that we could make an informed choice in the stores."

Not all performers were upset about labeling. 2 Live Crew, which already voluntarily stickered its own recordings, saw sales soar after Florida Governor Bob Martinez called the album obscene.

Luther "Luke" Campbell, the gap-toothed leader of rap music's infamous 2 Live Crew, was arrested for an allegedly obscene performance, and the lyrics of the group's raunchy *As Nasty As They Wanna Be* sparked legal action in five states. Campbell, who is 29, beat his obscenity rap on October 20, when a jury acquitted him of all charges stemming from 2 Live Crew's show before an adults-only audience in Hollywood, Florida, in June. The panel included a 76-year-old woman—who said the cuss words weren't anything new to her—and another jurist so moved by Campbell's poetic licentiousness that she suggested delivering the verdict in rap.

Campbell, "relieved" after the trial, maintained that he was a victim of racism as well as politics in his native Florida, where a conservative governor and sheriff helped spearhead a campaign against him.

He was quick to admit, however, that controversy had its rewards. "*Nasty* was a dead record until all this came up, then it sold another million copies," he noted. In fairly short order, Campbell not only became a figurehead for millions of anticensorship partisans but also managed to sell a quick 500,000 copies or so of his LP *Banned in the U.S.A.*

Campbell's life is a surprising dichotomy. The fifth son of a janitor and a hairdresser, he grew up in Miami's riot-torn Liberty City ghetto. Today, Campbell lives in G-rated suburban Miami splendor with his girlfriend of two years, Tina Barnett, 20, who is expecting his child in December.

Campbell can be found most days at Luke Records, the two-story Miami headquarters of a music empire that includes four record labels, 16 acts, a warehouse, a construction company and three local nightclubs. His game plan? "Diversify," said Campbell. "My mother told me not to have a one-track mind." So Campbell reads FORTUNE and spreads himself around, evidently to good effect considering reports that say he brought in $11 million last year.

"Rap music today is what rock and roll was in the '60s with the Stones," Campbell said. "It's considered the most rebellious music ever. Fifteen years from now," Campbell predicted, "2 Live Crew will get together for their reunion tour, and the stadium will be filled with black and white doctors, lawyers and politicians."

Axl Rose wasn't making any such predictions. One of rock's brashest bad boys, Rose is a man who attracts trouble both onstage (his songs have been attacked as, among other things, racist and homophobic) and off (he has been arrested for disorderly conduct and public drunkenness). Guns N' Roses 28-year-old lead singer was arrested for assaulting his next-door neighbor in a West Hollywood condominium complex. According to Rose, Gabriella Kantor, 37, the woman who claimed Rose hit her over the head with a wine bottle, was just an obsessed fan.

The title of Guns N' Roses platinum album, *Appetite for Destruction*, might spring to mind when considering some of Rose's actions this past year. Rose—frustrated over wife Erin's miscarriage and problems with Kantor, as well as strained relations with his family—visited the two-bedroom home he and Erin have been preparing in the Hollywood Hills.

"I had a piano, which I bought for $38,000," he said, "and there's a $12,000 statue in there and a $20,000 fireplace, and I stood there and I just snapped. I'm standing in this house going, 'This house doesn't mean anything to me. This is not what I wanted. I didn't work forever to have this lonely house on the hill that I live in because I'm a rich rock star.' So I shoved the piano right through the side of the house. Then I proceeded to destroy the fireplace, knock all the windows out and trash the statue and everything. The damages were about $100,000. What's wild," he added, "is that the next day Erin went to the house and she trashed the three rooms I didn't." ("I had my own different reasons," said Erin.)

The incidents seem to have helped the Roses' six-month marriage. "Erin and I hadn't been on the best of terms during the pregnancy," said Axl, who has briefly separated from his wife several times. "The miscarriage brought us closer together." Erin, 25, daughter of rocker Don Everly, said the arrest for assaulting Kantor was "the last thing we needed." On December 5, Rose and Kantor entered into an agreement to keep away from each other.

*Axl Rose.*

# DREAM STREET

**T**o an unsuspecting viewer, the backdrop for the opening titles of *The Cosby Show*—row upon row of primary-colored apartment houses peopled with smiling kids and parents—looked like the result of some high-priced animator's exercise. But to one contingent of underage fans, Mr. Cosby's neighborhood seemed distinctly familiar. It was, charged Manhattan's Creative Arts Workshop for Homeless Children, a near copy of *Dream Street*, a 50- by 100-foot mural painted in 1989 in a Harlem neighborhood by 63 homeless kids, ages 11 to 15, as part of a project to brighten the landscape of decrepit city streets.

According to project head Brookie Maxwell, she was first approached in August by *Cosby* representatives seeking permission to adapt the mural. "We were totally excited, not just for our kids, but for all the kids in East Harlem," she said. "We said, 'Great.'"

When negotiations broke down before final legal clearances could be granted, *Cosby* decided to design its own mural, which added the antidrug graphic of a hypodermic needle with a slash mark through it. When Maxwell saw the painting on the show, she enlisted a law firm to help fight for compensation.

*Cosby* producers then offered to give the Harlem kids a credit for having inspired the backdrop, but only if they signed away permanent licensing rights. Maxwell refused the offer, requesting instead that *Cosby* establish academic scholarships for her charges. "Part of what we try to teach our kids is to stand up for their rights in the world," she said. "We had to fight back."

Described by his publicist as "furious," Cosby apparently felt that 63 scholarships were excessive and said in a statement that he had copied the art with only the noblest of intentions: "I thought utilizing the mural would give a resounding cheer for the children throughout the community.... Instead, there is a woman who is saying, 'We want money for what you've done.'"

With negotiations at an impasse, *Cosby* producers announced that beginning with its October 18 episode, the controversial mural would be removed from the show's opening credits. "It has saddened us," said a spokesman for the producers, "to see something which began as an attempt to create a sense of community pride turned against these children and against us."

No one seemed sadder than the mural's young artists. "The wall was supposed to be our dream of what life should be," said 11-year-old Josie Menzies. Instead, it turned into a hard lesson in reality.

# THE PATRIOTS & LISA OLSON

**B**oston Herald sports reporter Lisa Olson drove away from the New England Patriots' stadium as fast as she could, shouting, "How dare they? How dare they?" She was angry and bewildered. "'Give her what she wants!' they yelled. What I wanted was an interview. What I wanted was to be treated as a professional."

What the 26-year-old Olson got, as she attempted to talk with cornerback Maurice Hurst in the locker room after a practice in September, was allegedly sexual harassment so extreme that it shook the macho world of pro football. Patriots tight end Zeke Mowatt, she said, stood naked in front of her and said, "Is this what you want? Do you want to take a bite out of this?" (Mowatt insisted he said only, "You are not writing; you are looking.") Two or three other naked players, Olson says, crowded around her making lewd gestures. "I didn't know whether to scream or break down and cry. It was a premeditated mind rape," she said. "After a few minutes, I gave up trying to interview Maurice, thanked him and walked away. I felt total, blind rage."

That was only the beginning. Patriots owner Victor Kiam II seemingly decided that the best defense was to be offensive. "I can't disagree with the players' actions," he said, arguing that the *Herald* "asked for trouble" by assigning a female reporter to his team. The Remington magnate acquired the Patriots for $92 million in 1988. He was perhaps unaware that some 500 women work as professional sportswriters and that it has been NFL policy since 1985 to provide equal access to journalists regardless of gender. Kiam went on to falsely accuse Olson of following a player into the Indianapolis Colts' shower (he later retracted the charge) and reportedly called the writer "a classic bitch." (Kiam denied it.) *Herald* columnist Gerry Callahan delivered an angry riposte: "We discovered that you can make millions in the razor business and own an NFL team without possessing the class or courtesy of the average pimp."

After the Boston chapter of the National Organization for Women urged a boycott of Remington products, Kiam spent some $100,000 on full-page newspaper ads protesting his innocence and apologizing to Olson. He also met with her for more than an hour. "He expressed remorse, and I believe he is sincere, but actions are needed, not just words," Olson said. NFL Commissioner Paul Tagliabue launched an investigation by a special counsel, Harvard Law School professor Philip B. Heymann. (Tagliabue's suddenly crowded docket also included Cincinnati Bengals coach Sam Wyche who was fined $35,000 for barring a woman reporter from the locker room in October.) Yet even after the uproar, many Patriots players seemed not to understand the seriousness of the incident. "If she can't take a joke, she ought not to be down here," running back Robert Perryman told a reporter. Running back John Stephens demanded, "What kind of woman wants to be in a locker room?" Olson, for one, always did interviews elsewhere if possible. "You put up with a lot of crap covering the locker room," she said, "the 'Hey, baby!' and 'You wanna go out some time, baby?' stuff. You learn it's part of the job."

Olson dreamed of being a sports reporter while she was growing up, the oldest of four children, in Phoenix. She was sports editor of her high school and college papers. With the *Herald* four years, Olson first covered high school sports and then some games of the Red Sox, Celtics and Bruins. "I never had any problems with any of them," she pointed out. "The Patriots are a different bunch."

Churlish behavior was not limited to the players. In September, as the reluctantly famous Olson walked towards the Patriots' locker room after their 37-13 loss to the New York Jets, the New England fans unleashed a torrent of abuse, chanting, "Lisa sucks!" Olson pressed onward to do her job.

On November 27, the National Football League fined Patriots tight end Zeke Mowatt, defensive back Michael Timpson and ex-Patriot running back Robert Perryman a total of $22,500 for the locker room harassment of Olson. The team itself was fined $50,000. Olson, whose current assignment is covering Boston's Bruins and Celtics, said she felt "optimistic about the future of every female sportswriter."

# lu·na·tic fringe

n., the members of a group espousing extreme, eccentric, or maniacal views; grim, grisly, macabre and dangerous bigots, crazies and fanatics.

# JEFFREY LUNDGREN

Neighbors in rural Kirtland, Ohio, welcomed Jeffrey Lundgren when he, his wife, Alice, and their four children rented a rundown 100-year-old farmhouse on Chardon Road in October 1987 and promptly began fixing it up. After a group of young men and women from the town's Reorganized Church of Jesus Christ of the Latter-Day Saints (RLDS) moved in, residents assumed they were starting a farm like the Mormons' in nearby Hiram. But this religious commune was soon up to something more sinister. Under Lundgren's fanatical leadership, it nurtured an apocalyptic vision that ultimately led to murder.

In July, 40-year-old Lundgren went on trial in Ohio's Lake County Common Pleas Court for the slayings of Dennis and Cheryl Avery and their three young daughters. Alice, 39, was tried for her part in the crimes later, as were son Damon, 19, and three other commune members. Four others pleaded guilty. The grisly killings stunned quiet Kirtland (population 6,500), where Joseph Smith Jr. built the first Mormon colony in 1836.

For Police Chief Dennis Yarborough and the Reverend Dale Luffman, pastor of Kirtland's RLDS church, the killings confirmed long-held forebodings. Yarborough had been troubled by Lundgren's growing arsenal, while Luffman had watched the burly lay minister become a self-proclaimed prophet who exercised a hypnotic hold over his faithful. "Lundgren came into this community with an agenda," said Luffman.

Lundgren and his family arrived in Kirtland in 1984. A native of Independence, Missouri, he married Alice in 1970, while the two were attending Central Missouri State University. In 1983, after four years in the Navy and stints at menial jobs back in his home state, Lundgren became a lay minister in the RLDS, founded after an 1860 reorganization of the Mormon Church. In Kirtland, Jeffrey and Alice volunteered as guides at the Kirtland Temple.

But Lundgren's brand of piety soon began to disturb church officials. According to former followers, Lundgren claimed only he could interpret the truth of holy books. In late 1987, Lundgren's increasingly heretical views—and suspicions that he had stolen money from the temple—prompted RLDS officials to fire him as a tour guide. The couple and their four children—sons Damon, Jason, now 15, and Caleb, nine, and daughter Kristin, 11—moved out of the house the church had provided and rented the 15-acre farm on Chardon Road. In January 1988, Lundgren's ministerial credentials were withdrawn, and he and some two dozen followers left the congregation.

Lundgren ruled his commune with dictatorial powers. He monitored phone calls and took group members' paychecks. He put the men through weapons training, ambush drills and target practice. And he told his followers that women could gain salvation through sexual rituals. According to court documents, he forced women to dance naked while he masturbated. Children who misbehaved were allegedly beaten on the buttocks and legs with poles, according to a 13-year-old who briefly lived with her mother in the cult. Most nights at nine o'clock, Lundgren harangued his followers, promising to lead them to God. He warned them that a "blood sacrifice" must occur before they could go to the promised land.

"It's only now I realize I was in a cult," said ex-follower Sharon Bluntschly, 31. "A web was wrapped around you slowly, and you didn't see it coming. Jeff was very methodical and started with very logical things. We were supposed to go on faith in him and one another. People were not allowed to ask questions."

Among the followers were Dennis and Cheryl Avery, a quiet couple whose lives revolved around their faith. Dennis, 49 when he died, worked as a computer operator for a bank in Kansas City, while Cheryl, 42, taught preschool, sewed her family's clothes and diligently supervised the education of their three daughters, Trina, 15, Rebecca, 13, and Karen, seven. In 1984, upset by the RLDS decision to

*Alice, Damon and Jeffrey Lundgren, after their capture.*

ordain women, the Averys left one Independence congregation and were attracted to Lundgren, who upheld a fundamentalist view. In the spring of 1987, after Lundgren had moved to Ohio, the Averys quit their jobs, sold their home and followed him to Kirtland.

For the Averys, life in Lundgren's flock was less than utopian. Dennis moved in and out of minimum-wage jobs, while the family lived in sparsely furnished rented houses. The girls could not afford to have class pictures taken or to participate in after-school activities. According to Cheryl Avery's friend Marlene Jennings, Rebecca lost her appetite and appeared gaunt and malnourished, while the oldest girl, Trina, told other children her life wasn't worth living. In March 1989, Jennings, not a cult member, noticed that Cheryl was becoming increasingly withdrawn. On the morning of April 16, 1989, Dennis told Jennings, who had phoned, "Cheryl will call you if she wants to talk to you." Then he hung up.

That same day, perhaps believing his family would be leaving with the group, Dennis accompanied Lundgren to a gun store in Chagrin Falls, where Lundgren picked out .380 and .45 Colt semiautomatic handguns and an M-1 carbine. Avery put the $1,300 purchase on his credit card, but Lundgren signed his own name to the registration forms, telling the salesclerk that Avery was repaying a debt with the purchase. The following day, the Averys' daughters were withdrawn from school with no request that their transcripts be forwarded. That night neighbors were awakened by the keening of a chain saw from the Lundgren barn. Former cult member Keith Johnson told the *Kansas City Star* he was at the apartment of two fellow cultists when an ashen-faced Alice Lundgren appeared at the door and said grimly, "The fog is blood-red at the house."

Two days later, Lundgren, his family and followers had vanished from the farm, and it was not until January 4 that police, acting on a tip from Johnson, unearthed five bodies from a grave beneath the barn. Cheryl, Dennis and the girls had been bound and gagged with duct tape, dumped in the pit, then shot with a .45 caliber handgun. Cult member Gregory Winship, 29, admitted running a chain saw to muffle the sound of the shots that killed the Averys, whom authorities speculate had fallen from favor and might have been planning to defect.

The Lundgrens and the others fled first to a campground in West Virginia, then to a farm south of Chilhowee, Missouri. In the months that followed, the band slowly disintegrated, rent by dissension over Lundgren's misappropriation of group money and his affair with Johnson's wife, Kathryn. In December the group scattered, and Lundgren took Alice and their children to California. Within a week after the bodies were found, a nationwide manhunt for the Lundgrens and 10 followers ended. Lundgren was captured in a phone booth outside a motel near San Diego, where he and his family were living. In their motel and in a rental locker nearby, police found an arms cache including a .50 caliber rifle with sniper scope, automatic pistols, revolvers, gas masks and enough ammunition "to ward off an army," said a federal official. Jeffrey Lundgren was convicted and sentenced to death; his sentence is being appealed. Alice Lundgren is serving five consecutive 150-years-to-life sentences for aggravated murder and kidnapping. Their son Damon was sentenced to four consecutive 120-years-to-life sentences. Cult member Daniel Craft was sentenced to 50-years-to-life, five other members await January sentencing and one other, Ron Luff, is currently on trial.

# ELIZABETH CLARE PROPHET

**S**et amid the splendor of Montana's Paradise Valley, the headquarters of the Church Universal and Triumphant seemed almost too beautiful to be true. Apple orchards and hay fields flourished on the 30,000-acre ranch, and rippling trout streams meandered through the forest meadows, but a closer look at this peaceable kingdom revealed a network of 46 fallout shelters gouged out of the hillsides. A gun tower sat along the perimeter of the spread.

High on a hill, a church follower showed off a fallout shelter capable of holding 30 people. The 1,400-square-foot sanctuary was equipped with a six-ton, steel-reinforced concrete blast door, as well as a state-of-the-art Swiss air filter to keep out radioactive particles. Inside, church members had stockpiled provisions, including cabbage seeds, lentils, millet, 5,000 gallons of water for drinking and washing, and enough Q-Tip cotton swabs to last 30 people three years.

What accounted for these threats to paradise? No less an event than the end of the world. That was the very real catastrophe anticipated and predicted by the leader and spiritual head of the church, Elizabeth Clare Prophet. Early in the year she announced that the world was entering a period of "particular danger." On March 15 the 3,000 or so faithful who live in the valley got a chance to try out the facilities when a practice drill for nuclear war sent them scurrying to their bunkers. Some did not hear that it was just a drill until dawn's early light. "About seven A.M. someone went outside with a radiation meter," said church follower Eleanor Schieffelin, 65, who had rushed for cover with her 91-year-old wheelchair-bound mother. "Then we all looked outside, and the sky was blue."

The church's neighbors saw red. For them, the Church Universal and Triumphant—or CUT—brought unaccustomed turmoil to their quiet valley, which stretches along the Yellowstone River 60 miles northeast from the boundary of Yellowstone National Park. To longtime locals, it became increasingly clear that the church's preparations for the apocalypse were not just bizarre, but also posed an environmental threat to their sylvan valley.

The church is certainly unorthodox. Prophet claimed that Jesus, Pope John XXIII, Confucius, the saints and all the angels in heaven spoke to the world through her. She supposedly took "spiritual dictation" from Buddha, Shakespeare, Christopher Columbus and Merlin the Magician, as well as someone named Cosmic Master Ray-O-Light. She also believed in reincarnation. "As a child I walked and talked with Jesus," she told PEOPLE. "We've all lived thousands of times." She referred to herself as Mistress of the Universe.

That sort of talk raised more than a few eyebrows in the small towns around the ranch. But what really alarmed the citizenry were Prophet's preparations for Judgment Day. An ardent anticommunist, she ordered not only the construction of the fallout shelters and a gun tower on the property but also the installation of 35 underground fuel tanks.

Then came evidence that CUT ranch members were stockpiling more than provisions. In October 1989, Edward Francis, Prophet's fourth husband and the church's vice president, pleaded guilty in Spokane, Washington, to using an assumed name to try to purchase $100,000 worth of ordnance, including armor-piercing ammunition and semiautomatic rifles. Francis served a month in jail and three months under house arrest on the ranch.

Prophet acknowledged that her adherents were armed but insisted they were no more dangerous than other Montana gun owners. "It's your constitutional right to keep and bear arms," she said. "If the people in China in Tiananmen Square had had guns, they wouldn't have been massacred by the Communists." She professed bafflement at criticism from the church's neighbors. "We never harmed anyone," she said. "We're not aggressive. I have never quite totally understood human hostility or hatred."

Francis's conviction was not CUT's first brush with controversy. Originally known as the Summit

*Prophet with children of CUT members.*

Lighthouse, the church was founded in 1958 by a former insurance and vacuum cleaner salesman named Mark Prophet, who claimed to be the reincarnation of Sir Lancelot. While operating out of a Washington, D.C., storefront, Prophet met Elizabeth Clare Ytreberg. At the time, she was a student at Boston University, the daughter of a strict German father who worked as a yacht builder and a Swiss mother who dabbled in the occult. According to Elizabeth, early on she had visions of heavenly things. By age nine, Elizabeth has written, she had visited every church and synagogue in her hometown of Red Bank, New Jersey, seeking spiritual enlightenment. Mark Prophet provided just that. Divorcing their respective spouses, the pair wed and eventually moved their burgeoning flock to Colorado, where Mark died suddenly in 1973 at the age of 54 of a stroke, said Elizabeth.

Prophet found herself the keeper of a sprawling spiritual empire. By then CUT was reportedly worth about $50 million, amassed, church officials said, by donations from followers, who customarily tithe, and profits from a lucrative printing plant. After Mark's death, Elizabeth headed for California, where she settled on a 257-acre estate in the hills above Malibu.

The church continued to grow despite major controversy, including the defection of Randall King, Prophet's third husband. After divorcing her, he accused his ex-wife of forcing him into "involuntary servitude" and sued her and the church for $23 million. Prophet settled out of court for an undisclosed amount three years ago.

It was about this time that Prophet received a message from an 18th-century European occultist and magician named St. Germain, one of a group of spiritual beings whom she calls the Ascended Masters. He told Prophet that nuclear war was imminent; she decided to move to Montana. As it happened, Prophet already owned land in Paradise Valley—12,000 acres she had purchased in 1981 for $7.35 million from the late publishing tycoon Malcolm Forbes, whose willingness to sell to her now infuriates the locals. "You've got to hope Malcolm Forbes rolls over in his grave every time a fish dies," said Yellowstone's chief ranger, Dan Sholley, referring to the environmental damage he believes CUT is causing. "Forbes is the real villain in this thing, the greedy bastard," he said. By buying up other parcels of real estate, CUT quickly expanded its empire to 30,000 acres. With the original 250 CUT settlers came bulldozers and

121

ranch sits astride prime range for elk, bison and the threatened pronghorn antelope; where once the animals could forage through the valley, they were now thwarted by fences, buildings and roads.

When talking about her rights and rebuking her enemies, Prophet can be persuasive. But when discussing her theology, she often lapses into new-age rhetoric. "If you could see the chart of the presence, it shows each individual's relationship to the presence of God," she began. "The 'I am,' that 'I am' that Moses saw in the burning bush...this direct line of crystal cord going up to the Christ and to the Father." When speaking of past lives she has supposedly led, Prophet was more understandable, if not more believable. "I recall being embodied as Marie Antoinette," she said. "I remember being guillotined. I remember the crowds. I remember leaving my body after being guillotined."

By radiating an intense and, it would seem, utterly sincere belief in her own righteousness, Prophet managed to convince her followers that she would be able to foretell the end of time. And though she has prepared for the apocalypse at least six times, CUT continues to attract converts. As the head of CUT, she said she draws a monthly salary of $1,900; husband Edward receives $500. The couple live modestly, residing in a trailer home and driving a Chevrolet Suburban. Followers who choose to live in Glastonbury must buy lots from the church. They are also able to buy into the shelters; CUT member Eleanor Schieffelin, for instance, paid $5,802 for her space.

The number of CUT adherents is hard to determine. Prophet said that only about five percent of the membership live in Montana and that tens of thousands of others are scattered throughout the United States and Western Europe. Whatever their number, church members are unquestionably devoted to the woman they refer to affectionately as Guru Ma. As Prophet emerged from a church-owned restaurant in Park County one day, a female worshiper who stood nearby instantly said, "Hello, Mother," and dropped to her bare knees in the gravel.

Members are from all walks of life, everything from doctors, lawyers and bankers to blue-collar workers, and learned about Prophet through church literature or one of the many lectures that Prophet gives around the country. Schieffelin, a retired secretary who once worked at the United Nations in New York City, recalled hearing Prophet speak in New Jersey in 1979. "At first I wasn't sure Mrs. Prophet wasn't faking it," she said. Schieffelin prayed over the question, then began subscribing to Prophet's weekly *Pearls of Wisdom* newsletter. In 1985 Schieffelin sold her retirement home on Mount

other heavy construction machinery. Huge aluminum barns and mobile homes, many of them bought from Bhagwan Shree Rajneesh's disbanded settlement in Oregon, appeared on what had been pristine meadowland. Prophet also built a 4,500-acre subdivision, which she named Glastonbury after the ruins of the legendary burial place in England of King Arthur.

Local residents were already angry over CUT's construction projects when it was discovered in April that underground tanks had leaked more than 30,000 gallons of diesel fuel and gasoline, prompting the state to seek a $50,000 court-ordered fine. In the meantime the ranch was caught dumping raw sewage in its fields. According to Steve Pilcher, chief of Montana's water quality bureau, all the waste leaches into the ground and into Yellowstone River. And Yellowstone Park officials complained that the

*Prophet and fourth husband Edward Francis; right, the gun tower.*

Desert Island, Maine, and moved with her mother to the CUT ranch.

Prophet denied that she had brainwashed anyone. "I don't control my members in any way," she said. "I don't tell them what they have to think." Two of her four children, daughter Erin, 24, and son Sean, 25, work for the church, while her youngest daughter, Tatiana, 18, has started college. However, daughter Moira, 22, a born-again Christian who broke with the church about a year ago, no longer speaks to her mother.

Life on the ranch is anything but cushy, especially for the 756 staffers, many of whom work cultivating the 58 types of vegetables and greens grown on the property. There are endless group prayer services, as well as ritual chanting, called "decreeing." The food served is mostly macrobiotic, and there is no drinking or smoking allowed. Prophet is also strict about sex. "You either lead a celibate life, or you are married," she said. "There isn't free sex here."

All in all, Prophet professed to be perplexed that people in Paradise Valley had taken offense at her teachings. "If I'm doing something wrong, I'd like the government to tell me so I can correct it," she said sweetly. "But we don't quit, and we don't run. Why should we? This is our land. We bought it, we paid for it, we pay taxes. We're Americans. We have a right to build fallout shelters. This is our home."

# ex·traor·di·nary

adj., uncommon; exceptional; singular: heroes, martyrs and remarkable people.

# EXTRAORDINARY

# GLORIA ESTEFAN

**F**inishing up the first leg of a global tour, Gloria Estefan felt on top of the world. The Miami Sound Machine had sold 10 million albums worldwide; their LP, *Cuts Both Ways*, was sitting comfortably on the charts. The tour had sold out everywhere. And then, in one awful moment, it all changed.

Six people, including two Sound Machine staffers, her husband, Emilio, her son, Nayib, and Nayib's tutor, were on board when Estefan's tour bus, stalled behind a tractor-trailer on Interstate 80 in Pennsylvania, was struck in the rear by a speeding semi. The tour bus slammed into the truck in front. "The next thing I knew, I was on the floor," Estefan said. "I had a black eye and a strange, metallic taste in my mouth. "I tried to lift my legs, but they would only go so far. I remember thinking I would rather die than be paralyzed. But I told myself, 'No way. I'm not accepting this, I'm gonna get through this.' Then I realized, 'As long as I can move my feet even a little, I'm not paralyzed.'"

Early bulletins reported the singer in critical condition and possibly paralyzed for life. Emilio, 37, Nayib, nine, and three other passengers were also injured, but none as seriously as Estefan.

Flown by air ambulance to New York City's Hospital for Joint Diseases Orthopedic Institute on March 21, Estefan underwent delicate spinal surgery. The operation lasted four hours and required a bone graft from Estefan's hip and insertion of steel rods to shore up the fractured vertebrae. Although the rods are permanent, they are located in a section of the spine that flexes very little anyway, and will not inhibit Estefan's movements. The operation left a 14-inch scar down the middle of her back.

The dynamic Cuban-born singer is one of the Miami exile community's triumphant American dream stories. In her teens Estefan helped nurse her father—an ex-Batista family bodyguard, Bay of Pigs invader and Vietnam vet—through multiple sclerosis. He died in 1980. Her mother, Gloria Fajardo, still teaches fifth grade in Miami. Estefan earned a B.A. in psychology from the University of Miami in 1978 and worked as a customs interpreter—she speaks French too—while pursuing her musical career. In 1979 she married Emilio, founder of the hot local band she sang with. Renamed and relaunched as Miami Sound Machine, Estefan's band sold millions of records throughout Latin America before crossing over to English-language success with the monster hit "Conga" in 1985. Emilio quit performing in 1986 to devote himself to managing and producing.

Three months after breaking her back the Miami Sound Machine star was working hard at getting herself in shape to return to performing. Emilio stayed home from the office to care for her after their return to Miami. At year's end, Estefan was finishing up an album and working toward a March 1991 tour.

*Emilio and Gloria Estefan.*

# PETER WILLCOX

**L**ong after dark, Peter Willcox scanned the calm South Pacific from the deck of the new *Rainbow Warrior*. His presence there, at the helm of the ship, was a statement of unshakable purpose. This was the first time Willcox, 37, had been back in the South Seas since 1985, when he lost the first *Rainbow Warrior*—and nearly lost his life.

Willcox and his crew were docked in Auckland, New Zealand, before heading out to document the effects of nuclear testing in French Polynesia. To deter them, the French secret service planted two bombs on the *Warrior*, which detonated around midnight on July 10. Willcox, who had been sleeping, stumbled naked and without his glasses through the foundering Greenpeace vessel to guide 11 shipmates to safety, but photographer Fernando Pereira was killed trying to save his equipment.

Greenpeace has been an effective pain in the afterdeck to those who pollute the ocean or destroy marine life. Since the first *Rainbow Warrior* was launched in 1978, the Greenpeace fleet has grown to seven ships, which patrol the world's waters from the Mediterranean to the South Pacific. The organization boasts nearly four million members worldwide, with offices in 22 countries. Willcox helped supply the evidence that eventually forced the French government to pay Greenpeace $8.1 million in reparations.

A native of Norwalk, Connecticut, Willcox dropped out of Antioch College in 1972. He declared himself a pacifist and took a government-approved conscientious objector's job as first mate of the sloop *Clearwater*, an environmental advocacy boat on the Hudson River.

Willcox, who is paid $20,000 a year, signed on as skipper of the *Rainbow Warrior* in 1981. Most days, he spends eight hours on watch and a few more helping his crew run the *Warrior*'s state-of-the-art communications equipment. "It's great to continue the work that was interrupted by the bombing," Wilcox said. "I know we can make a difference."

*Peter Willcox aboard the Rainbow Warrior.*

# EXTRAORDINARY

# NELSON MANDELA

**D**uring the more than 27 years he spent in prison, his words could not be printed legally in South Africa or his face shown in public. But his fame and reputation only grew, until he became the world's most celebrated political prisoner and the embodiment of the struggle against apartheid.

When South African President F.W. de Klerk finally set Nelson Mandela free on February 11, the stirring sight of him walking out of Verster prison—gray and thin but commanding—triggered a wave of rejoicing across South Africa. "I was completely overwhelmed by the enthusiasm," Mandela said. "It is something I did not expect."

Few of Mandela's followers know much about the early years of his life. Born in the rural village of Qunu, in what is now the black homeland of Transkei, he spent his days tilling fields and herding cattle and his nights listening to tribal elders talk of the time before the white man came to that part of South Africa. Even as a youth, Mandela showed signs of leadership. In 1930, after the death of his father, Henry Gadla Mandela—a farmer who was also the main adviser to the Paramount Chief of the Tembu tribe—12-year-old Nelson was sent to live in the chief's Great Place, where his intelligence quickly marked him as the heir apparent who would someday rule the tribe.

But Mandela—whose tribal name, Rolihlahla, means "one who brings trouble upon himself"—instead chose the path of political activism. In 1940, while studying at Fort Hare College in the Eastern Cape, he was expelled for helping organize a strike protesting administration efforts to limit the power of the student council. The next year he headed for Johannesburg, where he worked briefly as a guard at a gold mine before landing a job as a clerk in a white law office. At the same time, he began studying by correspondence for his law degree from the University of the Witwatersrand.

Along the way, Mandela married Evelyn Ntoko Mase, a nurse with whom he eventually had three children—son Tembi, who died in a car crash in 1979, son Makgatho, now 38, and daughter Maki, 35. But the marriage was troubled. Evelyn wanted her husband to concentrate on his career and forget politics, while Nelson felt deep anger at the discrimination—great and small—that he witnessed daily. In 1944 Mandela and two close friends, Oliver Tambo and Walter Sisulu, both now leaders of the black nationalist movement, formed the Youth League of the African National Congress.

"It was a time when we talked about nothing but politics," recalled Amina Cachalia, who helped organize protests with Mandela. "But there were times when merrymaking was going on. Mandela was a very likable person who made friends easily and liked to laugh and joke a lot." An avid amateur boxer, the six-foot-two-inch Mandela, who at one point weighed 245 pounds, often went down to local gyms in Johannesburg to spar a few rounds with other heavyweights. He also began spending time with a social worker named Nomzamo Winnie Madikizela, then 20, who was 16 years his junior. Mandela separated from Evelyn in 1955, and they were divorced two years later. (Maki contends that her mother learned of the divorce in a newspaper article, which left lingering bitterness.)

The courtship between Nelson and Winnie was far from routine. In December 1956 police arrested Mandela and 155 other activists and charged them with treason for staging strikes and protests in opposition to apartheid laws. Their marathon trial ended five years later in acquittal, but within months of the verdict, Mandela had gone underground to form the military wing of the ANC, which then launched a series of bombings on power plants, rail lines and other strategic targets. Thus began a life of separation for Nelson and Winnie, whom he had married in 1958 and who bore him two children, daughters Zeni, now 31, and Zindzi, 29. Mandela was captured by police after more than a year on the run; while in jail on other charges, he was convicted of sabotage and treason in June 1964 and sentenced to life in prison.

Mandela was sent at once to Robben Island, a craggy, windblown Alcatraz near Cape Town harbor. Mandela tried to make the best of the 18 years he spent on the island. Denied newspapers until 1980, he and

*Mandela greeting children at a meeting near his home in Soweto.*

his ANC comrades kept abreast of developments in South Africa through smuggled messages; in the evening they talked politics and proselytized new prisoners—so effectively that the place became known as Mandela University.

The psychological toll of confinement was relieved only by Winnie's visits. (Initially, she was allowed a half hour with him every six months.) "Had it not been for your visits, wonderful letters and love, I would have fallen apart many years ago," he wrote her in a 1979 letter. "I pause here and drink some coffee, after which I dust the photos on my bookcase. I start with that of Zeni, which is on the outer side, then Zindzi's and lastly yours, my darling Mum. Doing so always eases the longing for you."

Later there were tensions in the relationship, largely because of Winnie's more recent controversial activities. In a notorious 1986 speech she endorsed "necklacing," the gruesome practice favored by certain black militants of putting gasoline-filled tires around the necks of suspected police informants and setting them alight. She also formed a bodyguard detail of unruly young toughs, known as the Mandela United Football Club, who were allegedly responsible for numerous beatings and the murder of a 14-year-old activist in Soweto. Though Nelson never publicly commented on the actions, he reportedly told Winnie to disband the gang, which she did.

In 1982 authorities transferred Mandela to a maximum-security block in Pollsmoor Prison in Cape Town to prevent him from indoctrinating inmates at Robben Island. He spent much of the next six years without access to his political comrades and in 1988 was hospitalized with tuberculosis. After he recovered, he was taken to the Victor Verster Prison Farm near Cape Town, where he spent the next two years.

At the same time, the South African government began signaling its desire to open negotiations over South Africa's future. Last year President de Klerk stepped up discussions between Mandela and members of his cabinet and started allowing the black leader visits with antiapartheid activists. Finally, De Klerk set Mandela free.

In July, Nelson and Winnie made a triumphant 12-day U.S. tour. Thousands lined the streets to catch a glimpse of the spiritual leader of black South Africa. He received a standing ovation from a joint session of Congress. Harvard psychiatrist and civil rights activist Alvin Francis Poussaint noted: "Mandela is a small man who has taken on the giant forces of evil, and it looks like he is going to win. All of us, black and white, need to know that David can still beat Goliath."

When Nelson was released from prison, Winnie stood at his side, sharing the victory. In October, the Mandelas entered a courtroom in Soweto together. With Nelson, 72, sitting stony-faced in the first row, Winnie, 56, stepped forward to face formal charges that nearly two years ago she and a gang of toughs kidnapped and assaulted four young black men. Winnie denied having anything to do with harming the victims. Nelson angrily accused the government of fabricating the allegations against his wife in order to appease whites. Her trial is scheduled to begin in February 1991.

Having endured the rigors of martyrdom with consummate dignity, Mandela was left to fill the awesome role of statesman with an equal measure of skill, helping to bring democracy and equality to a deeply divided country. It was a task for which he had been preparing for 27 years, without any assurance that he would ever have the chance to attempt it. Mandela cautioned that solution would not come easily.

# EXTRAORDINARY

# QUINCY JONES

**Q**uincy Delight Jones Jr. has risen to heights he never imagined when he arrived in Los Angeles 25 years ago. A music legend long before he attained hyperfame as producer of Michael Jackson's *Thriller*, Jones, 57, lived among the trophies of his remarkable life. In his terraced house in Bel-Air, oil paintings of the big-band masters with whom he apprenticed, Count Basie and Duke Ellington, hung on a wall. Nearby were framed photos of his other mentor, Lionel Hampton, and the kings of bebop cool with whom he came of age, Bird Parker and Dizzy Gillespie. Another wall was lined with platinum albums for producing Jackson's zillion sellers. There were posters from some of the 40-odd films he had scored and, resting on the baby grand, a 1977 Emmy for his *Roots* score. There was a framed group photo from the 1985 recording session he conducted for "We Are the World."

Artists from every era of popular music, from bebop to hip hop, had dialed Q for success: Dinah Washington, Sarah Vaughan, Nat King Cole, Frank Sinatra, Andy Williams, Peggy Lee, Aretha Franklin, Ringo Starr, Donna Summer, George Benson and Barbra Streisand. "He's Doctor Fixit," said Dizzy Gillespie. "People go to him because he knows what he's doin'. He knows the sound you've got in you, and he's got the experience and the know-how to get it out. If I knew how he does it, I'd be a millionaire."

Now the world's most successful record producer was working on his career coda: Quincy Jones,

Hollywood mogul. Bankrolled by a multimillion-dollar Time Warner contract, Jones's fledgling Quincy Jones Entertainment Company already had one sitcom, NBC's *The Fresh Prince of Bel-Air*, and his talk show with Jesse Jackson was in syndication. With plans for an epic film on the life of part-Ethiopian Russian poet Aleksandr Pushkin and a comprehensive, multimedia history of black music in development, Jones joined the growing group of black Hollywood rainmakers that includes pal Bill Cosby, Eddie Murphy and Oprah Winfrey.

When inspired or distressed, he rubbed his broad brow, which is grooved by a big, vertical, troughlike scar left by two brain operations he underwent in 1974 after suffering a near-fatal aneurysm. "This is one helluva reality potion," he said, running a finger the length of the scar. "It will level your ass out real fast."

With six children bobbing in the wash of three failed marriages, Jones admitted that his personal life had been a bit rockier than his career. His first wife, childhood sweetheart Jeri Caldwell, split in the mid-'60s, and Jones took up with Swedish model Ulla Anderson. He and Anderson divorced in 1974 after Jones moved in with his third wife-to-be, *Mod Squad* actress Peggy Lipton. Starring in David Lynch's *Twin Peaks* as a heart-of-gold waitress who cheats on her heart-of-dross husband, Lipton has lived nearby with the couple's two teenage daughters since the split with Jones in 1986; she remains a friend.

Jones has recently been forced to relive his past, thanks to *Listen Up: The Lives of Quincy Jones*, a documentary film and a book. "Seeing the film kicks

my butt," Jones said. "I was such a dog." A scene in which his eldest daughter, Jolie, described how "the life just went right out of the house" when her parents divorced, "rips me to pieces," Jones said. "I go through all these changes, these feelings about the price my kids had to pay for me to do my thing. I was 20 when Jolie was born. I didn't know what I was doin' at all. But it wasn't as bad as it looks in the film. I didn't abandon my kids. Not even close." Jones was trying now to make amends.

His own childhood taught him nothing about being a family man. His Southern-born father, Quincy D. Jones Sr., a carpenter and semipro baseball player, met his mother, Sarah, in Chicago's vast black ghetto, where Jones was born in 1933. Jones eventually traced both their families back to a Mississippi plantation. His mother, the daughter of a former slave who still spoke an African dialect, was prone to erratic behavior and was eventually institutionalized for an emotional disorder now routinely controlled by vitamin injections. "I never really knew what it was like to have a mother," said Jones, who remembered a birthday party ruined when Sarah smashed his cake in the backyard.

In 1943 Quincy Sr. remarried and moved the family to Bremerton, Washington, outside Seattle, then in the midst of a wartime boom. Jones took up the trumpet. A quick study, he turned pro at 13, playing in local nightclubs. There he met 16-year-old Ray Charles, who would become a lifelong friend.

Jones won a music scholarship to Berklee College of Music in Boston, but he had done his real learning at the Seattle's Palomar Theater. "Count Basie used to come and play the Palomar," he said. "That's where I met him, Billy Eckstine, Sammy Davis. I'd sneak in and just sit and watch those guys. Oh, I was like buzzy, man; full of energy, nosy and curious. Basie was like my daddy. I don't know why he took me in like he did. I guess he liked me because I was thirsty to learn. Ray and me, we were just totally dedicated. Our aspiration was not about stardom. To be good and recognized as a good musician, that's what we lived for."

After dropping out of Berklee to tour with Lionel Hampton in 1951, Jones settled in New York City, where he arranged, conducted and played for his childhood idols. Eventually winding up in debt, he was forced to take a job with Mercury Records, becoming the first black vice president of a major record label. It gave him an insider's view of the ripoffs and racism that victimized the rhythm-and-blues artists who had invented rock.

Entranced by Hollywood after scoring *The Pawnbroker* for Sidney Lumet in 1963, Jones quit Mercury in 1965 and moved to Los Angeles. The producers left the room when he showed up for his first job, scoring *Mirage*. "They didn't know I was black," he said. Henry Mancini remembered getting an anxious call from the studio. "They wanted reassurance that he could do the job," said Mancini. He vouched for Jones.

Jones kept his recording hand hot, arranging and conducting the historic Sinatra-Basie collaboration, *Sinatra at the Sands*, in 1966, and winning a Grammy for his own *Walking in Space* in 1969. But he spent most of the '60s and early '70s at the movies, scoring more than 40 films. "I was doing eight movies a year," Jones said. "I was under a lot of pressure. I wasn't working out. I was staying up five and six nights writing scores. I was smoking tons, four packs a day."

Retribution came in August 1974, when Jones was 41. "My head exploded," he said. While operating, doctors discovered a second aneurysm ready to blow. With an eight-week wait between operations, Jones married Lipton, with whom he was living, in a ceremony at her parents' home in Los Angeles.

Determined since then to "inhale life," Jones grew rich and famous in the ensuing 16 years—his rise fueled by caring, not conniving. Now living alone, but well, Jones spends most nights at home, sharing meals—prepared by a French chef—with friends from a large circle that includes Marlon Brando, Oliver Stone, Sidney Poitier, Michael Caine and yoga classmate Kareem Abdul-Jabbar. Jones recently split from Verna Harrah, ex-wife of the casino owner.

Helping on a film project with rap-music impresario Russell Simmons, Jones was a big fan of the new form. "Young music has always been designed to irritate, to make you squirm," he said. "Look past the profanity and listen to what they are saying. Rappers have a heritage that goes way back to the African *griots*, the oral historians and troubadours who would sing the history and legends of the tribe in rhyme."

Jones saw a similar role for himself. "I'm hearing music in my head all the time," he said. "I hope it never stops. When I get to be 80, I want to write street ballets, street operas. Oh, yeah, man. I've got a whole lot of shit to do."

# VACLAV HAVEL

**I**n the West, playwright Vaclav Havel's work is known as theater of the absurd. From the vantage point of his native Prague and his personal experiences, the plays were more like socialist realism. This year, in the ultimate irony, the lifelong dissident and former political prisoner was named Czechoslovakia's President in spite of himself.

Havel, 53, emerged as his nation's most potent symbol of reform—an intractable opponent of the regime who chose to make a stand rather than follow many of his fellow artists into exile. He had been jailed repeatedly since 1968, when Soviet troops moved into Prague to replace the maverick Dubcek regime with reliable Communist hard-liners. His phones were bugged, his friends harassed, and his papers confiscated time and again. When Joe Papp invited Havel to be playwright-in-residence at his Public Theater in New York City, the Czech authorities, eager to get rid of him, said he could go. But Havel was adamant. "The solution to the situation does not lie in leaving it," he declared. "Fourteen million people can't just go and leave Czechoslovakia."

Havel learned always to carry toothpaste, razor blades and his favorite unfiltered cigarettes in case he was seized by the police. He stashed pages of his work in various hiding places and then smuggled it out to the West—each new play a biting indictment of the status quo.

The son of a wealthy Prague restaurateur, Havel was sent to the best schools and pampered by maids and governesses. But when the Communists came to power in 1948, the family's assets were seized. Because of his bourgeois background, Havel was barred from attending college. He took a job in a chemical factory and managed to attend a technical school at night, writing essays on poetry and drama in his spare time.

In the late '50s, Havel became a stagehand at the Theater on the Balustrade, the leading avant-garde troupe in Prague. Enthralled by the works of Ionesco, Kafka and Beckett (who later dedicated a play to him), Havel began writing drama.

When Soviet tanks rolled through the streets, Havel's work was outlawed, and he—like most Czech intellectuals—was consigned to manual labor. Yet, inexplicably, he was able to collect his foreign royalties and enjoy some material privileges.

In 1977, after he helped launch the human rights group Charter 77, Havel's house was robbed and ransacked by government agents, and he was jailed for four months. In 1979 he was convicted of subversion and imprisoned again for four years.

Some of his prison correspondence with his wife evaded the censors and appeared in the West as *Letters to Olga*. Olga Havel, 57, was romanticized as the heroine of the widely read *Letters*. The real Olga is more complicated, less romantic. Havel has described her as "a working-class girl, her own person ... even somewhat mouthy and obnoxious."

In many ways, the Havels seem to be an unlikely couple. Olga, who did not see why Vaclav had to be President in the first place, is an intensely private person. Havel often travels without her on state visits since she prefers to stay at home. The Havels, married in 1964, have no children, reportedly not by choice. Vaclav, who has two attractive female bodyguards, is known to have extramarital liaisons. "Olga and I have not professed our love for each other for at least 200 years," Havel has said, "but we both feel that we are probably inseparable." According to Havel, Olga is the steadying force that counteracts "my own mental instability.... All my life I've consulted her in everything I do. The wags claim I even require her agreement to the sins through which I hurt her."

Havel is unlike any leader in Central European history. The state's endless persecution made him a national hero. Catapulted almost overnight from being Czechoslovakia's foremost dissident playwright to its President, he is the political utopian's dream come true: a poet statesman, the harbinger of the new humane politics of Eastern Europe.

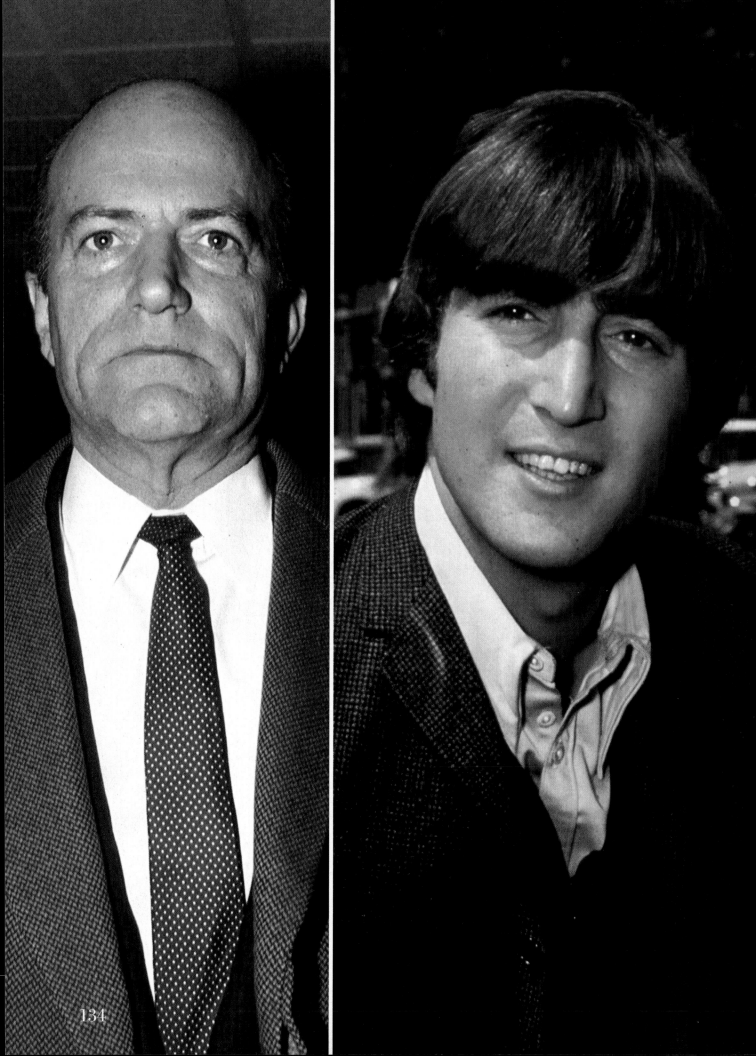

Polly Bergen and perennial Waters actress, Mink Stole. Said Waters of Hearst: "She's an American legend, and I'm her fan. She was the only one I was starstruck by."

JAMES DEAN—At 5:45 P.M. on September 30, 1955, James Dean was a 24-year-old actor with moody good looks and a promising future. Minutes later he was dead in a car wreck and on the way to becoming a legend.

His remarkable cultural status was reaffirmed again when nearly 30,000 old faithfuls, new fans and former chums of the actor gathered in Dean's hometown of Fairmount, Indiana, for a weekend marking the 35th anniversary of his death. Deanophiles, some of whom had come from as far as Holland and Japan, watched floats, marching bands and a look-alike contest, visited the James Dean Gallery and his grave and listened to a speech by Dean's former high school drama coach, Adeline Nall, 84.

Dean, who was killed instantly when his speeding silver Porsche collided with another car near Cholame, California, made only three films before his death: *East of Eden*, released five months earlier; *Giant*, which he had finished working on just days earlier; and *Rebel Without a Cause*, which was about to open. *Rebel*, in which he played a brooding teenage loner, set the image that would endure for decades.

*John and Yoko, 1980; Patty with daughters Lydia (top) and Gillian; James Dean, 1954.*

# good·byes

n., farewell gestures: tributes
to those now gone.

141

# STAGE & SCREEN

**E**VE ARDEN—She was every leading lady's best pal—the wisecracking second banana who never got the guy but always got the laughs. Eve Arden, who died of heart failure November 12, routinely stole the show with her stringently ironic tone, arched brows and bull's-eye timing.

Arden was born Eunice Quedens, 83 years ago in Mill Valley, California. She began her professional career at 16, quickly finding her niche as a comic stage actress. Despite her success in films, Arden truly became a national institution on CBS's *Our Miss Brooks*, a comedy series that began on radio in 1948 and then moved to TV. As crisp-witted Connie Brooks, America's most popular English teacher, Arden was a rare workingwoman among such television homemakers as Lucy, Ethel and Gracie.

Her private life included an eight-year marriage to literary agent Edward "Ned" Bergen. In 1947 she divorced Bergen and in 1951 wed actor Brooks West. In 1984 West died of a stroke.

Arden's publicist and manager for 35 years, Glenn Rose, said, "She kept being cast as this sarcastic, acid-tongued lady with the quick retort and put-down. In real life, Eve would have never put anyone down. She wasn't that kind of person."

HOWARD DUFF—Tough-guy actor Howard Duff died July 9 of a heart attack in Santa Barbara, California, at age 76. Born in Bremerton, Washington, Duff started in theater and then came to public attention as detective Sam Spade on the 1940s CBS radio series of the same name. He made his movie debut in 1947's *Brute Force*; more recent movie appearances included 1978's *A Wedding* and 1979's *Kramer vs. Kramer*. On television he was a regular in such series as *Mr. Adams and Eve* (in which he co-starred with his then wife, actress-director Ida Lupino, from 1957 to 1958), *Felony Squad* (1966-69) and most recently, *Flamingo Road* (1981-82), where he portrayed Sheriff Titus Semple.

JACK GILFORD—The 82-year-old actor, whose rumpled face kept him in juicy character parts in TV, movies and the theater for 55 years, died June 4 of stomach cancer in New York City. His best-known recent role was as the practical codger who elects to remain on Earth in 1985's *Cocoon* and the 1988 sequel, *Cocoon: The Return*. Gilford appeared in 18 movies, 14 Broadway shows and guest-starred in countless TV shows. He was nominated for a Best Supporting Actor Oscar in 1973 for his role as a demoralized older businessman in *Save the Tiger* and was nominated for Tony awards for supporting parts in *Cabaret* and *A Funny Thing Happened on the Way to the Forum*.

IRENE DUNNE—She was one of the great stars of Hollywood's Golden Era of the 1930s, equally at home in dramas, musicals or screwball comedies. When Irene Dunne died of a heart attack on September 4 at age 85, film buffs knew they had lost one of the most underrated actresses of all time. She received five Oscar nominations but never took one home.

Dunne may have lacked the cachet of her more flamboyant celluloid sisters, but her 41 eclectic films included some of filmland's most entertaining: *Cimarron, Back Street, Roberta, The Magnificent Obsession, Show Boat, Theodora Goes Wild, A Guy Named Joe, The Awful Truth, My Favorite Wife* and *I*

*Clockwise from upper left: Eve Arden, 1952; Irene Dunne, 1946; Vic Tayback, 1980; Jack Gilford, 1978; Paulette Goddard, 1936; Howard Duff, 1982.*

*Remember Mama.* Trained in music, the Kentucky-born Dunne first played in a touring company of the musical *Irene.* After several years on Broadway, she switched to movies in 1930.

Despite Dunne's elegant looks and shining screen presence, her life lacked two essential ingredients for a movie queen: temperament and scandal. A devout Catholic, she was married only once, to a dentist named Francis Griffin, who died in 1965. They had one adopted daughter, Mary Frances.

Dunne didn't drink and was always impeccably turned out, even refusing to wear slacks. A staunch Republican, she was appointed a delegate to the United Nations under Eisenhower, and she was one of the recipients of a Kennedy Center Honor during the Reagan administration.

---

## PAULETTE GODDARD—She died at age 78
(or as old as 84, depending on the source) on April 23 at her home in Switzerland, following a short illness. Goddard is likely to be remembered as much for the one movie part she didn't get as for the 40 or more parts she did. She had all but signed for the coveted role of Scarlett O'Hara in 1939's *Gone with the Wind* but lost the part, at the last minute, to Vivien Leigh.

Goddard, who was born Marion Levy in Great Neck, New York, arrived in Hollywood in 1931, having already married and divorced lumber magnate Edgar James. She soon captured the heart of Charlie Chaplin, co-starring with him in 1936's *Modern Times* and taking him as her second husband, she claimed, in a secret at-sea ceremony the same year. In the '40s Goddard became a top star at Paramount, but her career petered out by the mid-'50s. She was married twice more, first to actor Burgess Meredith from 1944 to 1950 and then, in 1958, to Erich Maria Remarque, author of *All Quiet on the Western Front*, who died in 1970.

---

## VIC TAYBACK—The acerbic cook, who flipped
burgers at Mel's Diner in CBS's *Alice* series, died at age 60 of a heart attack in Los Angeles. Tayback, whose father was a short-order cook, created the role of Mel in *Alice Doesn't Live Here Anymore*, the 1975 film upon which the TV series was based.

---

## JOEL McCREA—The lanky, low-key McCrea,
who ambled through such classics as *Foreign Correspondent*, *These Three* and *The Palm Beach Story* before saddling up as one of Hollywood's most enduring Western stars in *The Virginian* and *Ride the High Country*, died of pulmonary complications October 20, at age 84, in Woodland Hills, California. McCrea fashioned his life into something of a horse opera, buying up acres of land and listing his occupation as "rancher."

---

## MARY MARTIN—If the American musical had
a guardian angel, it was Mary Martin. She created the roles of Nellie, one of the dames there was nothing like in *South Pacific*, and Maria in *The Sound of Music*, but she was best known for *Peter Pan* (above). In the nation's imagination she *was* the boy who wouldn't grow up, perhaps because she believed it herself. "Never-Land is the way I'd like real life to be," she wrote in *My Heart Belongs*, her 1976 autobiography, "timeless, free, mischievous, filled with gaiety...."

"She was heaven," said Carol Channing, who sat at her old friend's bedside in Rancho Mirage, California, less than an hour before her death of liver cancer on November 3, at age 76.

Martin didn't like movies (she made nearly a dozen forgettable features), and the big screen never telegraphed the fresh-faced insouciance she displayed on Broadway. She made the stage hers in Cole Porter's 1938 hit, *Leave It to Me*, when she won raves for a comic striptease while singing her signature song, "My Heart Belongs to Daddy." But she would lay her claim to a generation of TV viewers in 1955, when NBC broadcast the first of three TV adaptations of *Peter Pan*, in which the 41-year-old actress performed a daring aerial ballet. Although she slowed her pace in recent years, Martin kept working. In 1987 she toured with Channing in *Legends!*, a nonmusical about a pair of bitchy Hollywood battle-axes. Contemplating her own end, she said, "It's been a fabulous life and a wonderful career. I'll keep living until it's time. Then I'll just go on to another stage."

## ROBERT CUMMINGS

ROBERT CUMMINGS—The eternally boyish, swinging bachelor of the 1950s sitcom *The Bob Cummings Show*, died of kidney failure at age 82, on December 2 in Woodland Hills, California. Cummings began as a stage actor in 1931 and landed supporting roles in more than 100 movies, but he was best known for his starring TV role from 1955 to 1959 as the photographer who dated all the studio models. Cummings, a devotee of health food and astrology, never made a move without consulting his horoscope and traveled with 30 pounds of vitamins. He was married five times.

## JOAN BENNETT

JOAN BENNETT—Movie star Bennett, who had a second career as the mistress of the Collins mansion on the 1961-71 TV series *Dark Shadows*, died at age 80 of cardiac arrest on December 7 in Scarsdale, New York. Bennett starred in the first of her 60 movies in 1929, appeared as a blond ingenue through the 1930s, then switched to sultry brunet in the '40s, when she took on tougher parts in such film noir classics as *Scarlet Street* and *The Woman in the Window*. "My change of hair color made a definite difference in my career," she said. "My voice dropped, and I smoldered all the way from the South Seas to Manhattan ... I got awfully sick of it after a while." Scandal cut her film career short in 1951 when her third husband, producer Walter Wanger, shot her agent Jennings Lang in a jealous rage.

## MARTIN RITT

MARTIN RITT—Socially conscious film director Ritt, 76, whose more than 25 movies included *Hud, Sounder, The Front, Norma Rae,* and *Stanley and Iris,* died of complications from heart disease on December 8 in Santa Monica. Blacklisted in 1950 because of liberal leanings, Ritt spent six years teaching at the Actors Studio, selling magazine ads, playing poker and betting on horses before producer David Susskind defied the blacklist by hiring him to direct the racial drama *Edge of the City* in 1956.

## RAY GOULDING

RAY GOULDING—Funnyman Goulding, who brought inane characters like cooking host Mary McGoon and the mawkish Charles the Poet to the airwaves, died of kidney failure at age 68 at his home in Manhasset, New York. His death marked the end of the peerless radio comedy team, Bob and Ray. Goulding met partner Bob Elliot in 1946 at WHDH in Boston, where Ray was reading the news and Elliot was morning deejay. They launched into impromptu skits on the air, and soon after, the half-hour *Matinee with Bob and Ray* was born. The comedy duo went to NBC Radio in 1951 and became known for their commercial spoofs such as "The Bob and Ray Home Surgery Kit." Bob and Ray performed together on TV, on Broadway in 1970, and continued working until 1988, when Goulding's health worsened. Legions of fans will always remember their patented sign-off: "This is Ray Goulding, reminding you to write if you get work ... and Bob Elliot, reminding you to hang by your thumbs."

## JILL IRELAND

JILL IRELAND—For six full years, Ireland resisted a virulent cancer with a grace and fortitude that was inspiring. On May 18, at the age of 54, she finally succumbed to the disease. The London-born actress trained as a dancer and began her career at age 15. After performing with the Monte Carlo Ballet, she made her screen debut dancing in *Oh Rosalinda!* in 1955. After switching to acting, she began playing dramatic roles in British films and television productions. Ireland's ten-year marriage to actor David McCallum ended in 1967, and the following year she married Charles Bronson. She played leads opposite him in several films.

In 1984 doctors found a malignant lump in Ireland's breast, as well as evidence of extensive "lymph node involvement." Ireland underwent a radical mastectomy and a brutal, six-month round of chemotherapy. For three-and-a-half years, at least, she seemed to have beaten the disease into submission. But by the fall of 1988, doctors found not only that the cancer had returned, but that it had metastasized to the liver and bones. At the start of her illness, Bronson, who fondly called Ireland his "golden girl," shelved his own film career to stay by her side. It wasn't possible to take her along on location with him, and he refused to be away from her at all.

In November 1989, her adopted son Jason, 27, one of the seven children she and Bronson had raised, was found dead from the cumulative effects of a more than 10-year-long drug habit. By then her condition was grave, the cancer having spread through her body, filling her chest with fluid. Ireland continued a grueling, radical course of treatment at the Arlington Memorial Hospital in Texas. Ireland wrote two books about her ordeal: *Life Wish* and *Life Lines*. A month before she died, she received her own star on Hollywood Boulevard's Walk of Fame, three blocks from Bronson's.

In a private ceremony at a Beverly Hills hotel, her husband, their children and family friends gathered to carry out her wishes for an old-fashioned wake, with balloons, champagne and guests dressed in bright colors. It was, as she had wanted it to be, "a celebration of my life."

# AVA GARDNER
## 1922-1990

**S**he was the most irresistible woman in Hollywood. Ravishing, fiery and dangerous, she had a smoldering beauty and a sex appeal that led her into stormy marriages and affairs with millionaires and matadors. In part she was the flamboyant temptress whose beauty cowed even Elizabeth Taylor; another part was a country girl who went barefoot and disliked anything that hinted of pretension.

In the end, Ava Gardner said that she was tired of living. Struggling against lung disease and the partial paralysis that was the legacy of her 1986 stroke, the woman whose mesmerizing looks once defined the term screen goddess spent her last weeks inside a sumptuous flat off Hyde Park, London. On January 25, Ava Lavinia Gardner Rooney Shaw Sinatra died in her sleep. Four days later the 67-year-old actress

was buried in Smithfield, North Carolina, the rural town she had left behind half a century before.

Ava's kin never appreciated the story—ground out by the MGM publicity mill—that she was a sharecropper's daughter who made good. Her father, a tobacco-and-cotton farmer, not only owned his farm, he owned a sawmill and a country store as well. And though the family lost their land when the Depression hit, they were never dirt-poor. After Ava's father died, her mother, Mollie, took over a boardinghouse in Rock Ridge, North Carolina, and put her daughter to work in the kitchen.

In the summer of 1940, Ava was allowed to visit her married sister Beatrice in New York City. The trip altered her life. Ava's brother-in-law, a commercial photographer, sent photos of her to the talent office at Metro. By the next summer, Ava was in Hollywood with a seven-year MGM contract.

While she wasn't a smash on the screen in the beginning, she was a major success with Mickey Rooney—the 21-year-old who was one of Metro's hottest properties. Besotted with 19-year-old Ava, Rooney pursued her relentlessly. The two were wed in a quiet ceremony near Santa

Barbara. Sixteen months later the marriage was over. After a dalliance with millionaire Howard Hughes, she married bandleader Artie Shaw in 1945. A strong-willed intellectual with four marriages behind him, Shaw, then 35, worshiped Ava's body. "She was a goddess," he said. "I would stare at her, literally stare, in wonder." Ava's view of Shaw: "He was so god-almighty, I never stood a chance." In 1946 she and Shaw were divorced.

Then she met Frank Sinatra. Their courtship was an exercise in glorious excess: It took two years for Sinatra to extricate himself from his first marriage, and the press trailed the two from Las Vegas to Mexico to Madrid. The Sinatras retained few secrets after they wed in 1951: They drank hard, fought with abandon and sustained a sexual tension that was palpable even in photographs. With Frank's career in a decline and Ava's on the rise, the battles grew more barbaric. She called him a gangster; he attempted suicide. And while the marriage lasted only two years, the passion never waned. (The 3,000-odd visitors who streamed through the

Underwood Funeral Home whispered about the wreath whose card was signed, "With my love, Francis.")

Ava never married again. In Spain, where she lived after the mid-'50s, Ava threw herself into front-page affairs with matadors, learned flamenco dancing and tried her hand at fighting bulls.

After her career reached its artistic apex with *The Night of the Iguana* in 1964, she began to retreat; always uncomfortable in front of the camera, she accepted roles in only 12 movies in the 16 years before she died. It was not because she wanted to prove anything as a performer; instead, she told one reporter, "I do it for the loot, honey—always for the loot."

Those who were close to Ava in her final years say that, although she was in pain, she harbored few regrets. "Honey, there comes a time when you've got to face the fact that you're an old broad," she once declared. "I've had a hell of a good time, so my face looks, well, lived-in. You won't find me standing in front of a mirror, weeping."

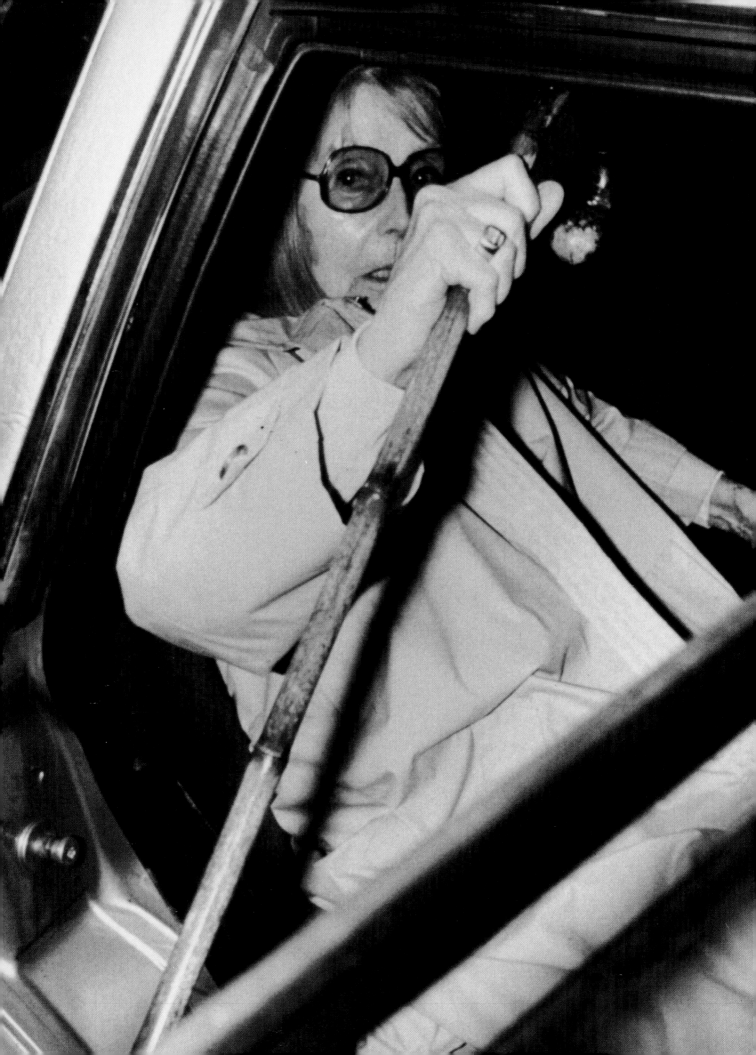

# GRETA GARBO
## 1905-1990

**She was born in Stockholm on September 18, 1905, to a family so impoverished that a benefactor made a salutary offer to adopt her. Young Greta Lovisa Gustafsson, third child of a privy cleaner who died of tuberculosis when Greta was 14, nevertheless managed to make her way in the world. Discovered by famed Swedish director Mauritz Stiller, she sailed with him at 19 to New York City and then went to Hollywood, where her luminous beauty lit 24 films, among them, *Anna Karenina, Camille* and *Ninotchka*. At 36, she abandoned her career, beginning one of filmdom's longest and most puzzling public silences.**

Greta Garbo's reclusive life ended at age 84 in a New York City hospital on Easter Sunday, 1990, of an undisclosed illness. (In death as in life, there was only informed speculation as to causes, though there was confirmation that Garbo was undergoing kidney dialysis.)

By the time of her last film, 1941's *Two-Faced Woman*, a box office failure in which she was disastrously cast against type, Garbo was falling out of moviegoers' favor. Yet she never meant her retirement to be permanent. In the 1960s she considered several films, including the title roles in *Hamlet* and *The Picture of Dorian Gray*, all of which collapsed from financial complications or her demands for artistic control.

For the last 37 years of her life, Garbo lived in the terraced fifth floor of a Gothic apartment building overlooking Manhattan's East River. All but three of its seven rooms were closed off, but her living room contained an opulent mix of 18th-century antiques, Aubusson rugs and dark damask curtains. On the walls was an impressive art collection, including a Renoir and a Braque.

Garbo was occasionally spotted at fashionable restaurants, and she often traveled, booking two seats on an airplane to isolate herself. Formal invitations, however, sent her into something just short of terror.

(Her MGM colleague, songwriter Howard Dietz, once asked Garbo to dinner the following Monday. Her reply: "How do I know I'll be hungry on Monday?")

Her favorite pastimes were long, aimless walks through the city; her stated preference was for quiet places. "I can't go to hotels because I can't stand noise. I have at least 40 earplugs," she said, but claimed that they enhanced her hearing.

Known as a recluse even during her Hollywood years, Garbo sometimes made exceptions. Her first love was Stiller. What she felt for him, she once said, was "the adoration of a student for her teacher, of a timid girl for a mastermind." Others soon followed. Though she briefly loved actor John Gilbert, she skittishly jilted him twice—once on their scheduled wedding day in 1926.

After Gilbert, Garbo boasted a glittering array of admirers, among them conductor Leopold Stokowski, Baron Erich Goldschmidt-Rothschild and nutritionist Gayelord Hauser, who became a financial adviser. Yet she married no one. Among the men who proposed, and were rejected, was photographer Cecil Beaton, who later bequeathed a painting to her—a picture of a solitary rose.

The steadiest male companion, until his death in 1964, was financier George Schlee, a neighbor in Garbo's apartment building, whose *haute couturiere* wife, Valentina, jealously referred to Garbo as "that vampire" or simply "the fifth floor." Once, when the two women met by chance in the building's lobby, Valentina shuddered and crossed herself.

Rumors long swirled about Garbo's sexual preferences, and with good reason. Silent film star Louise Brooks claimed to have been intimate with her, as did the cosmopolitan aesthete Mercedes de Acosta. Curiously, throughout her life, Garbo referred to herself in masculine terms, as a "strapping young boy" or a "bachelor."

Despite the public's undying curiosity about her, Garbo steadfastly refused to yield to it. "I was born. I had a mother and father. I lived in a house. I grew up like everybody else," Garbo told a movie magazine in 1938. "What does it matter?"

*The last photograph of Garbo, five days before her death.*

# BARBARA STANWYCK
## 1907-1990

**A**t Barbara Stanwyck's request, there was no funeral or memorial service. That was Stanwyck. Down to earth. Self-assured. No nonsense. A thorough professional who always got the job done and never, ever, gave a bad performance. She wasn't a great beauty like Dietrich or Garbo, nor was she an actress with the range of a Bette Davis or a Katharine Hepburn. But she had grit, sex appeal and vulnerability, in spades. No one played a saucy dame better or did more for a pair of ankle-strap shoes.

Perhaps Stanwyck's death from congestive heart failure at age 82 was such a surprise because the public never saw her fall apart. She aged regally, always trim and stylish, with her broad shoulders, long waist, narrow hips and pantherlike walk. But her last years saw a hard struggle to retain that star image. A robbery and beating at her Beverly Hills home in 1981, in which a cigarette case from her second husband, Robert Taylor, was stolen, started her decline.

Breathing special effects smoke while making *The Thorn Birds* in 1982, Stanwyck contracted bronchitis—an ailment compounded by a cigarette habit she began at age nine and gave up only four years ago. She was hospitalized periodically to have her lungs cleaned out. To a friend she said, "How could this happen to me? I never expected to become an invalid. I always thought I'd be trampled by a wild stallion or run down by a stagecoach. But never this."

On January 9, Stanwyck was admitted to St. John's Hospital and Health Center in Santa Monica, California, for back problems stemming from a slipped disk. Eleven days later her heart gave out.

Stanwyck's give-'em-hell manner was the product of a hellish childhood. Born in Brooklyn as Ruby Stevens, she was four when her mother was killed, pushed off a moving streetcar by a drunk. Destroyed by the loss, Ruby's father, a bricklayer, abandoned his five children. After a childhood spent in a series of foster homes, 15-year-old Ruby found work as a chorus girl in speakeasies, then advanced to Broadway. At age 18, she changed her name to the more glamorous Barbara Stanwyck.

While working on Broadway in the late 1920s, she appeared in two films made in New York. They were so bad, she said, they almost shut the door on her screen career. Undaunted, she went to Hollywood, where she eventually persuaded director Frank Capra to use her in 1930's *Ladies of Leisure*. She played a gold digger, and the role launched her on a steady climb to the top. With Bette Davis and Joan Crawford, Stanwyck formed a triumvirate whose film portrayals of strong women defined a Hollywood era. She could be a tomboy, as in *Annie Oakley*, the ultimate femme fatale, as in *The Lady Eve*, or the hard-boiled seductress with a heart of stone, as in *Double Indemnity*.

She was married twice, first, in 1928, to vaudeville comedian Frank Fay. His high living and heavy drinking reportedly plagued the marriage, which ended after seven years (he died in 1961). Her second marriage ended in 1951 when matinee idol Robert Taylor walked out after 12 years. After they divorced, she said, "There will be no other man in my life." He died in 1969, and Stanwyck broke down at his funeral.

Calling herself a "bachelor woman," Missy, as she was dubbed by her close friends, lived her later years alone. After Taylor, her name was never linked romantically to anyone. She preferred to work, saying that she hoped she could continue "until they shoot me." Her professionalism was legendary.

At the actress's request, her publicist, Larry Kleno, scattered her ashes from an airplane over an undisclosed California mountaintop.

*Stanwyck and Robert Taylor, 1940.*

# REX HARRISON
# 1908-1990

**T**he physical clues to an actor's disposition may be revealed in his gaze, his smile or even his walk, but Rex Harrison's character could be found in his eyebrows. Devilishly arched, they bristled with both irascibility and charm, as did he. They were haughty yet humorous, as was he. With one deft, skewering line he could deflate any pretender. And with just four precisely enunciated syllables—"Damn! Damn! Damn! Damn!"—Harrison, as the bachelor phonetician Henry Higgins in *My Fair Lady*, conveyed his endless chagrin that he had let a woman in his life.

Harrison, who died June 2, 1990, at 82, began acting as a teen near his hometown of Huyton, England. "I never wanted to do anything else," he once said. Performing in more than 40 films and scores of plays in the United States and Britain, Harrison won both a Tony and an Oscar for the role of Higgins, which he originated onstage opposite Julie Andrews. In 1989 he was knighted.

Unlike Higgins, "Sexy Rexy" romanced many women—and married six of them, including actresses Lilli Palmer and Rachel Roberts.

Just three weeks before he died of pancreatic cancer at his Manhattan home, with wife Mercia Tinker beside him, Harrison was appearing eight times a week in a Broadway revival of Somerset Maugham's *The Circle*. Many years ago, Harrison vowed, "I never intend to retire. Never." And as Higgins might have said, by George, he didn't.

*Rex Harrison, 1963; Pearl Bailey, right, in* Hello, Dolly!, *1966.*

# PEARL BAILEY 1918-1990

**O**ne of America's most beloved showstoppers, Pearl Bailey died **August 17, 1990, at age 72, of a probable heart attack. "She gave me one last look, and her head slumped down, and that was it," said her husband, 66-year-old jazz drummer Louis Bellson, who was with her in her Philadelphia hotel room. "I've lost my best friend."**

The road that eventually brought her to perform before seven U.S. Presidents began in Newport News, Virginia, where Bailey was born to a Pentecostal preacher. "From him," she once said, "I got the wisdom, the philosophizing, the soul." A career that included nine films, countless recordings and an impressive array of awards and honors (including a 1988 Medal of Freedom) perhaps had its brightest moments on the stage. Two decades after earning an award as the best Broadway newcomer, for 1946's *St. Louis Woman*, Bailey won a special Tony for her lead in the all-black cast of *Hello, Dolly!*, whose first night, with its string of standing ovations, prompted columnist Walter Winchell to call it "the greatest opening I have ever been to."

In private life, her fourth stab at marriage was the charmer: Pearl's union with drummer Louis Bellson lasted 39 years and included two adopted children, Dee Dee, 30, and Tony, 36.

# JIM HENSON
# 1936-1990

**F**our years ago, Jim Henson, the gentle genius who gave us Kermit and the Muppets, sat down to write a letter to his children, with the wish that it not be opened until his death. "I'm not at all afraid of the thought of death and look forward to it," he wrote. "I suggest you first have a friendly little service of some kind. It would be lovely if there was a song or two ... and someone said some nice, happy words about me.... This all may sound silly to you guys, but what the hell. I'm gone—and who can argue with me?"

It was like Henson—modest and unassuming—to ask only for a song or two and some nice, happy words. What was remarkable was that a man best known for his quiet gentleness left such a resounding echo in the world upon leaving it. Only 53 when he died, Jim Henson, along with his endearing collection of creatures, had undoubtedly secured a niche as one of the most universally beloved entertainers of his generation.

From the start, Henson was clearly onto something. As a University of Maryland student in the 1950s, he created puppets for a Washington, D.C., television show that were successful enough to allow him to pick up his diploma in a Rolls-Royce.

In 1969 the menagerie expanded to include an outsize creature of vaguely ostrichy persuasion. On *Sesame Street*, Big Bird and his buddies soon became a sensation. Seven years later British impresario Lord (Lew) Grade put up the financing for an even more ambitious project, and *The Muppet Show* became, with an audience of 235 million, the most popular syndicated series in TV history. Its temperamental star, Miss Piggy, danced *Swine Lake* with Rudolf Nureyev and, with Beverly Sills, trilled *Pigaletto*. In 1981 Henson shelved the show. "I wanted to quit while I was ahead," he later said. "I didn't want to get stale."

Over the course of two furiously creative decades, Henson parlayed his Muppet menagerie into a multimillion-dollar empire. If Henson's creativity and business acumen were singular, so, say associates, was the spirit that permeated his organization. "We were together 30 years without a contract," said his agent, Bernie Brillstein, "and he walked on this earth like no one else I know."

In the words of Carroll Spinney, who for over 20 years played Big Bird and Oscar the Grouch, "He would never say he didn't like something. He would just go, 'Hmm.' That was famous. And if he liked it, he would say, 'Lovely.' Everything was lovely—a place, a show...."

In recent months, the peripatetic, hard-working Henson divided his time between Los Angeles, New York City, Orlando and London. He had designed the computerized masks of the top-grossing Teenage Mutant Ninja Turtles and was preparing a new TV series (starring Ponce D. Lion) for its debut.

Though Henson's personal style was modest, the enormous wealth that had come along with creative success allowed for comfortable houses in London, Malibu, Connecticut and Orlando, an occasional Rolls or Porsche and such exotic pastimes as hot-air ballooning in France and camel riding in Egypt. "He was a modest guy in some ways," said daughter Heather, at 19, the youngest of Henson's five grown children. "In other ways he was completely over the top."

More than just an indulgence, the life-style served as a connecting bridge to his all-important family. "The houses," said publicist Arthur Novell, "were in large part so he had a place for his children wherever they visited; he wanted them with him whenever possible." He left his business to them.

Henson's death on May 16 from a severe but treatable disease, Group A streptococcus pneumonia, appeared unfathomable, but it was not. Its cause lay not entirely in the illness but, ironically and sadly, in his own character. Henson's humility, his desire never to bother anyone, became tragic flaws in the end. Not wanting to trouble his family, not wanting to trouble the doctors, he postponed going to the hospital until it was six to eight hours too late. By the time Henson was admitted to New York Hospital, his body was rapidly shutting down. Initial X-rays showed small pockets of infection. Several hours later they had spread through his lungs. After two cardiac arrests, his heart stopped beating for the final time.

Searching for some sort of foreshadowing themes in his life, Henson's friends and family recalled 1986 as a watershed year. The enduring Muppets had just celebrated their 30th anniversary, but his movie *Labyrinth*, a dark, Muppet-less fantasy, had fared poorly at the box office, as had *The Dark Crystal* before it.

It was also the year that the Hensons, wed in 1959, legally separated after living apart for more than two years. "He was working a lot," his wife Jane, herself an accomplished puppeteer, said of the breakup. "His attention was always on whatever projects there were. He'd just sort of grown on to another stage." Despite their separation, the two never divorced.

At Henson headquarters in an elegant town house on New York City's East Side, filled with tiny Muppets and Fraggle figures, a sympathy card rests on a grand piano in the wood-paneled library. A drawing from Disney's crew of designers—the Imagineers—shows Mickey Mouse sitting on a log before a magnificent sunset, his arm draped around a downcast Kermit. Before his death, Henson had been negotiating a deal to sell his business to the Walt Disney Company.

"There was a quality that I could never quite grasp about Jim," said his widow. "But he needed to accomplish something. He knew he could make a difference. It's not as if he knew he was going to die, but I think he realized he wouldn't be around a lot longer. He didn't think he'd ever be an old man—and it was time to put things in a place where they'd continue without him."

Henson's request for a "friendly little service of some kind" was granted in a vibrant celebration at Manhattan's Cathedral of St. John the Divine, where 5,000 colorfully dressed fans fluttered hand-painted butterflies, as a Dixieland band trumpeted "When the Saints Go Marching In."

At the end, Henson's own simple words, recited by his daughter Cheryl, best explained what had driven him. "I believe in taking a positive attitude toward the world," he once wrote. "My hope still is to leave the world a little bit better than when I got here."

# MUSIC

ART BLAKEY—A powerful jazz drummer whose influence ranged far beyond pounding out the tight propulsive beat that came to be called hard bebop, Blakey, 71, died of lung cancer in New York City October 16. Over the past 35 years, Blakey's band, the Jazz Messengers, served as an evolving showcase and proving ground for young, up-and-coming talents, including Branford and Wynton Marsalis, Freddie Hubbard, Chick Corea and Keith Jarrett.

AARON COPLAND—Composer Copland, 90, who wrote "Fanfare for the Common Man" and hundreds of other musical pieces, died on December 2 in North Tarrytown, New York, of respiratory failure. Considered the dean of American music, Copland once said that he wanted to establish a "naturally American strain of so-called serious music." A Brooklyn native, he wrote for the concert hall (1944's *Appalachian Spring* won a Pulitzer Prize), the dance stage (1942's *Rodeo*) and films (his score for 1948's *The Heiress* won an Oscar).

XAVIER CUGAT—Rumba king Cugat, the flamboyant bandleader who popularized Latin rhythms in America and taught a generation to tango, mambo and cha-cha, died of heart failure on October 27 in Barcelona. He was 90. The Spanish-born, Cuban-reared Cugat—"Cugie" to friends—came to fame in the '30s as a bandleader at the Waldorf-Astoria in New York City and the Cocoanut Grove in Los Angeles. He made a string of movies, many with Esther Williams, such as *Neptune's Daughter*. In his personal life, Cugat did little to undermine the Latin-lover image he cultivated onstage. His five wives included Dolores Del Rio's stand-in, Carmen Castillo; Abbe Lane, who sang with his band in the '50s; and the singer Charo, his last.

TOM FOGERTY—Rhythm guitarist for the seminal '60s band Creedance Clearwater Revival, Fogerty died of tuberculosis September 6 in Scottsdale, Arizona, at age 48. With his younger brother John singing lead vocals, Fogerty helped launch Creedance's six gold albums and eight Top 10 singles, including "Proud Mary," "Born on the Bayou" and "Bad Moon Rising."

DEXTER GORDON—Jazz great Gordon, 67, the tenor saxophonist who received an Oscar nomination in 1986 for his role as a battered jazzman in *Round Midnight*, died April 25 in Philadelphia from kidney failure. Beginning his professional career at 17, the Grammy-winning musician was known as one of the pioneering legends of bebop. After a successful comeback in 1978 following drug problems, Gordon continued to make records while turning to acting.

CORNELL GUNTER—A tenor with the '50s doo-wop group the Coasters, Gunter, 53, was shot dead in Las Vegas. Police said Gunter, who still performed with his own version of the Coasters, got into an argument with another man and was shot five times. Gunter joined the band in 1957 just before they became one of the era's most successful groups. The Coasters were a comic group, with such playful hits as their 1958 classic "Yakety Yak" and, a year later, "Charlie Brown." Another Coaster, Buster Wilson, was shot and killed in 1980.

BRENT MYDLAND—Keyboardist and songwriter for the countercultural rock band the Grateful Dead, Brent Mydland, 37, died suddenly at his home in Lafayette, California, on July 26. A toxicology report by the county coroner's office in Contra Costa, revealed that he died of a drug overdose. Although no drug paraphernalia was found at the time of his death, the report indicated that Mydland had injected himself with a "speedball," a combination of morphine and cocaine. Mydland, who

*Dexter Gordon, 1948.*

joined the group in 1979, is the third Dead keyboardist to have passed away. Ron (Pigpen) McKernan died of a perforated ulcer born of high living; his replacement, Keith Godchaux, died in a car wreck 10 years ago.

JOHNNIE RAY—The emotionally charged '50s singing idol who was called the Prince of Wails died of liver failure at age 63 in Los Angeles. Ray filled the post-Frank, pre-Elvis teen-heartthrob gap, winning screams of devotion for the catch in his voice and his onstage histrionics. Ray lost half his hearing when he fell and landed on his head as a child. His best-known record was "Cry," which became a No. 1 single in 1952. Ray's last hit, "Yes Tonight, Josephine" came in 1957, but he continued to sing in nightclubs here and abroad until last year.

SARAH VAUGHAN—Her friends called her Sassy, and she had the feisty manner of a kitten with dangerously sharp claws, but when Sarah Vaughan broke into song, she was never anything less than the Divine One.

"Boy, she knew some notes to hold," her friend Dizzy Gillespie said after Vaughan died on April 3 at the age of 66. "She approached the music like a horn player, and whoo-whee, was she *bad*." Even Ella Fitzgerald once called Vaughan "the greatest singing talent in the world today." Others were in awe of her improvisational skills. "We're talking about one of the finest vocalists in the history of pop music," said Frank Sinatra.

Born in Newark, New Jersey, Vaughan inherited her love of music from her father, Asbery, a carpenter, and her mother, Ada, now 87, a laundress and a singer in a Baptist choir. After winning an amateur-night contest performing "Body and Soul" at Harlem's Apollo Theatre, Vaughan toured with bands led by Earl Hines and Billy Eckstine, quickly learning to trade curses with the most incorrigible men in the band. She received national attention when she recorded "Lover Man" in 1945, backed by Gillespie and Charlie Parker. In 1989 she capped a sensational career by winning a Lifetime Achievement Grammy.

Doctors discovered Vaughan had cancer in September 1989. She responded well to treatment and even made plans to record a new album with Quincy Jones. "I'll do it," she said, "even if I have to sing on my back." But Vaughan never made it to that last session; she died in her home in the Hidden Hills suburb of Los Angeles. Married and divorced four times, Vaughan is survived by her mother and her adopted daughter Paris, 24.

*Sarah Vaughan, left, 1949;
Johnny Ray, 1952.*

# SAMMY DAVIS JR.
# 1925-1990

**P**erhaps more than most performers, Sammy Davis Jr. lived for the adulation of the public. His long career as singer, dancer, impressionist and actor had many incarnations—young black club performer, Broadway star (*Mr. Wonderful, Golden Boy*), Sinatra Rat Pack regular and Vegas fixture. Whatever the phase, the wiry, five-foot-four-inch, 110-pound entertainer was legendary for giving his all. "You've got to make them love you," he once explained.

Born in 1925 in Harlem, the son of a tap dancer and a Puerto Rican chorus girl who ran off while he was still a tot, Davis was only three when he began doing vaudeville turns with his father and his father's partner, Will Mastin. By the time he was eight, Sammy had earned equal billing. The young prodigy never went to school (he learned to read in the Army), and the stage was his only home.

It enraged him that while he could play in white clubs and hotels, he couldn't eat, drink or stay there. But the most glaring racism he experienced was in the Army during World War II, when, during basic training, he was assigned to one of the first integrated barracks. His white roommates broke his nose and painted I'M A NIGGER and COON in white across his chest and forehead.

After the war, Davis propelled the Will Mastin Trio into the big time. Boosts from such young celebrity fans as Frank Sinatra helped get the gigs, but the real turning point came on Academy Award night in 1950, when the Trio opened for Janis Paige at Hollywood's posh nightclub Ciro's. Sammy danced like he was "barefoot on hot sand," he later recalled. That night the Will Mastin Trio became the headliners, and Sammy Davis became the most famous black entertainer in America.

He began living that life with a vengeance. In 1954, when he lost his left eye in a near-fatal auto accident, the news pushed the Debbie Reynolds–Eddie Fisher courtship off front pages. A few months later he made more headlines by converting to Judaism, saying that "every question I had, the Jewish religion answered. It gave me solace." His romance with blond actress Kim Novak made the papers too. As a result, Davis took heat from her apoplectic boss, Columbia Pictures head Harry Cohn, who rankled the singer when he blustered, "I could understand Belafonte, but *him*! Short people, they ain't got no right!"

For flouting contemporary mores with Novak, Davis was threatened by the Mob, and for running with the white Rat Pack (Sinatra, Dean Martin, Peter Lawford and Joey Bishop), he was chastised by the black community. To defuse the situation, Davis embarked on what he called a "phony" marriage with black chorine Loray White in 1958. That union was dissolved the following year, leaving him free to marry sultry Swedish actress May Britt, then 24, in 1960. They had a daughter—Tracey, now 29—and adopted two sons, Mark, 30, and Jeff, 25, before divorcing in 1968.

Davis's Hollywood life-style tended to obscure the fact that even then, long before the heyday of the civil rights movement, he battled for racial equality. He was the first black to integrate the hotels of Las Vegas and Miami and the first to get a table at such elegant nightclubs as the Copa. Later he marched with Martin Luther King in Montgomery and even temporarily shut down his Broadway show *Golden Boy* in order to do so. He also performed at benefits for the United Negro College Fund, the family of Malcolm X and for '60s radical Angela Davis.

Those contributions weren't enough, however, to save him from later charges of Uncle Tomism. A onetime staunch Democrat and Kennedy friend, he appeared to grow more conservative. In 1972, when he threw his support behind Richard Nixon, Julian Bond, then a young Georgia legislator, called it "unbelievable, an irrational act." After a rally at which Davis leapt onto the stage to embrace the President, author Truman Capote observed, "When I saw him kissing Nixon, I thought he was the new Checkers."

Such impetuous behavior helped to create an image problem that plagued him for years. He affected the "groovy" lingo and garb of the day—the

Nehru jacket, miles of gold chains—but seemed to share the vision of the older white establishment. The breathtaking showman lost ground to an obsequious alter ego who seemed ready to warm any empty guest chair or barren stage, giggling at the host's insipid jokes, dancing himself into a frenzy, singing himself hoarse. Marlon Brando labeled him an "audience junkie."

His private life was equally desperate. After splitting from May Britt, Davis began a nonstop orgy of liquor, cocaine and swingers like *Deep Throat*'s Linda Lovelace.

"I didn't like me … I didn't like what I had created and what I had become," Sammy later admitted. But the party didn't stop until 1983, when an enlarged liver forced him to give up alcohol. Then came two hip replacement operations that threatened to end his career. The recovery was painful.

During those last years Davis managed to put his life in order. He reconciled with Sinatra after a three-year estrangement linked to Sammy's drug use. He cherished the love and loyalty of Altovise, his wife since 1970, "who went through the tortures of the damned with me." In 1989 the couple adopted a 13-year-old son, Manny. In August of that year, Davis felt at the peak of his form. A reunion tour with Sinatra and Liza Minnelli (filling in for an ailing Dean Martin) was winning standing ovations everywhere. One morning, the veteran entertainer awoke with a strange soreness in his throat. It was eventually traced to a carcinoma growing behind his vocal cords.

Thus began a descent into pain and a grueling passage through radiation therapy, chosen because of the fear that surgery would end his career. For a while it looked as though radiation had done the trick: The cancer was in remission, and by Christmas, 1989, Davis was talking optimistically about resuming the third leg of his worldwide concert tour with Sinatra and Minnelli. In January, however, Davis, down to a mere 90 pounds, entered Cedars-Sinai hospital in Los Angeles for what he thought was only a dental problem. The truth was much worse: The malignancy had returned.

Sammy Davis Jr., song-and-dance man extraordinaire, died at 5:59 A.M. on May 16, at age 64, after his eight-month battle with throat cancer.

It was only toward the end, when disease cruelly slowed him, that young black entertainers like Michael Jackson began openly to acknowledge how much they owed him. But most gratifying of all was the outpouring of love from well-wishers—the hundreds of get-well letters Davis received daily after revealing his illness and the calls flooding the Western Union hotline that was established during his final weeks. He was loved. And that is what he wanted most of all.

"There are only two things that count in show business," Davis once said. "Know when to get on and when to get off. Try to walk out with a little dignity." The night of his funeral, the Las Vegas strip went dark for 10 minutes.

# STEVIE RAY VAUGHAN
## 1954-1990

**H**e performed as he always had, as if the song of the moment would be his last. After the concert was over, guitarist Stevie Ray Vaughan found a chance seat vacant on a waiting helicopter and hopped a ride back to Chicago. The helicopter took off in fog around 12:40 A.M. with Vaughan and four others aboard. Moments later the chopper's remains lay spread across more than 200 feet of a man-made ski slope in a field dotted with bittersweet and Queen Anne's lace.

During the blistering, 20-minute rendition of "Sweet Home Chicago" that closed the show at the Alpine Valley Music Theater near East Troy, Wisconsin, guitarist Stevie Ray Vaughan was onstage with fellow bluesmen Eric Clapton, Buddy Guy, Robert Cray and Vaughan's elder brother, Jimmie. Shortly after midnight on August 27, the exhilarated musicians left the stage. Vaughan, 35, had planned to make the two-hour drive back to his Chicago hotel with his brother and sister-in-law, Connie, but at the last minute he chose to board a Bell 206B Jet Ranger, one of four helicopters waiting nearby.

All on board were killed instantly in what National Transportation Safety Board investigator William Bruce later described as "a high-energy, high-velocity impact at a shallow angle." A search for the lost copter wasn't begun until more than four hours later, after an orbiting search-and-rescue satellite picked up the craft's emergency-locator transmitter signal. At seven A.M. searchers found the bodies of Vaughan; Bobby Brooks, Clapton's Hollywood agent; Clapton's assistant tour manager, Colin Smythe; Clapton's bodyguard, Nigel Browne; and pilot Jeff Brown (who may have been unfamiliar with the hilly site's tricky take-off procedures).

The crash stilled the music of a man that many had considered on the verge of stardom. Vaughan's last album, *In Step*, had gone gold and won a Grammy, and a new LP, titled *Family Style*, had already been recorded.

A promising guitar player by the time he was eight, Stevie Ray grew up in Dallas, the son of an asbestos-plant worker and a secretary at a ready-mix cement factory. He abandoned high school at 17 and, with his brother, began haunting the all-night blues clubs of Austin, where his trademark bandito hat, tar-paper voice and potent playing became familiar. It was Vaughan's stunning set at the 1982 Montreux Jazz Festival that brought him both a record contract and the wider recognition he deserved.

Vaughan had been plagued for years by severe alcohol and drug dependency, and he chronicled his successful struggle to kick the twin sins with his album *In Step*. "He just went straight in the last four years," said a friend. "Since then he wouldn't even drink tea with caffeine. It's such a shame. He was such a sweet man." Five albums, countless tours and guest appearances—live and in the studio—with a pantheon of blues and rock performers like B.B. King and David Bowie had established the musician as one of the reigning kings of his genre.

Vaughan had bought a home in the Highland Park section of Dallas about nine months ago; killed four years to the day after the death of his father, he is now buried nearby. His death was a sad new addition to a series of similar aircrash tragedies that over the years have claimed such stars as Patsy Cline, Buddy Holly, Otis Redding, Jim Croce and Rick Nelson.

*Stevie Ray Vaughan, 1984.*

# DEL SHANNON 1934-1990

**I**'m a-walkin' in the rain.
Tears are fallin' and I feel the pain . . .

To fans of Pleistocene rock and roll, Del Shannon will forever be known for the plaintive falsetto of his 1961 hit "Runaway." But in the years since that bittersweet classic topped the charts, Shannon had become something of a runaway himself, trying to escape personal demons he imagined were just over his shoulder.

On the night of February 8, Shannon, 55, apparently gave in to his demons. His wife, Bonnie, who had been out shopping, returned to their home in the Santa Clarita Valley, north of Los Angeles, to find the singer slumped in a chair, a bullet wound in his right temple and a .22 caliber rifle at his feet. "Del had gone through bouts of depression," said Mike Crowley of the Los Angeles County Sheriff's Department. "We're pretty sure it's a straight suicide."

Yet the singer left no note, and family and friends, while acknowledging that Shannon sometimes grew dispirited, could not cite any event that might have sparked his fatal decision. Shannon's longtime manager, Dan Bourgoise, insisted the singer had no financial worries, saying that royalties and concert fees brought the former pop idol well into six figures annually. Shannon and Bonnie, 36, his second wife of just two years, had recently moved into a new $800,000, four-bedroom house, and he was planning a tour of England. Bonnie believes her husband's death was an accident. "Del was too loving, too considerate a person to do something like this," she said.

Others who knew him suggested that Shannon might simply have succumbed to a despondency that had grown slowly but steadily since his heyday. Born Charles Weedon Westover in Coopersville, Michigan, Shannon was working in a carpet store and moonlighting at the Hi-Lo Club in Battle Creek, Michigan, when "Runaway" soared to the top of the charts. And while Shannon followed up with a string of successful singles, including "Hats Off to Larry," "Little Town Flirt" and "Keep Searchin," he never felt secure in his success. With the British music invasion in the mid-'60s, various attempts to repackage himself as an artist failed, and a nascent drinking problem got out of control.

In recent years Shannon had put booze behind him, and the '80s had seen improvement in his professional fortunes. Friend and fan Tom Petty helped Shannon record his first LP in eight years, *Drop Down and Get Me*, in 1981, and in 1986 Shannon rewrote the lyrics to "Runaway" for the TV series *Crime Story*. He frequently played oldies shows and was in the process of recording another album.

But Shannon remained troubled. On February 8 he called his onetime manager and close friend of more than 30 years, Wayne Carter. "He was depressed, but I'd heard him sound that way many times," Carter said. "I told him we ought to get together for breakfast and rap about what was troubling him."

By the next morning, however, Shannon was dead, leaving behind Bonnie, her daughter, Shannon, 16, and the three children—son Craig, 33, and daughters Kym, 29, and Jody, 28—from his first, 30-year marriage to Shirley Nash, 53.

Following a memorial service, Bourgoise and Craig planned to scatter the singer's ashes over the desert. For now, Shannon's family and friends, like the character in the singer's most famous song, can only wonder why.

*Del Shannon, 1963.*

# LEONARD BERNSTEIN
## 1918-1990

A vivacious, versatile genius, Leonard Bernstein gloried in his huge appetites for music, knowledge, love, family—and the vices that finally caught up with him at age 72.

On his 70th birthday—a gala occasion at the Tanglewood Music Center in Massachusetts in 1988—Leonard Bernstein was honored by a grand chorus of admirers. Lauren Bacall serenaded him with a Sondheim composition called "The Saga of Lenny"—an irreverent song about his professional and sexual profligacy. Bernstein's 90-year-old mother, Jennie, gave the birthday boy a Chinese scroll. "The translation on the back says, 'Listen to your mother. Stop smoking. You'll live to be 120,'" she said.

Exuberant, willful, driven, Bernstein was too busy to take anyone's advice. He once said that making music made him feel immortal. He liked to boast that he had outlived the doctor who first diagnosed his emphysema when Bernstein was still in his 20s. On October 14 that reckless joie de vivre caught up with Bernstein. Struck down by a heart attack caused by progressive lung failure, he spent his last hours in his apartment at the Dakota in New York City, where he was attended by friends, relatives and assistants.

Six days before he died, he announced that he was retiring from the concert stage because of health problems. Still, it was a shock to many when Bernstein, hard at work on an opera and a chamber piece, lost the final battle.

It was hard to imagine a man of such extravagant energy and talents coming to rest. Bernstein would sleep only two or three hours a night when he was on a creative high, and he literally threw himself into conducting—churning his arms and occasionally falling off the podium.

Over his long career—in addition to performing with the world's great orchestras as a conductor—Bernstein composed symphonies and a violin concerto, wrote music for ballets, turned out Broadway hits (including *West Side Story* and *On the Town*), produced operas and an operetta, established himself as a piano virtuoso, wrote books, won Emmys, Grammys and Tonys and mesmerized TV audiences with educational programs such as the Philharmonic's Young People's Concerts. He also mentored dozens of young musicians and enthralled a legion of friends.

Bernstein came to music rather late. Born in Lawrence, Massachusetts, to Russian immigrants, young Lenny had been expected to take over his father's business supplying beauty shops. Instead, when he was 10, an aunt's old upright piano arrived at the house for storage, and Lenny, one of three children, demanded lessons. Sent to Boston Latin School and then on to Harvard, he studied piano and composition. In 1939, when he entered the Curtis Institute of Music in Philadelphia, he began to conduct.

Bernstein's life changed forever in 1943. By then assistant conductor with the New York Philharmonic, he was called in to conduct a matinee because conductor Bruno Walter was ill. Bernstein earned a thunderous ovation—and a front-page notice in the *New York Times*.

From that point forward, Bernstein was a celebrity. He was married in 1951 to Felicia Montealegre Cohn, a Chilean-born actress. The Bernsteins had three children (Jamie, now 36 and a rock musician; Alexander, 33, a teacher; and Nina, 28, an actress), as well as a high social profile. The couple separated in 1976 after 25 years of marriage, but Bernstein remained in close touch with Felicia until her death from lung cancer in 1978.

Although his bisexuality became public knowledge only in 1987, when Joan Peyser's controversial *Bernstein: A Biography* appeared, his involvements with other men were always an open secret in the music community. According to Peyser's book, Felicia was madly in love with Bernstein when she married him and hoped that at the very least he would use discretion. For many years he did. But a combination of events, including the gay liberation movement and his father's death, made him less circumspect in the '70s.

"Bernstein wanted it all," said Peyser. "And he got more out of life than most of us ever will."

*Bernstein playing Chopin's piano outside Warsaw, 1959.*

# MOVERS & SHAKERS

**W**ILLIAM S. PALEY—The founder and chairman of CBS died of a heart attack related to pneumonia at his home in Manhattan on October 26. He was 89. The Chicago-born son of Ukrainian Jewish immigrants bought several obscure radio stations in 1928 and built them into what eventually became known as the Tiffany network. Early on he signed such stars as Jack Benny, Burns and Allen, Edgar Bergen and Red Skelton. He also recruited a stable of journalists who pioneered broadcast news, including Edward R. Murrow. With TV, Paley's talent roster grew to include Walter Cronkite, Lucille Ball, Jackie Gleason, Ed Sullivan and Lassie. In 1947, immediately following his divorce from socialite Dorothy Hart Hearst, he wed beautiful aristocrat Barbara Cushing Mortimer, called Babe. The Paleys held court in Manhattan and in the Bahamas—often in the company of Truman Capote until, in 1975, he published the story "La Côte Basque, 1965," a veiled exposé of the Paleys' society world, which won Babe's scorn. When Babe was diagnosed with lung cancer, Paley used his wealth and influence to try to heal her. She died in 1978. For years Paley secretly supported silent-film star Louise Brooks, with whom he had had a relationship years before.

## THE REVEREND RALPH ABERNATHY
Dr. Martin Luther King's right-hand man from 1955 through the great battles of the civil rights movement, Abernathy died at the age of 64 after a heart attack on April 17 in Atlanta. In 1989 he angered black leaders and others with his book, *And the Walls Came Tumbling Down*, which discussed King's extramarital affairs. After Abernathy's death, however, Andrew Young, a former Atlanta Mayor and King aide himself, said, "There probably could not have been a civil rights movement without the contributions he made."

NANCY LADY KEITH—The lanky clotheshorse who was prominent on New York and Hollywood party circuits for 50 years died in New York City of heart failure at age 73. "Slim" Keith was born Mary Raye Gross in 1916 in Salinas, California, to middle-class parents, but she fell in with Hollywood's better social set by age 18. She married director Howard Hawks in 1941 and, through him, was partly responsible for Humphrey Bogart's marriage to Lauren Bacall. Slim saw Bacall's picture in a magazine and brought the unknown 19-year-old actress to the attention of Hawks, who cast Bacall opposite Bogie in 1944's *To Have and Have Not*. (Bacall's character in the movie was called Slim.) Keith, who professed to a "healthy interest in men," was married twice more, to producer Leland Hayward in 1949 and to a titled Englishman, Kenneth Lord Keith, in 1962. All three marriages ended in divorce.

*Keith with Leland Hayward in 1949; Haring, right, 1986.*

**KEITH HARING**—When Haring first drew his strange hieroglyphics in New York City subway stations in the early 1980s, he was arrested for defacing public property. By the time of his death from AIDS-related complications on February 16, his cartoon-like images had made the 31-year-old Haring one of the most widely known pop artists in the world.

Less than a decade after he sketched his first figure on the black paper that covers canceled subway ads, Haring was selling his work for as much as $350,000, decorating the hippest clubs and partying with the heartiest. "He was definitely the quintessential 1980s artist," said fellow painter and close friend Kenny Scharf. "He started with nothing but a lot of

ideas, devised a plan of getting his message out into the world and was relentless until he succeeded."

Haring battled AIDS with the same kind of energy, talking openly about his illness and meeting with groups of children to teach them about the disease. Until two weeks before his death, Haring continued to work—creating huge sculptures for playgrounds and public spaces, painting murals for inner-city walls and hospital wards, and teaching art to disadvantaged youths.

---

**ARMAND HAMMER**—Perhaps the greatest wheeler and dealer of the century died at the age of 92 on December 10 in Los Angeles after what a spokesman termed a "brief illness." Hammer was a globe-hopping fixture in his private Boeing 727. He amassed fortunes as an international industrialist, bequeathed tens of millions as a philanthropist, acted for years as unofficial diplomatic conduit to the Soviet Union—and still managed to earn a reputation as one of the most aggrandizing self-promoters of his time. Of his longing for a Nobel prize, former national security adviser Zbigniew Brzezinski once sniped, "If it can be bought, his chances of winning are quite high."

Born on New York City's Lower East Side, the son of a Socialist Labor party member, Hammer was named after a character in Dumas's *Camille*. (It wasn't until 1986 that he bought into the baking-soda manufacturer with which the public had long erroneously associated him.) After earning a medical degree at Columbia in 1921, he made a fateful trip to the Soviet Union. Sensing opportunity, the young entrepreneur stayed for nine years, representing dozens of U.S. companies—and began a collection of Russian art eventually valued at $400 million.

Back in the United States, Hammer's business ventures were not always beyond reproach. During Prohibition he sold a ginger extract that was 85 percent alcohol. Six decades later he was convicted of illegally contributing $54,000 to Richard Nixon's presidential campaign. What salvaged his reputation was his deal-making acumen, especially as chief executive officer of Occidental Petroleum, a modest tax shelter that he parlayed into the United States' 16th largest industrial corporation.

Publicly, Hammer donated millions to cancer research and a host of charities. His personal life included three marriages (his only child, a son, Julian, was born in 1929) and, in later years, a tangle of controversy. In 1988, after promising to bequeath his collection to the Los Angeles County Museum of Art, he instead decided to build a museum of his own in Los Angeles's tony Westwood section.

With the help of a 1989 pacemaker implant, Hammer remained active until his final weeks. His death, in fact, came one day before the planned celebration of a long-overdue rite of passage: the Bar Mitzvah that would mark his official entry into manhood.

# RYAN WHITE
# 1971-1990

**O**n Palm Sunday morning, minutes after Ryan White died in an Indianapolis hospital, his mother, Jeanne, hugged PEOPLE correspondent Bill Shaw and, sobbing, said, "Do a bang-up story. Tell everyone what you saw here this week."

What Bill and photographer Taro Yamasaki witnessed was the last valiant chapter in Ryan's life. They first met him in 1987 when they interviewed and photographed him for "Breaking America's Heart," PEOPLE's cover story on AIDS. In April, Taro and Bill were called again. Through them, PEOPLE's readers were made bedside witness to the sad, gentle passing of Ryan, perhaps now the best-known of this country's 76,000-plus AIDS fatalities. The Kennedy-Hatch Bill to appropriate $875 million for emergency AIDS care in areas hardest hit by the epidemic eventually came to be known as the Ryan White Bill.

Ryan White never surrendered—not to AIDS, not to despair, not to the fearful public passions that his illness once aroused. Diagnosed in 1984, he successfully challenged his school board in Kokomo, Indiana, for the right to attend classes—and became a reluctant celebrity. Later he moved with his mother to nearby Cicero, Indiana, in hopes of finding a more ordinary childhood.

Two years ago, when Ryan was talking about AIDS to students in Nebraska, another boy bluntly asked Ryan how it felt knowing he was going to die. Ryan replied, "It's how you live your life that counts."

Ryan White was unconscious, beyond pain and feeling, in that evanescent twilight between life and death. A heart monitor beeped quietly by his bedside,

two nurses in face masks silently monitoring its luminous dials. Beside the bed stood Jeanne White, a divorced factory worker from Kokomo, Indiana. Just a few days earlier, Jeanne, Ryan and his sister, Andrea, 16, were in Los Angeles for an Academy Awards–night party. Ryan later complained of a sore throat and said he wanted to go home and see his physician, Dr. Martin Kleiman.

They flew all night, arriving in Indianapolis at six A.M. Thursday, March 29. They went directly to Riley Hospital at the huge Indiana University Medical Center. By Saturday, Ryan's condition had deteriorated alarmingly. The next day Kleiman told Jeanne that Ryan's chances of pulling out of this latest crisis were 10 percent—and that was optimistic.

Now, at Ryan's bedside, Jeanne clung to the man beside her, the friend who stood by her throughout both grim and good times. Singer Elton John was one of the first prominent people to offer support shortly after Ryan, a hemophiliac, contracted AIDS from a tainted blood transfusion. AIDS was a new and alien specter then, and when the public fear and early ignorance led frightened parents to ask that Ryan be kept out of school, Elton John become a friend, writing, calling or visiting the boy every month. Now, standing in this hospital room, the singer looked ashen, his face a mask of anguish. He had flown all day from Los Angeles, slipped in a back door of the hospital to avoid the press and hurried to the bedside.

*Ryan and Jeanne White.*

"Ryan, it's Elton," whispered Jeanne, leaning over to smooth her son's spiked hair. "We put some mousse on it earlier in the day, Elton. I wanted him to look good." She sagged against her friend, sobbing quietly. Ryan seemed so small and helpless, swallowed up in the Donald Duck and Dumbo sheets the hospital had provided. Although he was 18, the ebullient boy was prevented by AIDS from growing beyond five feet and 90 pounds.

At first Elton was simply overcome, unable to speak. The superstar and the Kokomo factory worker hugged and stared. Only the thunk-thunk of the ventilator and the beep-beep of the heart monitor filled the silence.

Outside Room A-460, Ryan's friend and physician, Dr. Kleiman, a pediatric infectious-disease specialist, stood against the wall. He was the man who six years ago told Jeanne White that her son had AIDS and would die, probably in three to six months. Asked later to explain Ryan's longevity, he had said, "Because he's Ryan White. He's got a great attitude, and that plays a big part. He's optimistic, not a quitter."

It was Kleiman who Sunday morning ordered Ryan heavily sedated and hooked up to the ventilator to keep him alive while he worked to stabilize other medical problems. "It was Ryan's decision to be put on the respirator," he said. "I explained everything to him, why I felt it necessary, and he said, 'Go for it.'"

Inside a small waiting room at the end of the corridor, those few who were closest to Ryan sat and waited. His father, who was divorced from Jeanne in 1978 and had little contact with the family since then, had already come for a brief visit. Ryan's sister, Andrea, was there, herself an AIDS casualty of a different sort. She had been a nationally competitive, award-winning roller skater before his dreaded sickness forced a reallocation of her mother's time and the family's scant resources. With her were Ryan's grandparents Gloria and Tom Hale, who had rushed home from Florida over the weekend when Jeanne called. They were joined by Jeanne's brother, Tom, and her sister, Janet Joseph, who drove up from her home in Birmingham, Alabama. The Reverend Bud Probasco, pastor of the Center Chapel United Methodist Church in Muncie, Indiana, who has known the Whites for more than 14 years, was also there. Ryan wanted him to preside at the funeral.

Elton John filed hundreds of phone messages for Jeanne, cleaned up coffee cups and sandwich wrappers and distributed $600 worth of stuffed animals he bought for the other critically ill kids on Ryan's floor. "They're too sick to care," Elton said, "but I feel so helpless in this place, I had to do something. I did it for myself, I guess."

Late at night, after everyone left, Jeanne moved her rocking chair next to Ryan's bed and placed a little illuminated guardian-angel figurine by his side. Jeanne bought the angel when Ryan was stricken six years before. She stroked his hand and whispered to him.

"Baby, I love you," she murmured. "You're gonna do good for everybody who is sick. It's a shame it has to be you."

Elton had a new record coming out Monday. His Los Angeles office was going berserk because he was not there. "I'm staying here through the weekend and through next week and the week after that if I'm needed," he told his office during a tense phone call. Elton left only to sing a couple of songs for the Farm Aid concert that was in progress a few blocks away in the Hoosier Dome. As he walked onstage, there was a thunderous standing ovation from 45,000 people. "This one's for Ryan," he said shakily, inspiring a second, even more thunderous ovation. He returned by nine P.M. to join Jeanne at Ryan's bedside.

By midnight, as teams of nurses and doctors scrambled in and out of the room, Dr. Kleiman stood in the hall by himself. Ryan was dying. "I feel terrible," he said.

About one A.M. on Sunday, Jeanne took a call at Ryan's bedside from longtime family friend Michael Jackson. Michael bought Ryan a red Mustang about a year before, and the Whites were frequent guests at his California ranch. Michael wanted to come that minute. He was in Atlantic City.

"How long will it take you, Michael?" she asked. Jeanne looked at a nurse wearing goggles. "Two hours?" she asked the nurse. The nurse shook her head. "Michael, don't come, honey. Ryan isn't expected to last two hours." Jackson said he would be there in the morning, and he was.

By then Ryan had died, surrounded by close friends and family and Elton's bittersweet songs, which came from a bedside tape player.

"Just let go, Ryan," Jeanne White had said quietly. "It's time, sweetheart. It's time to go."

More than 1,000 letters were sent to PEOPLE after the story on Ryan's death. Back home in Cicero, Jeanne still receives 20 to 30 letters a week. Her phone rings constantly. She has kept up her friendships with the celebrities who rallied to Ryan's side. "Michael Jackson, Phil Donahue, Marlo Thomas and Greg Louganis are always there for me," she said. Elton even wrote from the Chicago clinic where he was battling alcohol and drug addiction.

Andrea, 17, has experienced a difficult period of adjustment. She wears Ryan's gold watch and drives his red Mustang but is unable to talk about her brother.

Pilgrims come every day to Ryan's grave in the Cicero Cemetery—and leave pennies, flowers, notes and candles. In September vandals tore out the two trees Jeanne had planted nearby, ripped up sod and stole a statue of Ryan's dog, Barney. When Jeanne put everything back, they did it again. Undaunted, she restored things for a third time. So far the vandals haven't returned.

Given a year's leave of absence from her factory job, Jeanne, 43, speaks at benefits and PTA meetings, has testified before Congress and has accepted awards on Ryan's behalf. "I'd rather be home," said Jeanne, "but as long as people will listen, I'll keep talking. I think this is what Ryan would want."

# MALCOLM FORBES
## 1919-1990

**A**s mourners gathered in the hushed sanctuary of St. Bartholomew's Episcopal Church in New York City, and gawkers and photographers clawed for position on the steps outside, the haunting screel of a lone bagpiper gave way to a rising thunder of motorcycle engines. Some three dozen leather-swathed bikers deafeningly gunned their hogs in an impromptu procession up Park Avenue. The discordant moment elicited little surprise from the arriving luminaries. For those who had passed through the orbit of Malcolm Stevenson Forbes, cultural clashes were commonplace.

Malcolm Forbes owned castles and yachts, ran with bikers and movie stars and almost proved his maxim "He who dies with the most toys, wins." The exuberantly extravagant publisher who embodied both the unapologetic spirit and style of capitalism died in his sleep of a heart attack on February 24 at his home in Far Hills, New Jersey, at the age of 70.

Many of the 2,000 who came to praise Malcolm later streamed through the limestone Forbes Building on lower Fifth Avenue for a New Society–style wake featuring cocktails, pâté and smoked salmon. On display were selections from Forbes's vast collections of art and artifacts, including antique model boats, toy soldiers and manuscripts. At the time of his death, estimates of Malcolm's wealth ranged from $400 million to $1.25 billion, though *Forbes* magazine itself coyly declined to pin down the exact total in its annual list of richest Americans. He owned eight homes, including Timberfield, a 40-acre Far Hills, New Jersey, estate; a palace in Tangier, Morocco; a château in Normandy; and the island of Lauthala in Fiji, where Forbes had directed that his ashes be buried under a marker with the epitaph WHILE ALIVE, HE LIVED. In addition to the family's feisty business magazine, which media analysts estimate may be worth as much as $600 million, Forbes also held 400 square miles of real estate, 2,200 paintings and 12 Imperial Fabergé eggs, more than even the Soviet government owns.

Still, it was not money that made Forbes a household name but the way he flaunted what it could buy. He entertained royalty on his 151-foot, helicopter-equipped yacht, *The Highlander*, and jetted around the world in his private 727 (named *Capitalist Tool*). He set six world records in hot-air ballooning and led "goodwill" motorcycle and ballooning tours to unlikely destinations, among them the Soviet Union, Thailand, China and Pakistan. In 1989, his two million dollar 70th-birthday bash in Morocco sparked an acrimonious debate about the morality of such conspicuous presumption.

Though he appeared to be a natural extrovert, Forbes's expansive personality was late in developing. Not until middle age did he make the metamorphosis from financial duckling to the flamboyant media prince the public came to know.

A Princeton graduate, Forbes received a Bronze Star and a Purple Heart after the Battle of Aachen, then, at the end of World War II, joined the family publishing business run by his taciturn Scottish immigrant father, B.C. "Bertie" Forbes. He also tried his hand at politics, winning the Republican nomination for Governor of New Jersey in 1957 but was soundly defeated in the general election by Democrat Robert Meyner. After the death from cancer of his oldest brother, Bruce, in 1964, Malcolm put politics out of his mind for good and took on the top job at Forbes, Inc.

It was then that his personal transformation began. Far from engaging in the lavish entertaining that became his trademark, Forbes was known at the time mainly for his conservative politics and solitary habits. His daily custom was to withdraw to a luncheonette across the street from the *Forbes* offices in Manhattan, accompanied only by a book. He gradually discovered a flair for self-promotion and warmed to the spotlight. By the early '80s, when Wall Street was booming, Forbes was ready to present his magazine—and himself—as the very embodiment of the limitless success possible in America.

The Forbes trappings—the yacht, the plane, the parties, the giant balloons bearing the magazine's logo—were all part of a strategy of megapromotion. Wherever he went, much of Malcolm's entourage consisted of potential *Forbes* advertisers, and the boss was known to sell a sizable percentage of the magazine's ads himself. Revenues increased enormously under his guidance. But *Forbes* editorial staffers complained that Malcolm sometimes overused the prerogative of ownership, engaging in the journalistically suspect practice of softening or killing stories to protect friends or advertisers. And there was persistent speculation—officially denied by the magazine—that Forbes's widely read "Fact and Comment" column was produced by a ghostwriter.

Upon Malcolm's death, majority control of the

Forbes empire fell to son Malcolm Jr, 42, who will receive 51 percent of the estate. The rest will be divided among the four other children: Robert, 41, who oversees the family real estate properties; Christopher (Kip), 40, who is curator of the many Forbes family collections; Timothy, 37, the president of the Forbes-owned *American Heritage Magazine*; and Moira Forbes Mumma, 34, who works with the physically handicapped. While alive, Malcolm had discussed his will freely. He said he feared that dividing his estate equally among the children would lead to infighting and leave the company rudderless. His offspring now insist they are all pleased with the way the pie has been cut, though some observers worry that the cerebral Malcolm Jr. (called Steve) may lack the panache necessary to fill his father's shoes. Others take comfort from the fact that similar criticisms were once directed at Malcolm Sr. And Malcolm's father had himself developed his more pronounced eccentricities—including growing his hair long—only later in life, suggesting perhaps that Forbes men become more interesting with age.

Malcolm Forbes's wealth and relentless self-aggrandisement made his personal life the object of considerable attention. In 1985 he and his wife of 39 years, Roberta Laidlaw Forbes, divorced. Sources close to the family say the split was due primarily to Mrs. Forbes's longtime disdain for publicity and Malcolm's increasing hunger for it. Forbes's subsequent friendship with Elizabeth Taylor was a source of endless fascination to the tabloid press, though the two announced often—and persuasively—that they were simply good friends. (At the memorial, Taylor took the place of honor—the aisle seat on the first row. Mrs. Forbes ended up buried in the middle of the row.)

In recent years, Forbes's exuberant nightlife generated persistent if unproven rumors of his homosexuality, especially on the New York City club scene and in the magazine publishing world. Family members have either denied such rumors or declined comment.

At Forbes's memorial service, the five children took turns sharing their memories of the man who raised them. Timothy, who is in charge of the company's pop-culture magazine, *egg*, described his father's unauthorized balloon flight over Beijing in 1982, which ended unexpectedly in the middle of a Red Army installation. Christopher spoke about his father's love of his Scottish heritage and his insistence on sharing it with his children. "If you and your siblings had had to go to church dressed in kilts, your friends snickering at the sight of you all in skirts... you could begin to understand why all of us are so close," he observed. Son Steve recalled some of his father's setbacks, including the painful divorce and a previously undisclosed cancer in the early 1980s. The most widely shared sentiments about Malcolm Forbes, though, were probably expressed by his son Robert. "It's been a hell of a party, Pop, my special friend, and such fun," he said, his voice breaking. "Thanks for the trip."

# HALSTON
## 1932-1990

**H**e lived so fast that his first and last names blew off in the propwash. The first American designer to rocket to international stardom put his middle name on the look of the '70s. Suave and gracious, he was a kind of Jay Gatsby of Manhattan nightlife, a mysterious, aspiring Midwesterner who re-created himself tanned, tuxedoed and elegant. It was Halston whose parties helped transform Studio 54 into the disco of the decade. It was Halston whose friendships with Liza Minnelli and Liz Taylor made him a fixture of the celebrity culture. Gushed *Women's Wear Daily*: "The 1970s belong to Halston."

In equally spectacular fashion, the '80s did not. A chain of business blunders cost him control of his empire and, eventually, the right to design under his own name. Depressed and embittered, Halston stopped designing professionally in 1984. He became increasingly reclusive, seldom partied and saw only a few good friends. In late 1988 he found he was carrying the AIDS virus. The revelations of drugs and debauchery in *The Andy Warhol Diaries* left him feeling embarrassed and betrayed. Like Gatsby, his dreams busted up before he did.

He was born Roy Halston Frowick in Des Moines—to a father who was an accountant and a mother who was an avid seamstress—and raised in Evansville, Indiana. After attending Indiana University and the Chicago Art Institute, he designed and sold hats in Chicago's Ambassador West Hotel, where his first celebrity customer was Fran Allison of the *Kukla, Fran and Ollie* TV show. He then migrated to New York City, where he landed a job with famed milliner Lilly Daché. By 1958 he was in charge of custom millinery for Bergdorf Goodman, where he received lavish attention from *Vogue* and where he began selling his own clothing designs eight years later.

In 1968 he left to start his own company, Halston Limited, which quickly attracted such clients as Liz Taylor , Liza Minnelli, Martha Graham, Margaux Hemingway, Betty Ford, Babe Paley and Lauren Bacall. In 1973 Halston sold his business to Norton Simon Inc. for $16 million—a princely price that sent gasps through the industry at the time. Halston stayed on as principal designer and guiding spirit.

His reputation grew as he created comfortable clothes in soft, luxurious fabrics, an antidote to the flamboyant styles of the '60s that preceded him. His cashmere sweater sets, Ultrasuede shirtdresses and strapless chiffon gowns rarely required a perfect figure.

In 1989 the ailing Halston put his beloved town house up for sale (it was sold in January 1990 for five million dollars) and unloaded his Montauk, Long Island, estate. In January he moved into a $1000-a-day suite at the Mark Hopkins hotel in San Francisco to be near his family and his doctors.

Halston, anxious to be remembered at his best and loath to be a burden, declined visits from even his closest friends. The thin duke of New York's nightlife, a Midwestern boy at heart, sought solace with his family. His older brother, Robert Frowick, a retired foreign service officer, another brother, Donald, 44, and sister Sue Watkins, 52, routinely made the 90-minute drive from their Santa Rosa homes to visit their sick sibling, whose "two biggest pleasures," according to Robert, had become "food and touring." To indulge the former, the family brought good china, nice silver and fresh lobster salad. To facilitate the latter, Halston purchased a $200,000 Rolls-Royce Corniche for family-chauffeured jaunts up and down the Pacific coast. He instructed his family to auction the car after his death and donate the proceeds to AIDS research.

The end came at 11:22 P.M. on March 26 in Room 670 at Pacific Presbyterian Medical Center in San Francisco. Halston, 57, succumbed to Kaposi's sarcoma, an AIDS-related cancer, after an 18-month struggle with the disease. An exceedingly private person, he had rarely discussed his illness, even with close friends. But Robert resolved to make the cause of death public. "We think it's best for all concerned to know the reality. We profoundly hope it has a positive impact on the public."

# MITCH SNYDER
## 1943-1990

**C**arol Fennelly had bad news to deliver. The longtime companion of housing rights champion Mitch Snyder, Fennelly, 41, stood in the street facing reporters. "This afternoon, at approximately two P.M.," she said, "Mitch Snyder was found dead...." Out of the crowd of homeless people milling around Snyder's Federal City Shelter, a few blocks from the Capitol, a woman's voice began to rise and fall, rise and fall, like the sound of an approaching siren. "Who will take care of us now?" she keened.

The fight for America's poorest will go on, but when Mitch Snyder wrapped an electrical cord around his neck and hanged himself, some of the fiery energy of the struggle died with him. One of the Reagan era's loudest advocates for housing the homeless, Snyder, 46, often resorted to dramatic gestures to highlight his cause, sleeping on street grates and undertaking highly publicized hunger strikes.

Snyder had known hard times himself. His father ran off with another woman when Mitch was nine; Mitch's mother, Beatrice, a Brooklyn, New York, nurse, was left to raise a family on her own. At 16, Snyder was picked up for breaking into parking meters and sent to reform school. He carried memories of that painful, troubled childhood with him all his life. "That wasn't a good thing to do to a kid, to leave him without a father," Snyder told a reporter decades later. "I grew up swearing never, ever to do to my kids what my father had done to me."

Yet that was exactly what he did. Snyder worked at all kinds of jobs, from construction to selling vacuum cleaners, but never for very long. In 1969, after six years of marriage, Snyder walked out on his wife, Ellen, and their two sons, Ricky and Dean. Within a year he and another man were charged in Las Vegas with auto theft, and Snyder ended up doing more than two years in federal prison, transferring to Danbury, Connecticut. There he met Philip Berrigan and his brother Daniel, Roman Catholic priests and Vietnam protesters who had been jailed for burning draft records. The Berrigans converted Snyder to their philosophy of nonviolent protest, and his life was transformed.

In 1973, after a brief attempt to reconcile with Ellen, Snyder moved to Washington. He went to work for the Community for Creative Non-Violence, an antiwar group in search of a new cause. He found his place in the CCNV soup kitchen, and as the army of homeless grew, so did Snyder's reputation for self-sacrifice. He lived at shelters himself and said he drew only a subsistence-level salary. On the eve of the 1984 presidential election, Snyder undertook a hunger strike lasting 51 days, forcing Ronald Reagan to donate a decrepit federal building for the 1,400-bed Federal City Shelter, run by the CCNV.

But in the last few months, Snyder's life seemed to fall apart. His planned marriage to Fennelly was called off. Fennelly refused to elaborate on the marriage plans, but told PEOPLE, "I think he got very tired. I think I failed him in that I wasn't there when he needed me. But Mitch didn't let a lot of people in." She also said that Snyder had been "deeply wounded" by critics of his recent tactics, which included banning census takers from the shelter to protest what he insisted would be an inevitable undercount of the homeless nationwide.

In the past Snyder had responded to such attacks by saying, "When you represent powerless people, you have to fight every step of the way." Last April, wearied by what he saw as the public's "psychic numbing" toward the homeless, he announced plans to take a leave and retreat to a Trappist monastery. On July 5 his body was found. For Mitch Snyder it was a most uncharacteristic decision: to leave the fight to somebody else.

# PHOTOGRAPHY CREDITS

# INDEX